1998

The Caribbean Writer is an international literary magazine with a Caribbean focus, published in the spring of each year by the University of the Virgin Islands and sponsored jointly by the components of Research & Public Service and Academic Affairs.

President: Orville E. Kean
Vice President for Research & Public Service: LaVerne E. Ragster
Vice President for Academic Affairs: Denis Paul

Cover design: M. Lisa Etre

Distributed by Ubiquity
Indexed by the Index of American Periodical Verse

The Caribbean Writer, University of the Virgin Islands, RR 02 Box 10,000, Kingshill, St. Croix, USVI 00850 ; Phone: (340) 692-4152; E-mail:qmars@uvi.edu

Judith King

CONTENTS

POETRY

SPECIAL SECTION: NEW POEMS BY OLIVE SENIOR

SHORT FICTION

PERSONAL ESSAY

DRAMA

SPECIAL SECTION:
POEMS BY CÉLIE DIAQUOI DESLANDES
Translated from the French by Peter Constantine

INTERVIEW

SPECIAL SECTION:
POETRY AND FICTION FROM BELIZE

THE CARIBBEAN WRITER 10TH ANNIVERSARY LITERATURE CONFERENCE (OCTOBER 25-27, 1996)
Selected Papers II

BOOK REVIEWS

This publication is partially supported by a grant from Virgin Islands
Council on the Arts and the National Endowment for the Arts.

Visit *The Caribbean Writer On-Line* at
http://www.uvi.edu/extension/Writer/carwrihm.htm

Poems by Cecil Gray, Geoffrey Philp, Margaret Watts and
others; **Short Fiction** by Jennifer Rahim, Jan Lo Shinebourne
and others, an **Essay** by Edwidge Danticat, Special Section
on **Surinamese Short Fiction in Translation**, a **Roundtable
Discussion on the Arts: The Caribbean as Muse**, and **Book
Reviews** of work by Kamau Brathwaite, Marina Tamar
Budhos, E. A. Markham, George Lamming, Evelyn
O'Callaghan and Bruce King. **Index** of Volumes 1-11.

POETRY

Lutheran Church, Christiansted, St. Croix   David M. Hough

shango music

Geoffrey Philp

beside broken axles, the pang, pang,
pang, slips under torrington bridge, climbs
over wareika into ital seasoning,
skitters over swimming pools
of beverly hills into the dub of jolly buses
grinding up cross roads, half-way-tree,
liguanea—the president meets the residents
of mona, hope pastures, and stony hill
at matilda's corner; my sister, outside
the post office, short of stamps, swollen eyes,
swollen fingers, sends a letter across the pond
to a cousin in paris, brixton, goteburg,
asking for money cause everything's late.
behind her a veil of rain: natty dreads
bubbling up from carib theatre, scene
of the first feel, casting shadows left and right,
to papine, hermitage, elliston flats: the drip,
drip, drip of sky juice into a cheese pan
by a door that opens into a bob-wired yard,
stitched from coast to cove, by a man
beating old iron into the shape of thunder.

sunset at greynolds park

Geoffrey Philp

"weeeee," my son's scream
unhinges an egret from the sea
grape's gnarled boughs, bitter juice
rises in my throat: his mother's station
wagon enters the parking lot filled
with minivans—young couples still naive
enough to believe in love—yet i wish it was
us, swinging higher into that arc that binds me
closer than the twin poles of the swings
that span the sandbox, our space,
where our children bloodied their hands
on the jungle gym, trampled now by raccoons,
awakened by the sweet stench of sapodillas,
the pups nuzzle the green mulch of their mother's
fur beside broken sewer pipes that connect
the park to the bay: the poison of sudden
blooming algae coming in under an orange sky
where 747's play tag over the barrier islands,
stranded in the gulf's reach toward guyana,
like our restless drive to renew ourselves,
coming in before the tug-of-war beween my jeans
and his mother's skirt, my son's small arms,
like a frail spider stitching the severed space;
coming in under the fingers of mangroves
pulling the tide, the retreat of hermit crabs
under sand, pulling me closer to us, closer to we.

Considering Bush

Jennifer Rahim

Profusion
is the sovereignty
of bush
that so loves its own society
E X P A N S I O N
is its mission

everywhere
          a green chaos
                    lives out
the native/ monster-
dream
to people his island
with himself

vanity or
          right
to glory
in the self
in the self to sing
of the self
these verses
          now swaying
     twirling leafy skirts now
stepping, straight-backed and
     slick as traveller's palms
moving   easy now
as forest granddaddies
stroking their beards and whispering
     knowing just how to spin a head
like fast falling leaves eager
for the business
on the ground
                    now
                    watch your step
raise those knees
in the wild tangle
of vines and shrubs
rubbing bodies

now with bush that can heal
or now make you
                    invincible
        bold
as this knot grass
that disrespects cast-
concrete directing paths
prodigious
as wild lilies sprung
from a dry crust
after night rain

give voice

sssssshake
                    make
noise

        say all
there is to say
in the breadth of this passing
wind
        touching tongues
of leaves with a language
seasoned in sea
                    and a landscape
served in variety

        announcing

no escape

        no escaping

this PRESENCE

misbehave

        spread

the ambition to sing
unheard melodies
to create

       choirs
where ever there is earth
and breeze

       unsettle
the eyes trained
to reverence order
in manicured lawns
and controlled hedges
because there is
dis
     order
     in
this wind
      in this
bushyanthem that plays
even along the straight lines
of highways
refusing to grow quietly
where told

not so
     this native
verdure
that multiplies
without blessing
      lives
and dies
     without ceremony
like douens

     push tender heads
push
   forward from wilderness
defy walls and fences
to reclaim space
      or simply find
community

     labelled parasites
they build
   startling kingdoms
in the armpits

on the shoulders
at the feet
in crevices of regal giants
whose extended branches
ride waves of glory
offering themselves - a shade,
like a civilization
to cool the nothing
that is really difference

push forward
        come out
of dark earth
           to sun
and wind and
        let them know
who don't know
let them see
only tropical splendour
in this verdure
that adds to its armory
even while they sleep

let them who reverence
the accomplishment of cities
see only a jungle
in the governance of trees
that hold the centre
more than they know

let them who see sloth
in the slow swing of the cutlass
or plain backwardness in yards
that house chandelier carili vine
ratchet, physic nut and verbine
never know
        the taste of healing
never know
        the peace of wild
tropical
        green

Carenage

Jennifer Rahim

i

Now there is a beach
where there was none
and the great seawall
that kept the Gulf
from invading her house
is only a waist-high hedge
along this new shore,
where the water lapping
my feet is murkier
than I remember.
The familiar boats are gone
except for a beached pirogue
called *Princess*, the hull
like the wall, half-buried in sand,
the oil-paint flaked,
its sheen now floating
on the sea's surface.

ii

I loved only the sea
not the house that grew
by some magic in August
to hold all twelve of us,
packed like fish on mattresses
that tortured our flesh.
The sea, not the woman,
kept us for weeks
becoming amphibian.
Her hands waved like flags
from the house that had eyes
on every side like God,
warning of depths and currents
we had no fear of,
measuring our pleasure
as the meals she miraculously
stretched to feed us all
equally, like love.

iii

This stretch of ocean,
rocking against the wall,
we endured long nights for
while the woman in her chair
marked the hours, back and
forth, tracing paths
through black hair, shaping
her head for dawn.
We slept wildly, dreaming
of giant fish and silver liners,
and woke to give ourselves
again to an ocean that released
Gorgons at the end.
Not the sea, but her pumice-
stone hands that rubbed our skin
with lime, raked through knots,
tugged at plaits and anchored
them with bubbles or ribbons.
Her bracelets rang like bells.

iv

I am told that the day
before she died a storm
raged and the seabed
heaved from the deep
to be at her side and
delivered this beach
where there was none,
and that the ocean wept
at her funeral and waves
were buried with her coffin,
that her house shrivelled
with grief and collapsed.

And much too much later,
I discover that she is gone
and the sea, a stranger,
not the woman, but this sea
I loved.

Celluloid

Cecil Gray

City-sewn, bound to concrete and asphalt,
I did not dream rustic romantic fancies
looking at the sea like a poet. White waves
were too distant, too scenic. Romance for me
was as fleeting and brittle as celluloid reels
spilling alluring places on a cinema's screen.
Seven times I went to see Now Voyager,
enthralled by the desperate love of Paul
Henreid and Bette Davis. The world was real
only in the dark of an auditorium. So all
of the Queen Anne Lace blooms on breakers
cannonading a shore lacked the power
to entrance me. What I dreamed could be seen
in the beams a projector relentlessly aimed
through smoke-filled air. I was Gary Cooper,
Claude Rains, Edward G. Robinson, James Stewart
in turn. I fought with the Bengal Tigers
subduing India. I shared Errol Flynn's
swordplaying glamour. And with C. Aubrey
Smith extended the British Empire. So
in the true life that I lived I did not
walk past gateways stench-filled with garbage,
did not hear any bitter, quarrelling voices
coming from hovels, nor have to find standpipes
to wash myself under. They were not in those reels.
Far away went stained mattresses with lumps like fists
knuckling your back, and the scratching claws
of brown fibre sticking from rips in the ticking.
I could forget flour-bag bed sheets, canecutters'
ajoupas, hookworm, the scourge of tuberculosis
and all the soul's famine the colonised suffered.
Without the sea I was doing quite well
weaving myself into happier dramas, swimming
like Johnny Weismuller, my favourite Tarzan,
out of the strong hunters' net we were trapped in.
Not having access to waves that nature
washes over the eyes to sedate the attention,
in the magic of celluloid I found my protection.

Leaving the Dark

Cecil Gray

When we emerged from the woods
with trees like the elm the cypress the aspen
and with birds like falcons ravens and pheasants
we saw our own samaan tree's branches
give broad spreading shade to the island
saw the hills' pouis yellow and pink
put on their plumes their lenten rosettes
in dry march and heard the picoplat
sweetly trilling a whistle high in the leaves
of morning when we walked from the dark
and opened our eyes there were no fierce eagles
here to admire no birches no daffodils
that dance in a field but before us instead
scarlet ibises glided as delicately as lean
lithe dancers in a cave of swamp water
and hummingbirds as swift as meteors
shot from flower to flower where heart-shaped
anthurium lilies with ivory-tongued pistils
held pink and white auricles up to the world

where blue-gray tanagers and yellow orioles
skipped lightly about knowing nothing
of robins and cardinals the ones we were taught
marked the seasons when here the canefields
we cut were not ours the poems we learnt
were not ours the places we loved and yearned for
were elsewhere so royal palms standing like kings
high and proud in the air lining gravelly avenues
kept vigil and waited but did not receive
our thanks the silk-cotton tree the flamboyant
the immortelle were passed by like squatters
not to be honoured in stories we read
for darkness had covered our minds
and all our thoughts fled northwards until
we came out into sunlight and our eyes
were filled with a beauty that then readily
patiently opened its arms and took us back in

when all of the rules had been kept
all the whips had been cracked
when all of the birds and the trees and the flowers
were ignored like strangers when we had taken
to heart all the lessons and obeyed every
commandment having learnt to spit scorn
on what might have been called ours
praising the nightingale and the wren
the oak and the yew and the ash
turning away from things too familiar
to win our respect and like lost orphaned children
we sought our parents in cold far-off countries
and the songs that we sang were only of places
unknown to us the verses we learned
to recite with fervour and overdone gestures
were of people unknown of dreams that were foreign
we knelt through our night of denial
of disowning and of being disowned
and pretended to all we were not the people
we were happily going on ardently thinking
an apple was better to have than a mango
the avocado was not a real pear

till we found we were faceless and no-one
recognised our islands in our low genuflections
to snow to yorkshire pudding to pallid
complexions gilbert and sullivan maypoles
cockney and yankee dialects so we knew
we were blind that our eyes should have seen
kiskadees before larks the frangipani before
weeping willows that the unacknowledged samaan
gave comfort the elm would envy
we had come from the dark woods into the sun
so we broke every injunction history's keepers
had issued as we looked all around us
and jumped up to see how blessed we were
how rich how lucky not europe not africa
not india could take from these islands
love and fidelity due our true parents
like the nutrient water given us when we kiss
coconuts so we let these islands course through
every thought every action let them soak through
the good earth we now know that we came from

Grete by the Pool

Susanne Kort

Squatting there, half off the chair, a cane between
her hydrocephalic knees, she stares at the girls
in their shiny bikinis, arching their midriffs like tenderloins
towards the sun
                The absolute absence of waste:
snug skin, the belly buttons of angels,
their lights & vitals as yet
unsprung. Young. Young.

Shame. Her gargantuan self
chides the varicosities the flesh is heir to
& particolored pouches, the ridges & gullies,
uncharted canyons, the disloyal hair:
turncoat, pubic & armpit
going sparser & greyer: the falling away:
the bunions. Some joke. Flesh's ghastly
transmogrifications. Who knew?

More decorous not to go on at all
than to dwell in this monstrous house.
Unbargained for. I'm fine she says, baring her dentures.
It's the neighborhood's gone to hell

Scaling Back (Caracas, 1994)

Susanne Kort

All our food is old food now, made
way before the day before, I do it

on distressed mornings,
I try to stay on top of things, I fry & defrost against

any of the many jokes of God, the
plethora of earthquakes of course, in this

blessed zone, but also blackouts, stickups, shortages, syncopes—
their coming in with their guns & knitted faces past

our *rejas* & *Perros Guardianes*,
past the waterless pipes:

I used to make up everything fresh
for us: cutlets, eggs, rice, when it was all

still bounteous & green here & we dared to park our car
at the market & roses had the nerve to trail up

over our lacy fences since replaced
by iron ones: fearless, brash

View from the Roof

Delores McAnuff-Gauntlett

Tonight the moon shapes
a whole delicious orange
which I will peel
and ribbon the skin
around my neck

I will slice it into halves and
quarters, then scatter the pulp
across the cloudless midnight sky
and watch the yellow flow
spill on the step of dawn

What Lies Beneath

Shara McCallum

The woman inside turns flour to dumplings
with the magic of water and salt.
Her hands move without thought.

Outside her window, girls gather,
whispering secrets in corners,
laughing at jokes she can't hear.

She is their age again, home in Trinidad—
swimming out to a nearby dock and falling
asleep in the afternoon sun. Night.

and the shore retreats from her reach;
the water fills with shadows. She hears
her father calling from land's edge.

Why doesn't she answer? Why is she afraid
with his voice instructing her path home?
She has forgotten this story a long time now.

Chopping carrot, her hands become the flashing knife.
Fingers dashing from bag to board, she pauses
to brush a loose hair from her eyes,

trying not to see herself shivering
in the cooling air, the sea beneath her
kept at bay by a few pieces of wood.

Not 'Nuff Respect

Zarina Mullan Plath

Calypso doesn't swing and sway like gentle foaming
island water, or the blissed-out heartbeats of steelpan.
It's full of noise, vertical motion, frantic
soca—sock-a—sock it to me ringbang hard.
When you're too *sweet* with rum and lime, when
you've been so *sweet fuh days* you don't know
can't think won't think don't care—*where is she body?*—
your body is carried by this ragga, this soca, this
rhythm of sex and gyration, *jooking, jooking*:
this sensuous grinding of hips that used to be
your flesh and your bone, but which now belong
to ringbang, to voices slamming, telling you
to jump up hands up while somewhere someone
is chanting *'bout respect, 'bout de bamboo man*
and when you pass by *wuk up wuk up* the tongues
lash like cane over snaps of rum—
but pay no attention, it never lasts long,
and you'll be forgotten by the very next song.

Poem for Sharon

Lynn Sweeting

I come again to the door I hope will lead
to the poem I was born to write, and know
this night will pass as too many others have,
full of words, yet empty of those words
that might shed a light, or open a fissure
in this barren limestone land, this rock
Luccu Cairi once walked and loved, and lost,
this island among seven hundred islands
poets struggle to define or name or mark
with signatures written in blood and painful dialect.
I write blindly, my eyes clouded in poems
an American woman friend wrote to a hard country.
Sharon wrote an epic of America
in a voice that trembled with the voices
of her Cherokee grandmothers, and her poems
were requiems for them and for the country
stolen from them and left to her as if the genocide
was meant to be. She wrote songs
as I would like to write them tonight,
telling stories of the native people lost,
telling stories of the motherland lost
to tourism and the lies of recorded history.
And the stories of all the people I know
so saturated in piety and morality and dogma
their spirits are dead as dust. I write blindly,
fatigued to the point of disgust and afraid
I am writing for no good reason at all.
The collective suffocation of spirit
can do that to a poet, or an entire nation.
The death of spirit will choke off all creation
and turn poetry to bones. But tonight I remember
hard country, Sharon's epic poem/song.
I take into myself the spirit she conjured then
filling for a moment all my empty spaces
and filling this page with a poem about all the poems
I will never write unless I am reborn
and unless I can stand the pain of being midwife
to my own rebirth, in my own name
and in the name of the Lucayan woman,

24

the last cacique queen who died at the point
of a conqueror's knife, who died without
leaving us even the memory of her name,
and in the name of the woman priest who
may never have a church or a congregation
because her body mirrors the Magdalene's,
and in the name of my mother Rosemary
and all my many grandmothers, known and unknown,
who lived and died and live again in me.
I write with a vengeance, in Sharon's way
because her poems are endless as the ocean
surrounding me, trapping me here yet opening
to a thousand ways out. I write echoing her rhythm
and the way her stories roll on, a river,
carrying me on to my own stories of my own country
a painted paradise, a harlequin country daring me
to name the music she dances to. Ten thousand names
could not begin to name this place, or who I am,
but this is the purpose of poetry - a naming ritual.
And so, on and on it goes, and I go on, deeper
into a night that does not embrace me, but shakes me,
wakes me, kneading the skin of my brain like bread,
pushing me to speak of things better left unsaid
for the sake of uneasy peace. On and on, until
I have smoked enough cigarettes to sink the Dolphin
and my poem runs like shed blood
across another cold blue computer screen
and the sound of my man snoring and the television droning on
begins to sound like music, other-worldly music, hiding
within itself a coded message about answers,
how there are no answers that hold true forever,
and my words move to the music, making discordant
harmonies only I can hear, as I am
the only person in this house who is awake.
But this is not unusual. Ever since early childhood I
have always been the last one to let sleep take me.
Back then, I was terrified when I found myself the only one
still conscious long after midnight. I used to cry.
These days, I love the freedom of solitude in the blackness
of the early morning hours. I love the gift given me
called space, and I love to pour my poems out like rain
or tears or sweat or bile or blood
because it means I am alive and the lies told about me

saying I am unholy and unwholesome and unwelcome
are belied once again, and not for the last time.
Because this too is the purpose of poetry, when you are a woman.
to prove at least to your Self that divinity
is alive in your finger bones and in your dreams
and in the voice that wakens after midnight.
And so Sharon this strange poem is for you, wherever you are,
with thanks for that letter you wrote to Paul about searching
for some transient poem and finding it at last
emerging in all its simple glory in your letter.
This poem is for you my lost sister, who took me by the shoulders
and shook me ten years ago in Napa, telling me,
there must be a way out for you, there must be a way
out from the prison of your birthplace where poetry
will always be a foreign language. This poem
is my letter to you, Sharon, to tell you that at last I understand:
the only way out, is through.

Three Diamonds in the Sky

Simon B. Jones-Hendrickson

(For George Beckford, Cliff Lashley and Carl Stone)

George, Cliff, Carl, you three,
selectively taken from the pages of
history, narrowed by
vengeance of the land
spiked by water, blows and smoke.
You have left us reeling in a
Blue Mountain coffee stupor.
George, you have marinated
consumption functions where
marginal propensity to
consume may be *bitter weed*,
wormwood and gall on a
rotten plantation economy of
persistent poverty.
And if Shakespeare were to meet
you, Cliff, you would have said
like Nelson Mandela in Brazil
"A casa e sua, irmao."
You had the gift of kings bundled
in an Oceana neighborhood
where a Central Bank was your view
and where others will not venture
Down Town, you knew Down Town
and Up Town were yours, too.
But whence does bitter weed
flow into polls of your
making, Petras, my Latin Stone?
Will you, Cephas, bring the two wayward sons together under an
ackee tree or will they wait
with guns raised to cease and settle
when the poui tree blossoms?
You tell me. Tell me if we must
have a faculty meeting at the
Graduate in Papine? Will there
be Marxian dialectics suffocating
through the pentameters of
assembled hard chairs in

SR4? Who will give me my
first opportunity to defend the
furrows of plantation economy
in the *alms* of Babylon on
a dry pitch next to Colly
Smith Drive? And when
will the polls ever ring
true again, so that you
can *trace* me for my idiocy
of disagreement? I will
miss your laugh that sirens
your coming and *castroes*
my time to listen to you
for hours. And what will
they say now? You three
selectively taken to make
hay in a land where sun does
not shine, where Atilla refuses
to do the bidding of Roman
peasants who believe they are
maroons in the kills of bondage;
where blood oozes from the
Kentucky massacred chicken
that you hated, that you
despised, that you knew was
taking over
Jamaica.
And when JAH-down shall
be no more JAM-down, and
the Love Birds shall no longer
fly high above the sky
with Love Girls fashioning
the latest dance-hall
bikini of indifference, we
shall awake to the
smell of jerk-pork, and cricket
shall be taught at UWI
for only then will you ask,
What do they know of Fern
Gully, who only *bami* knows?
Will we then ask that Irvine
Chancellor, Taylor and Seek
Hole march to one tune under

the watchful
idea of BOB
MARLEY?
Will we see three
ships sailing into the night
of finality like a Brian
Lara four taking him to a
century? Will Papine show
a three-dimensional figure
for those who seek socio-
linguists in a library crawling
with silence one day after
football week?
We sure will. You gave
us flowers. We were
scented in polls punctuated
in Shakespearean sonnets and
embellished in Walcotian
hexameters. Lest we forget,
you smelled your flowers while
they were in bloom. And while
your ships reached the Indies
too soon, you three knew
your journey; you were not
mistaken by some carto-
grapher who wanted East by
West. You three, selectively
taken, were stars in a firmament
of your own making. Your light shall
continue to shine on every granule of
persistent poverty, every
clientelism of a multi-party
and every Garveyism, Georgian
alliteration, wrapped in an anaphoric
assonance, like a diamond in the sky.

Powers and Boundaries (Jamaica, 1880)

Thomas Reiter

A rutted lane stretches through woodland
to a public wellstead, divides around it
and continues on. Women are drawing water
for callaloo soup and for laundry they hang
in the trade winds that came ashore
bearing the Spanish Crown and the last things:
death, judgment, heaven, and hell.

Two figures approach the well: an old man
on muleback followed by a boy on foot.
Eleven years old, he pushes an umbrella stand
mounted on a caster, steering with
a curved handle affixed to the rim. Jutting
from shadow there, a saw handle, T square,
claw hammer, and the knob of a brace and bit,
while the rider carries tools in saddlebags.

Now the man reins up. And while he's pointing
off into the forest and saying a mahogany
tree grows there, and that he remembers
—it was the year before Abolition—
watching craftsmen from England plane and mortise
that wood, building a sideboard for china
in the great house of the sugar estate
where, a young man, he was a kitchen slave,
ragling boys leaning against the wellstone
call this one's name and wave. He lifts his free
hand to them but continues looking into the trees.

Master carpenter and apprentice, they do not
pause for water, they go on past to where
the boy is learning to come into
the powers and boundaries of the common
tamarind, white cedar, and whistling pine.
He loves to set each grain and fragrance free.

Snug the studding in and toenail, so...
In framing out a dwelling, he has already
begun to take in what the man knows:
the discipline and beauty of angles made true,
the keeping quality of seasoned wood.

Fragments of a History

Maria Lemus

Cloth-bound manuscript discovered by wayward angler. Circa seventeenth century wood and gold coffer lodged in porous limestone bank, on edge of Atraves island reef, ink well-preserved, but parts missing due to salt decay. Translated by experts in native and old world hybrid speech: cultural and linguistic origin of manuscript unknown. According to documentation, the original manuscript of the first fragment burned the skin of its possessor, much as the man-of-war does when it comes in contact with human flesh. Manuscripts currently on display at Museum of Natural History.

Fragment I: Caliban's Dance

Long before our dreams, long before, a creature who could not speak spoke a language not of sound nor of writing but of movement. Asleep and awake he spoke the language of dreams before any sound echoed from his lips, before he traced the first word on sand. His dance was the dream. Asleep and awake the dream was the dance, the dream was his body sinking, the outline of his melting flesh vanishing beneath every passing wave.

This is Caliban, the first dancer, inventor of language, for whom language was not a dream such as ours but a dance

Long before our dreams, long before, now we only dance in our dreams.

This is Caliban, who moved, moved as the wind does when it barely stirs the whisper of skies, who moved as the tide does when it disappears to unknown places in the sea.

Some do not know the sea. Some have forgotten Caliban's dance, these are speakers of the dreams who have forgotten dreams asleep and awake. They do not speak, because they do not know the sea, they do not know memory

Between the blinding sun and gleaming sand the tide rose as it had never risen, thrusting Caliban fiercely, far from the shore. There, on the edge of the mangrove, the first awakening. Caliban saw his shadow. Caliban spoke the first word, our language. We who do not dream asleep and awake.

When he saw his shadow, Caliban spoke from his body, the first word a whirlpool spiraling. A sound from his lips embodied the sadness and hunger of his flesh.

We who no longer dream asleep and awake do not know the first word, but we know and forget that Caliban could not touch the sea, so vast and so distant. We know and forget that the first word contained the sea's betrayal, for in the gushing fall of blue, Caliban had never seen his shadow.

The sea, it had once caressed Caliban, dragging him nearer and nearer its faceless horizon. The sea, it had once cradled him with its lilting, winding currents. In the unfathomable liquid heaviness of the sea, Caliban had danced, spoken the language of dreams asleep and awake, long, long before our dreams

We know and forget as the sea forgets, retreating, swallowing the shallow waters. We know and remember as the sea remembers, returning the gift of memory through its redeeming pulse.

Caliban spoke the first word of betrayal, and his word shook the sea, glided across its depths, traced cursive symmetries on the sand, diluting sounds ever widening until the first word crashed against far away rocks and returned, the sea returning the first word and its gift of memory

The exhausted limbs of Caliban dreamed the first dream, a dream such as ours, a dream only possible after the first word, after the sea's betrayal

Years. . .the second awakening

Caliban picked up a mangrove seed and etched the sea's betrayal into the sand, now yielding, near the shore, where Caliban returned to ask the tides where it hid its language of dreams asleep and awake. The tide responded, its foam covering the sign Caliban traced into the sand. As the wave inhaled the sign, it hid the first word forever from Caliban's eyes

This is the first word, a word we forget, a word the mangrove seed dispersed as it sought root in the first book, Caliban's book

Fragment II, a scroll found rolled within a conch buried under an abandoned plantation. At the same site, archeologists discovered primitive navigational tools and a map of a stream stretching from the archipelago surrounding Atraves island, to the straits of the continent, marked by drawings of feathered fish in vivid hues. Conch was stolen from display case at Museum. Theft attributed to exhibition guard, who claimed that a faint breath and whispering voice distracted him from preserving the artifact's security, forcing him to return the conch to the sea.

Fragment II: The Air Spirit's Testimony

He lies buried somewhere, perhaps, under fans and anemones, his body nothing more than a coral city shadowed by sargasso clouds floating in the heavens. Yet another sky lies above this one, my sky, the air spirit's. I live these days in the empty conch shell that once saw Caliban sinking to death, after a storm, a mutiny, I do not know, sinking so slowly that his curved back touched the sea floor before his arms, his arms following his body gracefully, his palms praying upwards to indifferent frigate birds and gulls whose screeching the conch never hears.

The body weighs more than air. How I envy Caliban's body

Caliban's tattered clothes rose around him, muted man o'war tentacles reaching for air. I saw a belt buckle disappear into the sand, its sheen brighter, at these depths, than the sun's. I saw a fish poke curiously about his body, this fish with enormous eyes, its stare as empty and deadly as the scabbard that stuck out from Caliban's sleeve.

Those were not pearls that were his eyes. I never saw Caliban's eyes, but I saw his blood, as it poured from a salt-washed wound, a soft cradle for a dying body.

The blood stirs more than air. How I long for Caliban's body

A darkness swept above the sea's sky, its keel murdering below, its mast reaching the light in my sky, yet hopeless. The din of men's voices, hopeless. The sacks full of gold, hopeless. The skins full of wine, hopeless.

A mirage, a shoal, somewhere, perhaps, a shipwreck, a sea bounty. Those were pearls that were their eyes.

A river flows around the shoals, no ship can pass it without moving here, there, everywhere. the sea's raging arm a whip lashing into wooden beams of galleys.

I waited for Caliban's blood to disappear, before the sharks would arrive, before the frenzied feast of Caliban's body, but having no eyes of my own, my shell only witnessed this: that a current dragged me for thousands of miles, laid me on an island where psalms are read through leaves, through green and wind.

From above the sea's sky I see now the river formed by Caliban's blood, a stream from land's end to land's end, where whirling water sinks down to meet the earth's embrace. Caliban's blood murmurs endlessly through its endless return.

I am an air spirit longing for the sea. . .

Change, foretold and foreseen, from Sycorax's thighs to my pitiful lightness. A body twined about islands makes history, and even my tricks turn the tides against the hopeless din of men's voices.

The third fragment has continually vexed the translators, who have lost all hope of unraveling the fragile pages as they were found, torn, mixed, and unintelligible. After spending countless hours compiling and categorizing in logical archival sequence what appeared to be a collection of distinctive, separate sheets, the translators would rest their tired eyes, only to discover these fragments could reassemble themselves over the course of the night. Some magnetism between the dialects, perhaps, accounts for the chemical cohesion of the tattered papers, which, according to the translators, were of all the fragments most marked by oily fingerprints. The ashen color of the paper, marred by flames, conceals a marking some experts have likened to a stamp, and yet, despite these puzzling attributes, the translators believe this epistle was never sent because the postal system of Atraves island was constantly beleaguered by tempestuous weather and international conflict.

Fragment III: Powder Wig's Dance Lesson

Dear Sir --------,

We have buried the drums as you have recommended under the cane fields and yet we still hear them every night, without fail. Either our ears have succumbed to the effects of the heat, or the natives are deceiving us   quite docile since we implemented the security and vigilant measures you designed. Don't go into de circle, don't go into de circle, de circle of fire, burn you, dat circle, boy, move in squares boy dat is de way

Don't hear dose drums, boy, don't hear dem, dey will change you each night the supervisors bind them to their cots, and yet, inexplicably, the drums are unearthed   don't hear dem drums, dey will take you back, back, hear my voice boy, dat is de way the financial accounts have a mold about them sir, you see, the humidity   unreadable, but

we pray   you send the best doctors who are able to treat this condition. Failing that, send more supervisors to supervise our supervisors, as we have no way of knowing oui la la   what poison may linger in our foodstuffs that may effect our hearing so profoundly oui la la, oui la la   ,don't

35

A twitching of the muscles, accompanied by violent fits, unprovoked except perhaps by the ghosts who haunt and don't stomp on de earth wit you bare feet, don't let de heel beat de earth, don't let dat mud get into you boy get into you like part of you skin the cliffs are practically insurmountable given the profusion of ferns and bromeliads, the late sir --------- claims are carnivorous but   only the flora,   ,omit an offensive odor and don't let you voice sing, don't let you mouth smile even our most expert guides fall hopeless and helpless their limbs limp in the evenings to the deafening noise, a sound that drains the human spirit, sir, don't let you soul smile, don't let me know you be smiling, dat is de way, let me see you teeth, boy, dat is de way, sir,

With all due respect, sir, the enterprise we engage I teach you to dance boy, dat is de way, dat is de way, here may result unprofitable as the climate is under control by the natives whose drums   albeit an honorable condition of employment

You may find this hard to believe sir, don't listen to de drums, don't listen to de drums, don't listen, dey speak, dey move but I make no exaggerations. We found   and one of our women swallowing clay after the manner of the dey move you to speak

and a man with hands blistered by flower petals

Northeasterly winds have become cool, in contradiction to our sense   the chart maker confounded by the rift in the sea, it seems a stream dragging our sturdiest vessels   although the fear is an advantage in times of war, sir, with trustworthy mariners   , but twisted compasses

My superior, whose courage is admirable, has assured me that don't look at de sky, don't look at de earth the interview with   has proved ineffective. He has been exiled accordingly   According to the noise look at me boy, dat is de way, is nothing more than the copulation of crickets and don't cringe at de whip, boy, although   secrecy these are difficult times, sir,

Don't let de knee bend, don't let de hip sway, boy, don't heave de chest, don't let you arm swing, don't let de finger point, boy, the scarred keel of the ship was   mutilated bodies   beyond repair, but we could expect no more from her maiden voyage, oui la la her galleys pregnant with oui la la the men survived on rotting fish oui la la   your cargo was spoiled, boy, dat is de way, and we are remiss for this most grievous accident, sir, yet profits this year amount to

Others say that a man's body prevents us from leaving the island, but these fantastical stories let dose hands bind, boy, let dem bind, dat is de way, dat is de way   We know that storms have wrecked ships before we were able to make what was our own perilous landing. If you send doctors   the fog   unlike the mother country   please sir tell the navigators not to enter by the bay, rather tell them to skirt the peninsula, and seek the red current,

spilled by the current onto the shoal, his body was never recovered   my lady's coral necklace

I regret to inform you sir that my wife has disappeared since the first unearthing of the drums. Since that night her parrot no longer chatters don't drink de rum boy, don't drink de rum make you sing   ,but there is a silence about the home. Our servants look at me with suspicion, as if I, and not they, were responsible for her disappearance. As you know   sir, boy, my wife, was with child, and I therefore implore you to send more soldiers to protect our interests in order to drink de sweat off you brow, boy, dat is de way, dat is de way, sir,

Don't let you skin glow the coves   gulls' nests don't let me see dat light on you skin, black anhinga let dat skin be transparent so I read you like book, boy de   white egret   exports less   that is comforting news

We have nothing more than the interests of the boy, sir, dat is de way, sir, dat is de way, boy

accept the tortoise shell as   my

        dutiful servant,

The translators view the fourth fragment as evidence of their physiological effects. Most of the field notes about the archeological expedition were lost to a recent hurricane. The director of the expedition refuses to reinscribe these notes from memory, but he promises to write a book as soon as the feeling in his right arm returns.

Fragment IV: Caliban's Book

10 November 1996

Today we discover a skeleton. One of the assistants finds it lodged up against the maze of branches. We had been sleeping under this banyan for months and no one had noticed it. The skeleton is unlike any other I've seen, perfectly normal human structure, but its bones marked by strange hieroglyphs. Nonsense, the director says, the markings are nothing more than the tiny holes carved by insects that bore into bones and eat marrow.

I imagine a body made of skin, flesh, and bones, but no ordinary skin, flesh, and bones. This body is as white as the stars and as black as the sky illuminating them. This body is as smooth and taut as the distance between memories of laughter easily recalled. This body is strong, virile. This body frightens me, beckons me. It is not my job to imagine. I must sing myself to sleep.

12 November 1996

I haven't been able to concentrate since the discovery of the skeleton. The assistant who found him claimed naming rights, so now we affectionately call him boy. I say he's no boy, but the others shrug their shoulders. He's a man, I say, a man with words etched onto his bones, a man who was once beautiful, still beautiful. Look at the eye sockets, I say, they're focused, smiling. The director tells me to go home, I've been in the forest too long. Maybe the mosquitoes, but it's not the rainy season. The others say I need to climb up the banyan, and live in boy's tree house.

13 November 1996

So I do. I'm not leaving the camp. They need me, since I'm the only language specialist here. They asked me to join this expedition in case they met any natives. So far, we haven't, and quite frankly, I don't expect we will. The natives know about boy and his bones. They know about the banyan. They won't come here. They probably haven't been in this area of the forest for hundreds of years. The diggers, they're mocking boy now. Boy rests in a box by the director's tent. Boy protects us. They don't know that.

20 November 1996

I've been sleeping up in the banyan for a few days now. It's peaceful up here. I don't hear the snores and grunts of humans. I don't hear the incessant buzzing that kept all of us awake the first nights after we set up camp. I hear nothing. Only wind. I have made a bed on a splendid stump, not far from where we found boy. It is flat, and wide enough to accommodate my entire body. The wood is hard, but no harder than the ground on which the others sleep. I don't need a sleeping bag. Somehow the tree cradles me, even if I sleep with my legs and arms spread, hanging over the forest canopy. I'm not afraid to fall. Boy knew what he was doing. He knew this was a good place to die.

24 November 1996

They're looking at me. I can feel their breathing. Where have you been? I say I'm tired. You've been missing for three days, the director says, we've been worried, we're responsible for you. Look, let's just forget about all of this. Here's a clean, new notebook. Maybe you can write a chronicle of our expedition. I don't think you'll be doing much translating anyway, I mean we've been here for three months and we haven't seen anyone, so forget about all that boy stuff and play historian until it's all over. Thanks, I say, but I've been writing history all along. Is there any food left in the pot? Don't tell me cook stewed more iguanas. I'm hungry.

I spend more time on the tree now. I tell the director it helps me record history from a bird's eye view. Fine, he says, but don't forget to eat once in a while. We laugh. He's not a terrible man, really. You've got to be strong out here, so I've given up chronology, that's the director's job.

Boy is still resting in his box. They mean to take him back to the lab eventually, with the other artifacts from the dig. I haven't told them the hieroglyphs on boy's bones are also etched into the tree. I'm not really writing their history. From time to time I satisfy the director with a few paragraphs on the day's progress. He believes it. Anything I say he believes is history, a little fact, a little information, a little summary of events, this is history to him. They're finding history on the ground. They're not looking up, they're not looking at the tree.

I'm not digging, they say, I spend the day up here. What can I know about history? The director tells them to be quiet.

There's a sequence to the hieroglyphs.

Boy returns to me in my dreams. If I look at his body, he says, I will understand the hieroglyphs. They're not really hieroglyphs, boy says, they're not words either, but they speak all the same. Did you write them, I ask? He never answers my questions, and so I look. I see an arm as thick as these branches, sinewy, marked by blood vessels, rage, a back supporting the world, angry thighs clinging to speed, running somewhere. Boy, I say, you're not that skeleton, you deceive me, you deceive them.

My body is trembling. I wake up clothed in sargasso weeds, but we are miles from the shore. Salt crystals tangle my hair. The director says there are abnormal quantities of sodium in the lakes here. He says don't bathe in the lakes, they're full of piranhas.

The expedition ends in a week. I must say farewell to boy.

Last night, a snake, or was it a dream? The assistant director died of a snake bite after the first week. I feel strange, a warmth coming from me, it can't be poison.

I could hear them looking up and saying, didn't we just have full moon? My skin, glowing, I was licking the sap from the tree. It can't be poison. Now, boy says, I will never be hungry. Something is moving under my skin.

I am peeling the bark off the tree. The bark is tough, but if I work diligently I might succeed. Boy is angry at me. I know I'm destroying the tree, boy, but I'm saving your book. Stop it, boy tells me. You don't need the book, he says.

I stepped down to sit by the camp fire. I promised I would extinguish it before I went to sleep. I was the only one awake. Boy came before me, dancing. It wasn't a dream. I was afraid, but I understood. I no longer possess my body. The book possesses my body. The body is my book.

The fragments end here. Archeologists have requested assistance with recent discoveries, but the translators are exhausted.

Sugar Cane

Rosamond S. King

He treat me like I
sugar cane He
give me a long look
an wink an ask if
I want to walk a bit an we
walk an smile an he tickle
me lil bit and we en up
at my house. He say
he will come back de
nex day an when he
come he say he come
to stay me I say alright
to de sugar cane in he
mout an I fix up me lil
rooms to make dem
cozy for two an even
de fus night he ain
come home I ain say
nuttin I ain cry I ain
scream nuttin I jus lie
in bed and look
at de place I fix up so
it comfuhtable fuh two
an when he reach an don
answer me an try tuh
sweettalk an tickle an
tease me I jus roll over
an say is not long he could
treat me like dat I wuhk
an cook an clean for he too
an if he wan play games
he should fine somebody
else for sweettalk. He come
home every night for a week
well you know I cyan put
up wid dat I put he out wit
he ruck sack an put me place
back tuhgedda so it mine an
cozy for one he ain get over

on me atall I tell you he is treat
me like sugar cane he come to
suck out all my sweetness but
is me who spit he out first.

Mango Madness

Christopher Miller

A spoon just doesn't cut it
when you eat a mango.
You have to get down and
Slice
off a cheek and
Bite
into that yellow flesh
Allow
the juice to stream down your chin
staining your shirt
Pick
the strings out of your teeth,
Savor
those sinful juices
after you finish two cheeks,
take the seed and
Suck
it til it's dry.
Ignore
those who stare
They know not bliss
Slurp
up passion itself,
Revel
in ecstasy until the
seed is bald with strands of
yellow hair covering the sides,
Naked
of flesh
Stripped
of skin
Prime
for planting

Song for Caliban

Erik Turkman

for my cousins, all of them

What you call this color! I ask
Inez at the market, and knuckle
backside my wrist. *Café au lait*, she say.

What you call this color! I ask
Beulah at the bakery, and toe
against my knee. *Cinnamon*, she sigh.

What you call this color! I ask
Helena by the back street, and tongue
along my lip. *Tamrin*, she surmise.

What you call this color? I ask
Oliver at the rum shack, and palm
inside my elbow. *Baben Cour!* he bellow.

I dash home and bend back
over the computer forms sent
from the continental college.

Well now—

I ain' black, I ain' white, and I ain'
no Eskimo. I ain' no Chinee neither,
and I ain' never been to Honolulu.

I can't pack inside none of these boxes
so how I gon' get to school?
Mother see me sinking and fling out:

Oh bright boy, you can' figure dat yet!
Check dem all! And tro' in Carib,
and Arawak, and the old man

coming back from Denmahk. You holdin'
all God creation in your golden palm.
Go on now. Write your book.

So sit I here staring, looking back
on that sinking day. It slow in singing,
but soon, I think, a song beginning.

Night Crossing
Erik Turkman

My cousins, who we simply call—the boys,
my brother, and I, careen in crazy flight
through the last gasp of suburban light, chasing
fireflies in the backyard. My sister, the sole
maiden of our generation, and therefore the gem
in our diadem, scorns us from the back porch,
chiding our evil ways as we smash the glowing
insects with wiffle ball bats and tennis racquets,
even an old golf club gets its licks in. We strip
the bugs of their embers and smear the fluorescent
goo onto fingernails, transforming ourselves
into Draculas as we wail and stagger drunkenly.

When the summer wanes and my cousins must
return to their tropical island, they lament
that there are no lightning bugs in paradise,
so we contrive a plan to transplant the iridescent
insects by the stealthy employment of an old
peanut butter jar and some dry grass.
We gather hundreds of the blinking buggers,
pack them in like a tin of mackerel,
and shackle them down for the voyage.

My sister says they'll never arrive intact,
the glass will crack, or they'll suffocate,
or a customs agent will confiscate them,
but we punch holes in the metal lid with my
Swiss Army knife and conceal the throbbing
contraband deep beneath folds of clothing.

Erik Turkman

Much to our amazement, the cargo survived
its secret crossing, yet failed to populate
the night with its glistening offspring. Our West
Indian upbringing, with its reverence for mother
and matriarch, made it inconceivable to us
that within a divine plan, there could exist
a species in which only males were permitted
to glimmer. So now, deep into mid-life, we,
still the boys, wonder why the nights are void
of the luminescent promise of new life
as we swagger beneath the moon in solitude

and praise the wisdom of darkness.

Volcanic Songs

Patrick Sylvain

We used to sit underneath palm trees,
or on porches where the sun could not reach
our skin. Sometimes, we would sit on a long
marble bench leaning against the wall
of our house that grandpa had built
before calluses and arthritis
had found refuge between his knuckles.

We sat around Manno to watch
his long black fingers
conversing with his guitar strings,
as his colossal voice exploded
songs as hot as burning oil.

He sang about our bent-back parents
threading needles on cows' skin
making baseball. Foreign signatures
carving deeper into the land and
into their skeletal like frames.

I will never bury the images
of his back arched like a bow,
holding his guitar like an arrow
with its six strings and echoing
the messages of his fingers
in a theater where waves of macoutes
could not touch his shore.

He sings with a tidal energy against
the military who have broken the radios
and try to prohibit his songs,
still we kept singing
"je nou byen kale, n'ap siveye."
Our eyes well lit, we are watching.

We're from a dark town
where monsters' teeth glow
in the dark, and our light

is a torch from our ancestors
that we carry in our hands
like his songs.

My Grandmother Danced

Mirlande Jean-Gilles

My grandmother danced on duvalier's head
with one red shoe and one blue
I come from coconut groves
where men's heads hang like ripe mangoes
no matter what the season
My grandmother would sing these men down
bless the back of their necks with aloe and comfrey
but they would not respond

We watched public burnings,
embers blamed no one
but danced their fiery dance
Grandma had herbs, money and gun powder stuffed into her brassiere
Murder tucked demurely within the folds of her skirt
At five she sang me redemption lullabies
and I dreamt war, blood red

We were hungry
and papa doc was taking the food
from between our teeth
grabbing our real papas in the darkness
and the flames
and their screams
would illuminate midnight
outshine the moon

My grandmother danced on papa doc's skull
with one red shoe and one blue

We played on human bones in Haiti
death left on our swings
in our schools
random fingers as bookmarks in our bibles
And the white god laughed
his crucifix too heavy on our necks
drowned us during baptisms
we couldn't fly any more
couldn't astral project our bodies to tree tops or foothills
they got weapons for that now

Unlike past slave revolts
where entire cargo would disappear
(ya'll never heard about that)
lightening during sunshine
rivers and tidal waves
white babies speaking in tongues
after sucking black breast
did you hear of the slave master
trying to rape
woman black
and she laughed and laughed
turned to jackal, to donkey
then she turned into his own daughter

Men who knocked on doors with heads tilted far left
and cords still wrapped around their necks
tongues eggplant
eyes blasted
(ya'll never heard that stuff)
but you understand
transportation was provided
first class to Paris
to those that peeled the richness of their people
renamed our magic, voodoo
cloaked us in embargoes
signed over revolution and land
our families pay rent on homes that they own
they want our children to pay for the freedom their parents took
want to open Gap factories and Disney pays my aunt three dollars a day
for fourteen hours
fills my cousins with birth control
empties them with hysterectomies

They're not afraid of us anymore
now that they got their language tattooed to the roof of our mouths
got us singing gospels to heaven
we forgot we were heaven
they're not afraid of us anymore
got us running to bleach

but ain't all of us scared

We've got spirits forcing us off roofs
making us find our wing span
practicing camouflage on the A train
and finding herbs in Prospect Park at four a.m.

We've got little Clinton dolls in our coach purses
if we could only find some hair samples. . .
masking drum beats in hip hop
spells written between the lines of text books

I now dance on Clinton's head with one red shoe and one blue

Women's Legs
Mirlande Jean-Gilles

Women's legs are so skinny
Our legs like poles and sticks when you look at
all the weight we have to carry

But we walk

We teeter sometimes
when we first get back on our feet
Shaky like thirty year-old men in high heels
But miraculously we walk
Some of us even run on those pencil thin legs
that hold up hips that have been pushed open
Old ugly hearts held together with rubber cement
and chewing gum
but still work
still love

Raped on Monday
get up for finals Tuesday
Abortion Saturday
Sex on Wednesday
Beaten today, nursing tonight

cook dinner tomorrow
laughing in the morning

What tiny little legs we got
How do they hold us up?
And why aren't we resting more?

Eyes heavy with tears
Dams break from so much water
Voices that can shatter crystal
cause eardrums to pull into themselves

We carry back packs filled with our insecurities and past blames

How is it that we don't fall?
don't even trip

Women's legs need to be
tree trunk big
200 feet
3000 years old
Wrapped in bronze bracelets
golden anklets

A tropical desert of Joshua trees
Head wraps of apple, mango and gingko
Church bells would be our toe rings

Redwoods, Oaks and Sequoias

When we are tired
all would stop
We would shake our feet/roots
free of dirt
Soaking them in oceans together
Give each other pedicures with boulders
Paint our faces blue
make you think we were the sky
our eyes moon
cloudy eyelashes

We'd wear broadleaf dresses of coconut
palms and ferns.

We would not commence seasonal changes
until we are pleased
We would block the sun
with our leafy green Afros
Until altars have been placed at our feet

Heavy legged women with eagles nest in our ears
and wind in our pockets

Our menses would cause red tornadoes
and those watching would say
"and the sky turned crimson, contracted
and then it rained blood."
All would stop when oak tree women bled

Still, they would try to chop us up
cut us down
carve paper from our flesh
make living room furniture with our hands and backs
Suck syrup from our mouths

Then, we would turn into the Argentinean Ombu tree
whose wood cannot be burnt
bark cannot be cut down

What will the world do then?
With women who stand only as women
Not as dinner, not as skin for drums
or a convenient hole to lay your privates

What will the world do when we get the proper
fitting for our legs and name ourselves
Ombu

Awa/Ahwe

Gene Emanuel

Fresh footprint in the sand
Track of the asantewa
On Amina (Akamu) grain
Where bata steps in time
With the ageless bend of the river
Purple with Oshun's dye. . .

The running waters
Flow in pyramid heart
To the open door of the sea
When Nana walks on water
Back to the groves of Ife
Wrapped in swaddling robes
The baobab shields the rebirth of Sango
Oba Koso

The rains rain stones on the barracks of the long knives. . .
The pointed spears dyed green
Piercing the expectant air. . .
Kaskadees and feathers fluttering
The wet blood of the white cock
Sperming the dry earth
Like the answer of prayers
To the ancestors
In the dust to dust

To life. . .

The sky crimson
With the blood of childbirth
Flowing from the pools
Of beginnings,
The waterfalls cascading
To the sea
            And
The footprint now merged
                    With
The sand and the sea

And
The ageless movement of the
Elemental core. . .

Crucian Time

Jeanne O'Day

Summer's equinox passes
unnoticed like a shy girl
carrying sisal bound
to her granny's,
skirting Christiansted's
columns, and taxi drivers

flip dominoes
black and white
draped chiaroscuro
in shade and light
dust and sea.

Day and night share
their orbits split in two
by a minute's sunset
like an egg cracked
on an iron skillet;
life sizzles
around the edges.

Ishmael

Raymond Ramcharitar

You are going to have a son and
you will name him Ishmael. But your son
will live like a wild beast. He will be against everyone
And everyone will be against him.
Genesis 17: 11

For years you waited, looking for signs, and then,
Like a child, you wished it out of nothing.
Beginning, you fed it, stroked its joints with oil
To make them supple. The strength would come
As years and seasons passed, leaving their wholeness:
The completeness of a tree ascending the air:
A life artificing life. You did not
Know this at the start—that in creating it, it
Created you, as a child does; although
You knew it was not a child.

Still, you nurtured it, let your blood warm it;
You let your heart, in time, become its heart,
And listening to your heart, you heard its song.

It was not a child, but like a child you knew
The time was coming: its limbs had begun to grow,
Wings had formed, its life was slowly unfurling,
Separate from you, along a path you
Could not see or follow. Until you saw
The inexorable claws, and the heaviness
Of its existence draw it away from you.
You watched, like Daedalus, the fragile wings
Flutter, saw the hungry eyes imprison
The sunlight in its brutish memory.

And thus, when the time came,
Your knowledge was useless, for although you knew
It was not a child, you gave it your heart. Your blood
Was mixed with its brute's blood. And when it fell,
Your blood made the sea the colour of wine.

Listen, I have tasted the sea water:
The purple echoes of rage still resound.

Legacy

Elizabeth Veronica Best

Here in this corner of circumstance,
where children bear children,
and fathers abdicate
Grand Mammas still reign
sustained by peddling, trusting,
sacrificing and meeting-turning;
the cookup, the cuss-out
and the necessary balm
of redemption songs.

Fighting her war on want,
My Mamma fired peace-seeking prayers,
bombarding the courts of heaven
from her depression in the cuss-cuss bed.
Often, before the lamp oil burnt out,
or she swept fatigue into the Everlasting Arms,
I'd slip away,
her hollow hopes sprouting heart
in the womb of my dreams.

Dusk always closed in on attempts
to redeem the bitter pain
of orphaned youth
sown on sugar plantations -
those fertile loins of this land
conceived to spawn coppers
for a miserly crown;
ploughed and planted
to puff the chests of the dead.

Every foreday morning witnessed
that ancestral pride bending
with each starched fold of
"lilly white" belly-band;
tying itself into a calico tiara;
turning to the twisted resilience
of a common head pad-
ritual, survival -
preparing for the field.

Cutting, piling, loading,
heading to transport me
beyond her station,
this squat collossus
cleared sure-footed tracks
to alternative futures
in the wake
of each wall of cane
that fell to her bill.

Master of sickle and hoe,
jucking board and heater
serving the least among
Her Majesty's servants
communing in estate parlours -
protected seats of plenty
perched like ripened nipples
atop this island's choicest mounds—
she nurtured a vengeance quiet, constructive:

Brute tough she raised me for purpose.
Tamarind rods flayed in threes,
rained stripes of correction
on sins hinted and committed;
serrated glances trimmed experience
with a thousand "don'ts";
no hugs, no kisses softened my falls
"cawz, when yuh don' look whe' yuh duh guh
yuh bong to tumble upsided dong."

From the education seeping
through these cracks of wrath
this much I gleaned:
felled or fallen
I, Black Village Woman
must always rise
harvesting the dust,
hug my sore, battered selves
and dance despite the pain.

So challenging the odds
we managed,
she and I,

emotions and fortunes
see-sawing in time
until I, the child,
rose one unexpected dawn
to mother the woman
in her second childhood.

Never discarding embarrassment
with the bath water
I tip-toed solemnly
through the enclosing daze
of her eighth decade
in helpless vigil, pacing
the tread of consciousness
as it limped
towards the end of its route.

She leads me now along highways
she never knew existed,
cheers as I clasp the
chalice of independence,
prompts me to preside in halls
where her voice would have shrivelled
retreating to the threshold of silence,
her ancient, untutored self
fading to a shadow in the corner.

So as long as I live
My Grand Mamma shall never die:
I utter her name
from a well of tears
fly her memory
on every field of conquest.
Regrets constantly jostle gratitude
yet I know I've been blessed
for having lived with Mamma Hess.

Flute-man, Whey Part you Dey?

Mark Sylvester

> *In honor of poet Senya Darklight*
> *who perished while mountain climbing*

Flute-man, down-to-eart'-man
    de mountain still sing sankey
an' valley sleep
    while star play Peeping Tom at night.
humming-bird play accordion
    for lizard to dance de Trembles,
banana-quit skip from hibiscus
    to bougainvillea, lickin' pollen,
bee busy buzzin', while mother-in-law-tongue
    shick-shack, an' wind gustin'
force branch to rub shoulder an' moan.

T'under implodin' each time fly
    get tangle in spider-web,
de coo-coo bird still call de sun
    to rise in dreams of Kilimanjaro;
we still hear shouts of silence
    in de shade of de baobab,
school children still "walk de tight-rope
    wid no net below," an' babies
scream in teenage womb,
    prison door spin round an' round
an now job more scarce dan tortle-shell.

We miss de riddims of yo' flute
    dat mek burd'n drop as de breddren
stan' in ovation,
    we miss seein' de sun rise
in yo' eyes, an' hear dat laugh
    dat firs' start like a chokin' cough
den brekkin' loose like Niagara fallin'
    sprayin' mist of tikkle on each list'ner.

We miss de layman wisdom
    dat flow easy like ripe banana peelin'.

Mark Sylvester

Yo' voice still echo
     in each twis' of de wind!
Flute-man, down-to-eart'-man
     whey part you dey? whey part you dey!

miranda: the first voicing

Elaine Savory

i

"Europeans, you must open this book and enter it. . .it is you
who will feel furtive, nightbound and perished with cold."

> Jean Paul Sartre, Preface to *The Wretched
> of The Earth* by Frantz Fanon.

i am old now & burdened with memories.

four hundred years
& my young arrogance

& beauty merely
the salt bone of the wind
flaying my understanding.
no more balm of forgetting.
i look for pretty words &
find only a tunnel of mirrors.

this face-mask of old lies
i have never looked behind:
what is there left of me?
i can only hear caliban's
words in my words.
i am a small stone
on the parched floor
listening to the dam burst.

i am double-divorced from language
& an outsider. loss & denial
my brittle companions whose shapes
silently hollow out
my chill cell of remembering.
i speak without speaking
as through flowing water & dying
& i nurture my fantasy that some
bizarre & stubborn fragment of love survives
a frail leaf clinging to a withered stem.

i was careless once, i could speak
comfort, quietly lethal as butter.
i loved my coils of blonde curls;
dazzlingly shed & reclaimed my skin.
i was an ordinary petulant girl,
a doorway for the wind.

i want to tell now. & the
drawing of feeling. in a
language which has faced & understood.
i have no nation. no breathing language
only my father's words rotting in the shell
& my own brutal & inarticulate misgivings.

ii

> ". . .I have bedimmed
> The noontide sun, called forth the mutinous winds
> . . .graves at my command,
> Have waked their sleepers, oped, and let 'em forth,
> By my so potent art. . ."
> William Shakespeare, *The Tempest*

four hundred long & mostly lying years:
this island's green & turbulent graces
cut & remodelled in my father's hand.
four hundred years of silent masquerades.

like an old photograph, an old
self is a closed window, an old life
too easily lights as fable. if i believe,
i'll hear only the whores of language.

my voice is fashioned to celebrate prospero
& so i have long silenced myself
only one choice
i flower as betrayal
or swell as his savage fruit.

there have been centuries of my forgetting.
lifetimes of wandering after i betrayed my father.
i am half-crazy with lives i could never enter.

but as i stepped mischievously onto the
dangerous edge of motherless womanhood
my young skin glowing like a living marble
dusted with anticipated & unknown pleasures
i ruled my father & i tormented him.
barefoot & innermost
wielding the cruel imperative
of a young, full smile.
i grew princess of all princesses
in my father's loneliness
& no mother to rival me & jibe.

my choices always lines already interpreted.
my father sometimes conjured
me as a book & read my
unrestrained images of desires, read
longing and language hunted one another.

i learned division as i learned to speak
i was my father's son & daughter
fragile heir & summation
cause & explanation in the
guarded & fortressed name of miranda.

i harboured shrill & secret resentment
like the cruel blood of the manchineel
bitterness rooted in salt.
the motherless & wayward miranda
thought only to hold her hands empty & receive.

my father stilled the idea of his daughter
possessed it with the violence of injured spirits.

my father who smelled of spices & high rank.

iii

"You're trapped in this fantasy, that someone like him could
melt you and take you down to the thing you've lost touch
with. . ."
        Marina Warner, *Indigo*

Elaine Savory

we turned over unprotected palms
letting clear water run over back to the pale sand:
the island's sacred mornings, blue & delighted.
the coral slabs glistening greens & browns
and ochres & the crabs attentive.
caliban in his embrace & freedom of a voice
translating other worlds for me
morning after glorious morning.
the high surf shaped a barrier of sound
my father who delivered no possibility of
alternatives out of his great
magic could not hear our voices.

the skins laid down. hands over hands
scarred on sharp rock. we were copper
& sand. we were ochre & earth.
the harsh hard cliffs of the north
the island's point into ocean bare & callous
forbidden consciousness. i was constructed
freedom. my father slept on
images of my obedience.

i thought i could laugh then
enough to give the winds
sense of redrawing the
entire map of feeling.
i saw ideas turning their colours
a true anarchy in a shining air
owning themselves & nothing.

the wet cutting coral of the northern cliffs
a passage spiralled down to the mysteries
a cave the ocean devours every high tide
sweeping all sacrifices into its hungry mouth.
suddenly & all the colours of creation
the spray hot & brilliant in the uncanny sun
& caliban would draw in his breath
& bright complexities: his mother's
chest of word gems. sycorax
rainbow magician arching her brilliant
palette over the wounded &
ruined conception the island
erasing old failures

to begin new memory of endless
transformations. before the captivity of
thought, before my father jealous &
savage with half-decided fear.

iv

"She is the white light that paralysed your mind, that led you
into this confusion."
                    Derek Walcott, *Dream on Monkey Mountain*

just before flame & purple sunset.
caliban was tapestries of words figured
extraordinary silks of imagining full of singing
in his mother's words which i knew then
& which wrapped us in
possibilities of transition.
the moment lay on my tongue
& i began to taste its many fragrances.
but he said, first in his words,
then in my father's harsher fabric
i helped him fold into his inner sense

there is no more loss worse than this.
& i knew he spoke of sycorax.

& i demanded speak to me.
words cannot be demanded.
he looked for the rainbow & for
me every word was opaque & my tongue
sought weapons & i allowed a shadow
between the sun & my longing.
i spoke & sycorax held my words
smothered & tied &
dropped into deep water
carried on the high white waves
silent & divorced
& i could not
say.

v

"It was the Atlantic this side of the island, a wild-eyed, marauding sea the
colour of slate, deep, full of dangerous currents, lined with row upon row of
barrier reefs, and with a sound like that of the combined voices of the drowned
raised in a loud-unceasing lament—all those the nine million. . .who. . .had
gone down between this point and the homeland lying out of sight to the
east."

Paule Marshall, *The Chosen Place, the Timeless People*

outwards into memory sycorax
gathered her daughter. voices &
language singing through space. but
i only turned the shells that i was given,
turned them & turned them, listening.
i could not hear the echoes of the dead:
my silence was too brazen & too long.
i write their names where ocean
washes them: stiff fingers cannot
shape connection. i am brought here.
i come to this bare beach & beg for
words: the crowds of memories refuse them.

behind my life the ships furl sails,
there out beyond this violence of waves,
where poetry is ended. this is plain:
lives which i might have loved, cast overboard.
the ships glide on to market. veils &
gasps of tears do nothing. the dead
speak only as the waves can breach
masks & amnesia.
                              a faint voice a footfall.
who can bring back the dead? what
penance buries them with honour?

i set my white hand at the water's edge:
touching brings tears & in them maybe
history. i must wait here lonely & afraid
a novice of surrender ignorant of vows
my breath caught in the voices of the waves.

vi

". . .I pitied thee,
Took pains to make thee speak, taught thee each hour
One thing or other: when thou didst not—savage!—
Know thine own meaning, but wouldst gabble like
A thing most brutish. . ."
                    William Shakespeare, *The Tempest*

old i am now & burdened with memories.

harm reaps such unbridled interest
doubling & tripling & quadrupling its power.
i remember although for these numb centuries
i have refused to have to remember
my father's cobalt eyes clouded with
questions his voice razored with insecurity.
under the scarlet fire-tree's blossoms
under the warm dangerous kisses of the wind
amidst thin bush on the faded clay mountain
rivered with self-doubts. behind my father's cabin
his wooden palace: blinding authority:

i denied, with my own words, my brother.

miranda, palest and youngest & most dangerous
thinking to enter caliban's ancient knowledges
without surrender. to design new gods
without giving libation. i turned from
shadows thousands deep in my blue eyes
afraid of strong light. as if it were possible—
though i have bitterly learned
over many lifetimes
skin sometimes tells you
little of its stored secrets
we do not always serve
the new lifetime in the same surface
honour it or not.

Elaine Savory

vii

"So the god, / mask of dreamers / hears lightnings / stammer,
hearts / rustle their secrets."

Kamau Brathwaite, *The Arrivants*

strict white & starched jewels
out of the thin rain & the mud.
painted roof sheltering celebration
then the shone bell &
shell trumpet: so the belonging
is traced & signed

fragrance for cleansing
clove cinnamon glimmering nutmeg
bowled in a young girl's hand.
threads unwinding the step
back to first self unfolded
from the chill eyes of the week
only guarded by Sunday's freedom.
& the frangipani & oleander
for clear eye & fierce touch
when past centuries & promises
leap up in the incense smoke.
weary & divided child of the spirit
faded & weathered the blood diverted
brought for this witness.
i stand apart in unaccustomed
purity of garments hold
long fractured connections
buried shards of old angers
& the wound is empty & grey.
origins of silence lit like
candles with flames &
they know me through
spirit eyes hard laughing
not yet not yet not yet:
blessing only to strengthen.

consciousness drop by crimson drop
may bring colour & feeling
pain in the long-dead flesh
so they determine:

weave again alone the
long frayed hope of
rediscovery & so begin
the journey back to source

the ancient
smiles of
elders. &
i must speak:

i have been the raindrop
which contaminates the leaf
i have been the ray
which must devour the cell
i have been the silent
wishing to decipher
the lost alphabet of connections
half-erased with bloodstains
carved with names
there is dust on the world &
it no longer shines
& i am old & remarkably burdened with memories.
& worse i am always outsider
so i can only watch
the children of our savageries
nurture their stubborn plantings injured selves
until they are choked & exhausted
with the elaborate fatigues of hating
children of our cleverness
& failure gaming with words
hoping for signs & beginning
to despair of all signing

there is only
to testify &
to acknowledge
& finally to know
four hundred years of lifetimes
try as i might
to image easily enough
to escape.
there is
only to gather

scattered word
embers so they may
light questions.
dark & pale. a
thought who is a
woman holds my hand.

it is for me to turn &
confront that prison:

prospero's daughter.

Note

For those who may not know Shakespeare's play *The Tempest*, its Caribbean iconography or Kamau Brathwaite's important development of both, it is necessary to say a word about the characters in the following poems. Each one has an incarnation which is slightly different in England, Africa, the Caribbean and the United States. Some of these have been already established by other writers.

Prospero: Ruler of the island, which he took away from Sycorax and her son Caliban. The European prince and the great magician; in Caribbean iconography, the white colonialist and slave-owner.

Miranda: The daughter of Prospero, the European princess; in the Caribbean, the cossetted white lady of the plantation. Raised by her father alone, with Caliban as her companion, until as she claimed to her father in Shakespeare's play, Caliban tried to seduce her. In Marina Warner's novel, *Indigo*, Miranda also has several lifetimes, and most recently is an upper-middle-class English woman.

Caliban: In Shakespeare's play the eloquent slave, fully aware of Prospero's abuse of power. In the Caribbean, the enslaved and dispossessed but defiant and subversive African man, as in the work of Kamau Brathwaite, George Lamming and others.

Sycorax: In Shakespeare's play, merely a few mentions, but in Kamau Brathwaite's work, the powerful source of anticolonial creativity which sustains both Caliban, and also the African woman, Caliban's woman, Caliban's sister, named Stark. Sycorax is an important presence in Marina Warner's *Indigo*.

Four Sisters

Laurence Lieberman

Under fair sky,
taking my first hours-long brisk hike
from Carriacou's remote south beach northeast
back to Hillsborough, I set out just before sunset and clamber
past twilight into deep dusk
in so few minutes, it seems, and wouldn't you know, my flashlight
goes dead just as the road narrows.
Fear not, my friends had mocked. *If you but follow*
the main drag, you can't
get lost. But in tar-black dark, who can tell weed-riddled
patchup of road
from side paths
that fork off, at intervals. So I find myself coming upon
abrupt dead end,
and know myself for lost. . .Peering through woods-
brake, I can make out dim auto
headlamps in the distance. I cut through the little patch of forest
and make a dash to head off
the vehicle. The mercifully slow driver, so stunned to see
a lost foreign pale-skinned gent   bareheaded
in rolled-up trousers   come rocketing
from roadside brush

like startled quail
into his bearing-down-hard trajectory,
brakes to a snappy halt. The front sidedoor
flies open to offer me a lift before I can think to thumb-beg
for it, all welcome blurted
in the gravelly rasp of aged voice (*O if ever turn of tongue*
incarnated pure pulse of helper's
hand, the magic of utterance now felt so). . .Soon
installed beside one
very thickly bifocal-laden man bowed over the wheel,
those heavy specs
drooped so low
on his nostrils, a small miracle of balance keeps them
from sliding off
to the floor of the Fifties-style VW beetle.
Father Mulligan and Father

73

Sheehan, both Irish, are co-priests of the Roman Catholic Church, here.
What with Sheehan off-isles
this month, my new helpmate Mulligan divides his squeezed time,
about equally, between church duties
and building, he alone sole architect
and contractor

for all church
construction or restorative labors
in Carriacou and neighbor-isle Grenada,
but never too busy to rescue a lost lamb just strayed away
from the flock. *Yours truly,*
do you mean? No verbal reply, but he squints a yes-nod. Peeps,
at last, from two tiny women
hunkered down small in backseats, so noiseless
before now, I wonder
if they held their breaths. *Are you two with the Church?*
obtusely I ask,
two nuns, both
out of Habit, garbed in drab loose ash-colored smocks
and beige pullover
sweaters. More nods, in tandem. *And which Faith*
do you espouse?. . .O Roman
Catholic, this nation's passion and High Calling. Ours, as well. . .
Do you know Mother Theresa,
young fellow? Mulligan interjects. For all answer, my jaw
drops open. *These two are HER children,*
he exults. *O my, you're her DAUGHTERS,*
I sigh (holding

down a fluttery
gasp). *Indeed not, we're meer SISTERS!*
voices rising to a brittle staccato now.
They arrived here just last month, *Four Sisters* ferried out
together by cheap freight-
barge carrying huge cargoes of rice and beans direct from India
(that numberless bevy of sisters,
too, *a crop* of sorts), the other pair of Church
Ladies from their elite
small quorum now resting in the church annex that Father
Mulligan himself
built last summer
for their troop's harborage. *Where is your home?* I ask,

                    still not letting it
            sink in. *O here, wherever a challenge to our Faith*
                and Mission is strongest. We set
    sail from our City of Birthright, Calcutta, some six weeks ago.
                As it happens, these women
        had never before left their native Asian terrain, and given
            the likely scope of island-nurturing project
                    they've just begun, they may never go
                        back to Calcutta. . .

                        Father, don't miss
                your turn, murmurs the near loquacious
            Sister Esmeralda, tapping his shoulder
        to signal the precise instant for him to take a sharp left
                at the narrow side-road
    forking through a tall archway to the churchyard. *The entry gate*
                is just here, she softly chirps.
            More shoulder nudgings. He seems to look beyond
                        the gate, or above it,
            as if it's a blank void—but follows her lead, even so.
                        I hear a faint
                rustle & scrape,
            whilst he grazes front fender on the brass gatepost.
                        The two Nun zealots
            exchange wary glances. I can see they've muddled
                through such minor collisions
    before, though I sense Esmeralda's struggle to ward off an impulse
                to seize the wheel from him. . .
        Parting words, we four now standing in a circle beneath
            the bright streetlamp: Father Mulligan
                    turns my book over and over, squinting
                        hard to descry

                    tallish letters
            of my title. Those milky-white lenses
    magnify the print just enough. *Ah, GOD'S*
MEASUREMENTS, he rattles off, fondly inviting me to Sunday
                High Mass in the next breath.
Now the women are thumbing pages, asking a few routine questions
                    about my year in Japan—the size
            and beauty of the giant Buddhas. . .When they first
                    have some leisure time,
        they hope to read my poems, which cue prompts me to ask,

                    75

shyly, *How long do*
you mean to stay
in Carriacou? Forever! Dipa beams back, without pause.
We shall never leave
this place. Always there will be four of us here.
The whole flock—perhaps two dozen
Women of the Cloth—will be shuffled about, rotated from isle
to isle of the Grenadines
and beyond, like a portable lending library of Lady Clerics!
Always, others of the Faith will take our place.
In Fours. No matter which, we're all the same
One. Four in One.

Nearing Sixty

E. A. Markham

for Eudora

i

Two weeks here and time to depart. The 5 a.m.
cockerels, lurid as painting
at the start of the holiday, now stitch patterns
of sound round auditioning dogs and crickets
as if to stress some theme in this quilt of remembrance:
if they knew of your complaint, the hostess seems to say,
they'd mute this third world welcome. The illness, though,
sounds like a boast to prompt a chorus.

Nearing sixty: I imagine it in letters,
less threatening than numerals whose lack of flourish
and curtsy-like something harsh not softly
counting—prod you to revisit stretches
of life underlived. O, for Walcott's one-sentence poem
at nearing forty, managing, in the end without bitterness
or pity, to rhyme sleep with weep. There will be a party
when the time comes. I am packed now, again,
for England, looking neither forward, as in '56
nor backward through a life skirting comedy—
though the jokes, the jokes have gone missing!
England, then, for the *festschrift*, friends rounded up,
their forced cheerfulness making you stutter;
brave, greying heads, somehow lyric and dignified
as if saved from a wreckage. Here are the pioneers
who discovered no new land to rename
after decades of travelling. Drink, then, to the attempt,
to near-misses, and check that something which you might call
the ship's log is written up in our script.

I'm thinking sixty can't be where you disembark
with accountants from England and German bankers
whose native thrift balloon into magic Pacifics
grass-skirting young bodies, or in mind-swept tuscanies
beyond Provence where my poolside prejudice
twenty-five years ago rejected, in short lines
and in narratives more indulgent such late, life-weary

resting places. For I, too, may have planted a brick
here or there and watched it grow, like unearned income, into villa,
casual as the thought of travelling to Australia.
(A mistake, then, to have travelled to Australia.)
I can see us standing here, drink in hand, children
of friends itching to know when duty is, in duty, done.

So it must be here, back here, the island of origin.
A Sixty in good shape, to be remembered as simply fading
and distant, not gaga and twisted into some joke-recycling life-
form due to residence abroad. Not like Uncle George,
back from Panama in the '50s with his friend Rodney,
before we knew men loved men. Islands cannot sleep
in case they vanish in the night: watchdogs
will worry any bone seasoned abroad till the neighbours
flesh it new; and the story of our travels will stand
retelling. From Boston to Stockholm; PNG and the Forbidden
City, you bring relief from familiar Canada and Britain;
though the Brother who soldiered in Africa upstages you still.
Once, like a new comic, you did the rounds
seeking audience outside the rum shop or with yard characters
under a tree, folksy, as in a Selvon story. Now home is a test:
hurricanes and volcanoes have checked our progress, exxing
out certainties: this friend, well-housed in another's home laments
life in the shelters. This stains the talk. Gone is the League Table
of advantage for those who left the island, so we prick
the bubble of our ambition—and did you hear
the one about the girl in the supermarket, her hat at an angle?
Ah, it was worth travelling the world to see that hat!
Your stories of cervical spondycosis from 40 years of manual
typing (or from railway portering) maintain the post-modern note.

ii

But here is discovery, magical as Columbus, and
with hindsight, aiding us to treasure what is found.
I am here by accident, calling on someone elsewhere.
And there she is, a girl in a dress bleached
like washday making you nostalgic.
Her face, uncreased, should be our calendar, absence
of teeth not spoiling the line. Something for the journal.
She tells the story too perfect for a book.
Propositioned seventy years ago, she almost blushes,

by my father, she has survived the generation intact.
(She might have said yes, said yes too late.)
A found mother: no disloyalty to a mother who in winning out
must have suffered from her triumph; Wish you were here, too.
Two mothers; what luck, as if to renew my apprenticeship
as son—and this time it will be better, better.
She is like a flower ashed in the garden between Eden
and after-life. I balance flattery and apology;
(What precision of speech! 'I'm not too lonely, I listen
to the voices from the radio and the television') and recall
a dream of my sister, skipping, young, and of my grandmother
materializing as a baby yet to talk: This makes me cautious.
For my eyes are open; and this mother lives alone;
and you can't assume that friends, scattered on four continents,
will assemble for a birthday.

Special Section:
New Poems by Olive Senior

Olive Senior is the author of two books of short stories, *Summer Lightning and Other Stories*, (which won the Commonwealth Writer's Prize in 1987) and *Arrival of the Snake-Woman and Other Stories* (1989); non-fiction works, such as *A-Z of Jamaican Heritage* (1983) and *Working Miracles: Women's Lives in the English-speaking Caribbean* (1991); and three collections of poetry, *Talking of Trees* (1985), *Gardening in the Tropics* (1994), and *Discerner of Hearts* (1995). She was also editor of *Jamaica Journal* (from 1982-87) and throughout her life has been a strong proponent of women's literature and Jamaican culture in general. Most recently she has been living and teaching in Canada and England.

Moon

I'm walking on this dark path overhung with hibiscus, bougainvillea,
when suddenly, an opening to the sky, and in my face, this great, big,
overpowering moon, in silver. Thank you, Moon, for showing your most
dazzling self tonight, dimming the stars, seducing me from gloomy thoughts,
from citylight. I know it's your best face because each month
I watch you grow fat, then waste away on some celestial diet
before you disappear. No mystery there. I know your ways.
Soon a new you so svelte and trim will start coming round again
—until you lose control and gorge to almost bursting.
I can tell by your patina on what you are feasting. This month
it's the metallic you, with hint of quicksilver, pewter, antimony.
At other times, there's the warmth of liquid amber, of honey.
Though you have never failed us yet, you tantalize with the uncertainty
of never knowing how big you'll get. That makes you
almost human. Not like that Sun who acts as if he's so divine.
I know comparisons are odious, dear Moon, but such self-discipline
is hard to stomach. He comes showing the same predictable face
day after day: no fat, no shrinkage, no blemish. He does get a bit red
and wobbly some afternoons (bad-minded people say, from drink!).
I'd like to think it's just that sometimes the old fuddy-duddy
can't wait till he's out of sight to change into his old red flannel shirt
and relax by doing a two-step.

Blue Magic Carpet

Driving up
           mountain trails
                to Cinchona
I'm not feeling
          the punishment
                of that dirt track
I'm not watching
          the curves
                nothing scares me
nothing
          not the precipice
                falling away
look way down
          not altitude
                look up there
nothing scares me in these mountains
          not even
                you leaving
to rock bottom I've fallen already
          see down there
                through undergrowth
dark as umbra
          look down

Then at the last bend
          as we enter the garden
                slowing down by the sinister Blue Gum:
Look Up!
          The tone of your voice makes me look
                Can't stop
going Oh!
          I'd forgotten Agapanthus
                Hydrangea
famed blue hillside at Cinchona in May every year
          Now I'm touched
                Is that why you brought me
5000 feet plus
          up here?

Can't stop leaping out to fall on this carpet: Agapanthus
Hydrangea.   It's the acid that does it   turns it blue
they all say.   Can't stop my own acid leaching away
To blue up this carpet   some more

Thinking   (for the first time in my life)
Thinking   I'm going to be alright
Thinking   The higher I climb the sweeter the air
Thinking the blues are getting lighter year by year.

Missing

The last time I went home they told me you were missing.
For the first time since I'd known myself, you were not there.

For one so home-bound, who could have foreseen
such a dramatic ending: Missing Person. Presumed Dead.

Village fiddler, your playing was always out of tune.
Your choice of instrument that creaking violin: What

was it signalling? The ne'er-do-well? The one who failed
to make the grade? The only one who stayed?

Yet, your discordant life played out, I was amazed to find
you hadn't passed through like a false note, a broken string.

You remained a vibrating source of conversation
an endless susuration. With the police indifferent,

your poverty-stricken neighbours hired a van
to take them on their own investigation across the river

to the rumoured scene of the crime, for they believed
you had been murdered. Theories were rife:

- *You know how he facety when he tek up his waters.*
- *He did get money so he boasy that day.*

Why had you taken that bus at all?
Where were you headed?

In a life devoid of excursions did you know
you were finally setting out to be tripped up by your fate?

Leaving home like that, you have missed so much:
Mass Dick's funeral, Tennie migrating, Pearlie and baby too,

Miss Carmen's husband dead. So many departed.
The young ones sit and wait. Not in the expectation

of any return. Waiting has become an occupation.
A permanent state. Abandonment the theme of this new life.

One day, I thought I heard you, Jumbieman,
unburied wandering spirit playing an unstrung fiddle

headed our way. Miss D who is the oldest person I know said:
Nah, is you hearing bad. Ol' time sinting done weh

Not even duppy bodder wid we now.
Yes, it's Version Time. Lyrics and licks. A life too raucous

for anyone to hear ghostly fiddlers again. Not you. Not Tambu.
Not Jonkannu. Not silenced Gumbay.

O Tambu you come back
but wha de use?

You come back but
wha de use?

Olive Senior

Leaving Home

one day, strength (from
where, you don't know) to aim
for the opening, to say: I am leaving.
To walk to the edge of your feeling.
To load up with guilt (not a word
from the ones at the threshold). Not
a word! You keep walking. Down
the dirt track, to the lane, to
the street, to the highways of
the world. You alone. Not yet stunned
by the brightness. Not by hardness
of stone, of the pavement. No.
You say: I could get used
to the lightness.
                    Till the day
you're snared by another sensation:
on a hilltop, at that, you find yourself
drowning, a movement of ebbing
and flowing. You recognise early
(or too late) that you failed to detach
from that mooring.

Always, cruelty of choice.

Here's the knife.

Yourself:
        Executioner
Midwife

Rejected Text for a Tourist Brochure

"I saw my land in the morning
and O but she was fair"
        M. G. Smith. "Jamaica"(1938)

1
Come see my land

Come see my land
before the particles of busy fires ascend;
before the rivers descend underground;
before coffee plantations
grind the mountains into dust; before
the coral dies; before the beaches
disappear

Come see my land
Come see my land
And know
That she was fair.

2
Up here, the mountains are still clear.
After three weeks, I heard a solitaire.
Down there, the mountains are clear-cut
marl pits. Truckers steal sand from beaches,
from riverbeds, to build another ganja palace,
another shopping centre, another hotel
(My shares in cement are soaring). The rivers, angry,
are sliding underground, leaving pure rockstone
and hungry belly.

3
No Problem, Mon. Come.
Will be one hell of a beach party.
No rain. No cover. No need to bring
your bathing suit, your umbrella.

Come walk with me in the latest style.
rockstone and dry gully. Come for the Final
Closing Down Sale. Take for a song
the Last Black Coral; the Last Green Turtle;
the last Blue Swallow-tail (preserved behind glass).
Come walk the last mile to see the Last Manatee.
the Last Coney, the Last Alligator, the Last Iguana Smile.

Oh, them gone already? No Problem, Mon.
Come. Look the film here.
Reggae soundtrack
and all. Come see
my land. Come see my land and know, A-oh,
that she was fair.

Lost Tropic

Friend, I'm in a bad way, my skin
leaches out more tropic every day
like flood-prone mountain soil.

Left behind: uncompromised bones
like volcanic stones on hillsides.
Waiting. For Thunder.

Today, though, no rain. The Sky Shepherds
have corralled their flocks.

SHORT FICTION

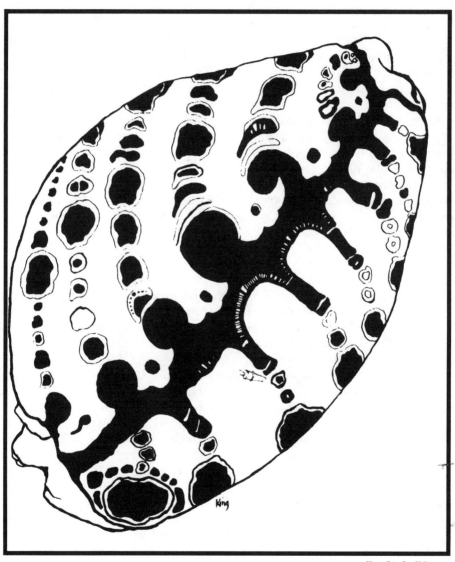

Judith King

The Horse at Albertine Hall

Susan Brown

The way we came to have a horse was because the boy known to us simply as Young King, lived at the low quarters of Albertine Hall on the west end of St. George Island, and stole our bicycle repeatedly, though the bicycle was close-chained and padlocked to the genip tree in our yard a mile up the hill road at Lookout Point. Somehow, Young King released and rode the stolen bicycle along the sea road everyday after school where we'd be sure to see him. We'd stop, accuse him of having our bike, and Young King would cheerfully agreed the bicycle was ours, but would not let go of the handlebars until we paid him 50 cents to retrieve it. This we did until one day, after we had paid more than the old bicycle was worth, we found it in the road outside Albertine Hall, run over by a quarry truck, and Young King himself arguing with the destroyed bike as if it was a live thing that had betrayed him.

At the low quarters of Albertine Hall, Young King lived in an exotic community of animals and people sharing a quadrangle of half-stone, half-wood, once slave quarters, where okra and plumbago, banana and mango grew against old walls smudged with cooking fires which sent up quite indecent smells. Even with eyes closed, you could follow your nose to Albertine Hall, lured by strange smelling smoke rising from compound fires burning the goat or young pig you saw trotting along the road only yesterday. For years, I tried unsuccessfully to trace the pungent smells floating out of Albertine Hall's low quarters to some imagined offensive place coupled with dangerous desire, where I might hallucinate while eating the darkly herbed meat turning on the spit, have it take me into the low rooms at Albertine Hall's old slave quarters where generations of immoralities would hysterically laugh at my white skinned innocence.

A cloud of possession enclosed the community along the sea road at the foot of the hill on top of which, on a combed and curried, well-tended lawn, Great Albertine Hall sat, secure behind its three-hundred year old wall.

Inhabitants of the low quarters often strolled, or sat on the sea road itself. They shifted to let our truck pass, for they knew who we were, but other than Young King, did not greet us.

A bit of sandy beach belonged unquestionably to Albertine Hall's low quarters. The beach was haphazardly guarded by a few sea grape trees and thin strips of barbed wire so light against the western sky as to be almost invisible and once, I answered a curious call to walk on the sand. Too late I saw the barbed wire, too late saw the beach peopled with men, some poking at sand mounded into small volcanoes, other men splayed seductively across overturned fishing boats, but I was already caught in the vortex of their primal atmosphere and spread apart the wire when instantly, a barb shoved itself into my shoulder, tearing my blouse and my arm ran with blood. I backed away, grimaced, said nothing. The dark eyed men flashed looks one to the other, said nothing, continued to poke at the pitted volcanoes where charcoal smoldered.

One day, on our way home from school, Young King rode out of the field at Albertine Hall on a lean white horse. Long of nose and dainty of foot, the horse was sort of white, not princely white, more crumpled sheet white, yellowing at the edges. Her mane was streaked dirty blonde as was her tail. She had a showgirl look, uncombed, windblown, free spirited.

Young King offered to sell her to us to replace the ruined bicycle.

We gave Young King ten dollars cash for her. The horse was gentle with the children, unexpectedly lovely in the moonlight on the hill up at our house on Lookout Point. In night air so quiet, while lying in bed, I heard the horse outside, cropping grass, heard her snort with satisfaction. So spectral did this horse appear, we named her Shadow.

While we were at school, Shadow was kept lightly tethered in the yard at our house. She seemed to enjoy life on the hill, until one day, we discovered Shadow carried within her some of the low quarter's primal blood, and every so often she answered its call, slipped her tether and trotted along the sea road back to Albertine Hall's low quarters. The horse seemed to need the scrubby fields below the Great Albertine lawn; fields alive with colts and mares, goats and chickens, crickets, children, dogs, shouts and laughter, all held in the mysterious smoke of Albertine Hall cooking fires.

Every so often, Young King darted out of that smoke, ran alongside our homecoming truck, yelling, "I got you horse. She run away. I got you horse," and we had to ransom Shadow. It became another small business for Young King until one day my husband objected, and was apologetically allowed to buy a bag of charcoal as restitution.

Albertine Hall's charcoal was not for everyone. It was not for sale in stores. It was a narcotic of dreams. Its knotty pieces, used sparingly, turned a meal of common food into a dream-like feast. It was as though Albertine Hall's charcoal was alive with stories held in branches stolen from sap filled trees, or broken from well-tended bushes flowering beside the Great Albertine door. Charcoal cooked in a cave of hot sand, sand older than time, sand which took in flowers and fish, snails and bones, flesh and membrane, reflections of sky, echoes of laughter, sand constantly perfecting itself just above the reach of crystalline waves. In those waves, Albertine Hall horses stretched beneath bodies of half-naked men gripping rope bridles punishingly tight, frothing the mouths of horses, as horses and men crashed and churned through waves rocking and splashing in a tick cleansing bath. Standing on the road, outside the barbed wire, women from Albertine Hall, wearing billowy skirts printed with small flowers, held the hands of little girls in pink, and watched frenzied men and horses bathe in the sea.

Shadow never went into the sea like other horses from Albertine Hall. Instead, Shadow got pregnant.

Up at our house, we watched Shadow's belly swell, fatten, though not as much as we would have liked. We watched over her, pulled a galvanized tub of water into the buttressed shade of the kapok tree. We talked to Shadow, encouraged her, rubbed her long nose. She snorted back. We cut and brought fresh green guinea grass, served it in a pile at Shadow's feet. The children were gentle, refused to ride her now. We did not keep her tethered. Somehow it seemed wrong.

But there was something in Shadow which kept her trotting along the sea road, returning to her birthplace in the fields at Albertine Hall, to be with goats and crickets and children, to eat spiney bush, to inhale the thick hypnotic smoke of Albertine Hall's low quarters.

One evening, it was a Sunday, we left Shadow in our yard with fresh guinea grass and water while we went across the island to the movies in the old theater in Saint Olaf town.

It was Continental night at the movies, that meant films shown in English, for continentals, statesiders, Europeans. Tuesday and Wednesday were films in Spanish. Thursday, theater closed. Friday and Saturday delivered wild and booming action films for the population demanding them. Monday, a repeat of Sunday, but nobody ever went. Sunday it was, to sit in the balcony with Paco, the manager of Ludwigson's Lumber yard, to greet the local senator who also owned Delicia's Wine and Spirits. Henry and Myra Slater were always there, Eric P., the realtor, was there with his wife and two boys; Rick from Ricky's Records; the Anglican priest and the Lutheran minister and his wife sat next to Ricky.

We saw *Lawrence of Arabia*.

After the movie, after thick milkshakes sitting outside under floodlights at the Paradise Cream and Soda Shanty just outside of town, after the half hour ride home through dark hills in the rough springed truck, the children in the open bed singing into the sky, we drove into our yard and found Shadow down on her side by the kapok tree.

At first we thought she was resting, readying for the birth. Her eyes were open, belly heaving. We ran to her, stroked her neck, cooed. We implored Shadow to say something. None of us knew what to do. The vet lived back across the island, near Paradise Cream. Telephone connections were sporadic, unreliable. We convinced ourselves the birth would be natural for Shadow, she came from Albertine Hall where things were birthing all the time.

Uneasily, we went to bed.

Sometime after midnight we heard the horse cry out. We ran outside in the moonlight and watched helplessly as Shadow danced in mad circles around and around, a small gelatinous sac hanging from her as she ran around in crazy circles trying to loosen it, screaming for help we didn't know how to give.

As we watched, the sac slid, fell free. Shadow walked away.

Inside the sac curled equus, a tiny ancient form shining in mucous. We waited, stupid, powerless for Shadow to do what was needed; maybe lick open the

90

sac, maybe just rest. We did not know. Maybe our presence bothered her. We retreated behind the buttress of the kapok tree, waited for Shadow to react. But she continued to walk around and around. Equus lay stilled in the sac.

At dawn, I was awakened by Young King climbing onto our sleeping porch. "Psst. . .psst," he whispered. "Come missis, come," and with him alone I went.

Shadow lay on the luxurious hilltop lawn of Great Albertine Hall. I dropped to her, stroked her neck, lay my face against her dirty, throbbing, almost human neck. Our eyes walled to each other in terror of what had happened. Beneath the strong hairs of her coat I could feel Shadow's heart racing. I called her name over and over, realizing Shadow had walked back to Albertine Hall, but on this walk she erred. Instead of using the sea road, careless of consequences, as if she already knew her fate, Shadow had climbed the fine grassy hill of Great Albertine Hall. A short-cut maybe, a dazed confusion perhaps, or a reunion with the stallion uppermost in her mind. Or, perhaps the horse was just going home.

In the silence before dawn, as Shadow crossed the magnificent cut and curried Great Albertine lawn, someone behind the wall raised his rifle and shot.

I called Shadow's name through tears of indignation, of sadness, of hate, of regret. Then, I pulled back, my eyes filled with wonder as Shadow, flat on her side on the soft grass, suddenly began to run. Her great white figure, flat flat on her side on the velvet lawn, like an enormous articulated horse, rhythmically pulled in her legs, stretched them out, again and again in perfect gallops. Shadow began to run as fast as a white horse can run to wherever white horses go. Pulling gracefully, smoothly, with greater and greater speed she ran in place, faster and faster, flat on her side on Great Albertine lawn, lovelier than ever she ran. Then she was still.

I fell across Shadow's body, stroked the coarse neck hairs where the bullet had entered. I called her again and again, my tears mixed with Shadow's dark blood. I told her unbearable secrets to take with her, to comfort her, as anguish choked my throat.

The maid from Great Albertine Hall, a full black woman, lifted me from the horse, gathered me to her, and with a tic of her head towards the house, muttered, "That man evil, evil." She cloaked me with her words, the strength of her arm, the smell of her starched dress.

I had thought landowner power was no longer in effect on St. George Island. I was wrong. A simple, errant horse had crossed old boundaries and was violently punished, yet I found myself incapable of fighting the power of this fury, of history, of affluence. I could only stand and weep beside the dead horse.

The groundsman who had orders to shoot Shadow, could not look at me, though he knew me by name. He was not beyond knowing certain spirits will come to belabor him as well as the man who ordered the shoot.

Six field hands appeared, pulled the horse onto a canvas sling, dragged her across the lawn, marking a bloody trail down the groomed and grassy hill, past bushes that dropped fleshy leaves and crimson flowers in its wake.

W omen came silently out of Albertine Hall's low quarters, threw wash on the bush, pulled pots from the fire, took the hands of small girls and stood wordlessly on the road. Showing neither judgment nor sympathy, the women simply watched.

Half down the hill, in a sudden slide, the canvas sling escaped. Men ran, stumbled, shouted, halted the sling just short of the sea road. Frantically, men scraped the dead horse onto the canvas, pulled it across the road, past women rooted in their dresses, past mute children. The groundsman cut the barbed wire, opened the beach, the men dragged the dead horse onto the old, old sand.

Then, in cyclonic movement, the groundsman shouted orders, the men lunged forward shouting louder and louder, quicker and quicker the clamor of their voices over-riding one another as if by sheer volume their outcries could save them from the taint of evil which was visited upon the horse this day.

Alone, I walked out onto the forbidden sand, walked away from the women, away from the men, away from every place I knew, as from a great distance I heard tiny words yammering, cursing, praying, bawling injustices, tiny words I hear but did not hear, tiny words that grew bigger and bigger assaulted my ears, louder and louder, until with overpowering grunts and heaves, the men, unable to bear the silence of their burden, slid the dead horse into the sea.

Retreat

Teresa A. Cardinez

I hadn't returned home as I said I would. I told them I was over-worked and needed the rest. The children, the noise from the neighbours, the heat and confusion of Port-of-Spain would simply be too much for me. I had not taken a holiday in years, so while this was untimely and unexpected, my boss did not complain. Samuel, the junior accountant was quite capable of taking over from me.

The company was one thing, but I knew my wife would not accept my fragile excuse, that she would demand to know more. I couldn't handle that. There was too much to explain. Apart from the present matter so much had changed between us. What could I say to her? What could I say to myself?

What really possess you, boy? The times I asked myself that question and could not think of an answer! I did not need the money, even though everybody could use some extra. But it was true, I did not need or want money, strange as that may seem. I'd long stopped listening to the boys and their chasing after this or that car, that position in the firm—when it wasn't some woman, that is. I'd also learned to ignore Sandra's sighs for yet another innovation to our home—this time she wanted to add a gym. And the children—I had to admit they were spoiled. I'd done a fine job on them, always begging for the latest toy, which they usually got. No, it had not been the money. It was more—ennui. I had swindled because I was bored. But you can swindle more than just money.

The guesthouse was deserted. March was too early for school vacation and too late into the winter season. At any rate, the establishment where I was hiding out did not seem to have much of a clientele. It was an adequate place, however; it suited my purposes. I could think, do nothing if I pleased. The owner was discrete; this I could tell from my observations of the weekend activities, the little liaisons which were probably the guesthouse's main source of income outside of vacation-time; the men needn't worry about anything getting back to their wives. I observed these goings-on and remembered my own encounters. The pros and cons of such activities had never been of much concern to me, and, under different circumstances, I would have been an amused on-looker, intent on recording those names and faces which would provide interesting conversation with the guys in the office later on. Instead, my thoughts, my past, kept intruding. I would have preferred the role of observer of other lives and to forget about what awaited me in the town. But I couldn't. The events of the recent past filled my days and nights.

I fell into a routine of sorts. I would wake up early, walk on the beach, watch the jetsam left behind by the tide and the occasional crab scurrying on tiptoe across the wet sand. I liked to sit on a particular rock on the cliff and enjoy the morning from that vantage point. Eventually, when hunger began pestering me, I would have breakfast in the dining room. There were no other guests and Mrs. Panchoo, the cook, housekeeper, etc. had long given up making conversation with me. I was not the most congenial guest, especially in the first two weeks or so after my arrival. After breakfast I read, usually on the veranda, often looking up from my reading and losing myself in the ever-changing sea. That time of year the sea was soothing. It was my refuge, the respite I needed from what had surrounded me in the town, from what I had become part of. . .

II

Two a.m. and I was on my way home. The books were as balanced as they would ever be and I sat in the back of the taxi hugging my briefcase, the dry air-conditioned air settling on my skin. I was more tired than I'd realized and glad that I'd left the car at home. Still, I began now to feel a vague disquiet, which I sensed would grow into something louder, something I could not ignore. When I arrived home, the children were asleep; so was Sandra. In the bedroom the air-conditioner hummed quietly and it was cold, like the chill in my own soul. I switched on the bedside light and by its soft glow I saw that Sandra had pulled the blanket up to her neck. I looked at her as I undressed. Her hair was disheveled from sleeping but I could tell she'd had something done to it again: it was shorter and she had put curls or waves or something in it. I used to like it when she wore her hair long. I found myself thinking that she was still an attractive woman. Relaxed in sleep, the unguarded quality and softness of her expression reminded me of when we'd first met.

How fascinated I used to be by her! It was her smile that got to me when we first met at the same company, those eyes, almond-shaped, very black, teasing but uncannily astute. She knew at once the effect they had on me. Then she was an attractive brown-skinned, twenty two-year-old, with a flair for short skirts and high, very high-heeled shoes. Now she was the sophisticated executive's wife who dressed elegantly in designer clothes, knew how to accentuate her high cheekbones, and indulged in expensive haircuts.

She was sleeping soundly, her lips slightly parted, holding the blanket tightly around her. It was colder than she would have liked it to be, if she had been awake to feel it. I did not bother to turn the air conditioner down. I showered and got into bed and felt something sharp, metallic. I swore softly and threw the wretched toy onto the floor. How many times had I told Sandra I did not like the children playing in our room? I had felt tired on my way home, yet now I was wide awake. Sandra slept. I turned the radio on softly but the music was not to my taste and I did not feel like reading. I looked at Sandra and thought of waking her up. Like misery, restlessness loves company. But I dismissed the idea. What was the point?

I reached for my briefcase, which I usually kept under the bed for moments like this and took out the papers. I found the sheaf I was looking for and glanced at the list of names on the top page. Martin Fernandes. The name jumped out at me as it always did although I knew it was there and had seen it there a dozen times—a dozen times too late. I turned the page, examined the numbers, did some quick calculations, and found them correct, as I knew they would be. But I went on from page to page, working through the figures, jotting down points to draw to the attention of my secretary the next day. It was nearly four before I began to feel sleepy. Sandra would be stirring in about an hour's time, and by 5:30 she would be up and beginning her chores, getting the children up, making sure they showered before dressing, fixing breakfast and then lunch for them and herself, before she herded them into the car and off to private school and before she headed off to her job. Sandra didn't need to work, we both knew that, but she insisted and I couldn't be bothered to make an issue of it. The children needed her less and less now that they were both at school. And another child was out of the question. If having a job kept her happy, why should I complain? I was probably going to sleep through all that this morning since I planned to go in for nine. I put away my papers, turned off the light and went to sleep.

III

I was struggling with a wave. The water was dark; it was dark all around but I could see things in the water as I went down. Somehow I was able to breathe. I saw other people, heard their accusing voices: the children, Sandra, Jones, Samuel, some of the boys from the office—I didn't know them but somehow I knew who they were—and Mr. Briggs, my boss. I was being pulled away from them by the wave, protesting their accusations. Water filled my mouth, my lungs. . .

I awoke and gulped air. Sandra must have been in one of her bad moods; she had turned off the air conditioner and the room was stiflingly hot. The digital clock said 8:15. I had hardly slept and felt more tired than ever. I lay back, trying to decide whether to go in for 10 a.m. instead. No one could complain after the hours of overtime I had put in. Mr. Briggs knew me and knew my reliability. I had worked my way up on reliability—and a few right moves here and there—and had got to the position where I could take such liberties, where I could come in an hour late once in a while. Still, I dragged myself out of bed.

As I drove to work I thought out the points that would be raised at that afternoon's meeting. . .

IV

The job had been a routine one with nothing extraordinary about it, normal business practice and quite legal. We were taking away a man's livelihood but we had done this so often in the past few years. We were the receivers, simple as that.

95

"Paul, boy, I really in a bad way, try and see if you can't help me nuh. . . for the old times."

Martin had never been one to beg; this was a clear sign that he was desperate. I did not see there was much I could do. The conversation, his visit to the office embarrassed me a great deal. I suggested we go out for an early lunch: my treat.

I hadn't seen Martin since our days at university. I'd heard that he'd gone into business but it was only now with him sitting in front of me that I made the connection between him and the bankrupt company which we were about to move in on. Martin rambled on over his beer, going over the reasons why his small carpeting firm had got into its present difficulties.

"When I found out you worked for Multifinance, boy, I tell myself there might be some hope." He waited. I said that there might not be much that could be done at this stage. "I don't really know too much about your account," I said. This was untrue. After another silence, I said something about seeing what I could do.

"Just a little more time is all I need. People owe me too. As soon as they pay me I'll be able to get things back together."

"Isn't there someone who could bail you out?"

His company owed us a lot of money. Only a miracle could save him— a miracle or a big favour.

"I'll see what I can do," I said again.

It was unavoidable, we all agreed. Business was business and we had to make good on our loan to Carpet Delight. Collection would begin as soon as the arrangements could be made with the bailiffs. We moved on to other items as I shuffled my papers, shifting the accusing file out of sight.

V

The suicide still haunted me. I tried to imagine his anguish as he took that last step. He had always been intense even when as children we walked to school together, and then in secondary school when we shared desks. At university we had remained friends. Later though, we lost track of each other. He went to the States to do a business administration course; I moved from one accounting job to another until I found my niche at Multifinance.

I told myself that there was nothing I could have done. Martin had taken the way he'd felt would be least difficult for his family to face. The coroner ruled accidental death, as most drownings are ruled. I knew it was suicide. I had not been able to look him in the eye when he stopped by the day after the bailiffs moved in, his eyes red from sleeplessness, hands shaking, to find out whether there wasn't something we could still do. But there was nothing and he knew it too. Defeat was written all over his face. Leaving, he'd not even had the spirit to accuse me of not trying to help a friend.

I did not go to the funeral. His death had been too real. I imagined how it must have felt walking into the water that windy night, with the day's red flags sticking out of the sand, warning of the dangerous swells. Yet cautious Martin had gone swimming. What did it feel like as the water swallowed him, pulling him down? The thought preoccupied me. Cautious Martin had gone swimming.

VI

The phone rang shrilly. It was Mr. Briggs' secretary. Someone must have informed him I was back in town, even though I had not yet returned to work. I was wanted urgently at the office. I knew what the matter was before I got there. Samuel, that young upstart, had discovered the mistake. Someone—who?—had succeeded in hiding it with great mathematical wizardry. The payments by Carpet Delight had been in arrears, but not nearly so much as Multifinance believed. Martin's firm had not deserved those threatening letters. Receivership had been premature. Someone had diverted funds going to Carpet Delight's account. Who?

"Why hadn't you noticed this, Paul? Mr. Briggs fumed. "That's not the way this firm operates. Can you imagine if someone in the press finds out? Heads can roll over this one." Then he added, "I'm counting on you to work this one out."

VII

Maracas Bay was packed with the usual Sunday crowd. It was a blisteringly sunny day, with hardly any breeze. The sea was calm. We'd chosen a good day to bring the kids. It was our first outing as a family in a long time. Sandra was right, it was a good idea to do this once in a while, for the children, and at least they seemed to be enjoying themselves. While she busied herself getting lunch unpacked, I sipped a beer and kept an eye on them. They seemed content enough to play together on the sand now that they'd had a lengthy splash in the water.

The water still looked inviting and I decided I would have a swim by myself sometime before lunch, but not just yet. I looked over at Sandra. She was humming softly to herself as she pulled out some plastic plates from a bag, getting ready to fill them with pelau for the children. Something about her reminded me of when we first knew each other and I thought of those long-gone days when a day at Maracas was almost de rigueur for us two. Once or twice we'd sneaked off—sick-leave or something—in the middle of the week to have the place all to ourselves, to be gloriously alone with each other. She glanced up, caught my stare and returned a puzzled gaze. She started to say something, but changed her mind. It was my move. But I averted my eyes and returned to looking at Marcus and Sharri, pushing all thoughts of what used to be out of my mind. She went

97

back to putting out food for the children. While she called them for their meal and sat down to eat with them, I helped myself to another beer from the cooler and looked out at the sea once more. . .

"They ever found out who was to blame for that fiasco at work by you?" Sandra had finished her lunch and was sitting near me.

"No one is to blame, it was a genuine error."

"That's strange. . .I thought everyone was so sure that someone had swindled?"

I shrugged, looking at a group of teenagers who were playing soccer ahead of us. "So we thought, but there wasn't anything that could be pinned on any individual, so it had to have been a mistake."

"A terrible mistake. Either that or somebody covered his tracks very well. . .And that poor man. . .Didn't you used to know him?"

I took a few rapid gulps of beer before I answered. "Slightly, we were at U.W.I. around the same time."

I waited for the next question. But she spotted some friends walking by and stood up to call out to them. She walked away. I finished off the beer and headed toward the water for my swim.

The water felt good around me and I swam briskly in its welcome coolness. I swam out into the deep and paused, treading water, looking at my wife and children on the beach. They were still with Sandra's friends and seemed to be enjoying a joke or something. Sharri, that precocious daughter of mine, was busy making friends with a little girl who was with them. I floated on my back and looked up into the clear blue sky. The sun warmed me up, or perhaps it was the beer, and I began to relax. I thought about Martin. There'd be no more questions at work. Then, tired of the stillness of floating aimlessly on the gentle waves, I turned over and dived deep into the cool, clear water.

Honor

F. W. Belland

The old man, Domingo was his name, heard the argument through the partition. His daughter Caridad stridently defended him; the husband, Jorge, responded with modulated statements of reason. They spoke in English, but the old man knew enough to understand. Caridad wanted him to stay; Jorge did not. A family of five in a small apartment did not need an old man taking one of the children's rooms. Ay, the old man thought, I would sleep gladly in the broom closet. God knows I've been kept in worse places. All I wish for now is a little peace. When I begin bringing money home, perhaps Jorge will relent. It is right that I should contribute and I am a good worker.

Domingo covered his face with his arm and rolled in the child-sized bed to face the wall, aching for the disruption he had caused. It was quiet now, the argument finished as quickly as it began. Domingo's brain filled itself with an explosion of pictures. Hardly a month had passed since he'd drifted across the Florida Straits alone, mad with hunger and thirst. He came to a daughter and a land he had not seen in twenty years. Perhaps he should have stayed in Cuba. No. They would have killed him. They always killed men like him. First there was the *Brigada* and the humiliation of capture. Then the years working for the Americans until they'd caught him again. They'd starved him and beaten him with sticks like a dog. He'd grown old in the prisons of his own land.

Domingo thought then perhaps it had been for nothing, that his whole life was merely a cypher. The thought lingered only a moment. No, it was not true. God has blessed me. I have Caridad. And I have my honor. Never in all the time he had been in the struggle had he broken. Never once had he failed to keep faith with his comrades. The love of Caridad and his honor were the currency that would sustain him. Tomorrow he would go out and begin again. He would begin work and his life in this strange place. He already had a plan and a job. It was his secret.

Domingo rose early. He was used to it. In the dimness he dressed in the school crossing guard's khaki shirt. Like some sort of policeman. He smiled at that. Domingo, the policeman. In a small cardboard box under the bed, he reviewed his fortune: a rosary, three tarnished quarters, a five dollar bill, a box of matches and half a cigar wrapped in a plastic bag. Domingo removed the cigar, matches, and the three coins.

In the bathroom he cleaned what teeth remained in his mouth and smoothed the white strands of hair over his skull with a damp palm. He did all this in the gravest of silence lest he wake anyone in the household. Holding his worn shoes in his hand, he tiptoed to the kitchen.

Coffee would be good, but there was no time and he did not dare make the noise of brewing it. Instead he drank a glass of water and ate a lump of bread. He held the water glass to the light of the dawn. He marveled that water could be clear without a trace of color. And its taste was so much like rain that it made him shiver.

"Papi." Caridad stood in the doorway in a terrycloth bathrobe, a lock of her long, silver-streaked hair across her forehead.

"Caridadcita." She came to him. She reached out and touched the material of his uniform shirt.

"What is this, Papi?"

Domingo tried to smile at her and became self-conscious of his missing teeth. "It is nothing. Only a little thing." He was terribly proud. "I have a job. It was to be a surprise, but you've discovered me."

"Oh, Papi." She caressed his face with her palms. "It's not necessary that you work." Her eyes were no longer young.

"I wish it. And it's not much. Just a few hours until noon at the school up the road." The woman sighed. "I need something. I will be able to help you and Jorge."

"Papi," she said again and the voice came out sad.

Now it was he, Domingo, who reached out and placed his hands upon his daughter's face. "I never had the chance to be the father to you that I wished to be or a good husband to your mother, God rest her soul." Caridad began to protest. "No," Domingo went on, stopping her. "It is the truth. But now I can atone. I want to help. I want to be with you and the children. And I have heard there is a job cleaning at the very same school in the evenings. I plan to take that too. In a year, if I save, we'll have enough to put down on a little house."

"*Dios*!" Caridad struck her forehead with the flat of her hand. "You cannot do so much, Papi."

"We shall see," he told her brusquely. "Now I must be off. We'll speak of these things later."

Caridad took his arm. "At least let me make you breakfast."

"I've eaten. Let me go. I don't want to be late." But Caridad maintained her grip. In the new light Domingo saw that tears welled in her eyes.

"*Cuidate*, Papi. Care for yourself. I love you so." And then she let him go.

The bus stopped in front of the apartment. Domingo held one of his three quarters in his hand so that he would be ready. The bus came and he counted the blocks and sometimes looked upwards at the tall buildings. And such buildings! How Miami had changed in his absence.

The school was not far, but the luxury of the bus would permit him to be at his post ahead of time. Domingo was given a bright flag and vest and stationed at the traffic light on the corner. By pushing a button he could cause the light to turn red. He was then to usher the children across.

Because he'd come early, there were no children yet and Domingo amused himself by watching the automobiles. He did not recognize them. They were new and shining and the well-dressed men and women behind their closed windows sometimes spoke into telephones without cords. Domingo had never seen the like.

Soon the first children began arriving in ones and twos. They were quiet and waited patiently until Domingo caused the traffic to stop so that he might escort them across the road.

More and more children came. With the greater numbers they became rougher and unruly, some darting through the traffic before Domingo could make the light red. Waves of them, little things who came up only to his waist, surged about him like schools of colored fish and when a gap appeared in the flow of automobiles, they ran pell mell to the other side of the street. Domingo called to them to wait but his English failed him. One girl child with blue eyes and hair in a plait down her back made an obscene gesture which shocked Domingo. He followed, waving his flag. Cars honked and tires squealed. With relief the old man saw that the light was red. He urged the children across and they moved in a sea. When the last child had reached the far side, Domingo felt a burden lift. But just as quickly, the blaring horns began again and the traffic roared past him. Domingo realized the light had turned green, leaving him alone in the middle of the street. He skipped to the sidewalk, barely avoiding being run over by a truck. The driver yelled in Spanish and made a gesture even more obscene than had the little girl.

In the next hour Domingo experimented with different ways to make the children mind him. Some worked; most did not. By 8:30, when the bell rang and the pupils were in class, Domingo was sweating and the backs of his legs ached.

I must learn to be more patient, he told himself, and not worry so. If the children cross against the light when there is no traffic, what's the harm? But he had the concern that they had been entrusted to his care and that he bore a responsibility. It was a matter of duty. Well, he would work at it and overcome what obstacles came in his way .

Domingo took the half cigar from his breast pocket and extracted it from the plastic bag. He lighted it, his fingers brittle like an old woman's. The cigar was good but not as good as a freshly lit one. Still, Domingo enjoyed it. It was a fine cigar of Cuban stock, and well made. He smoked slowly and walked down the block to a small café. Outside the café Domingo allowed himself one more draw on the cigar then carefully stubbed it out and replaced it in the bag. He would save the rest of it for later.

The warm food smell of the café caused Domingo's stomach to rumble and he felt a little faint. He seated himself and studied the chalkboard menu behind the counter, remembering that he had only two twenty-five cent pieces. *Café con leche* and an order of buttered bread were the cheapest. Forty-five cents. A little more with the tax. He regretted he would have nothing to leave the server. A plain *copita* of coffee would be a dime less, but Domingo yearned for the *con leche*

101

with half a lifetime of want. He would make it up to the server tomorrow.

The server came. He was a disinterested young man, a boy really, with a fine black mustache and several gold chains about his neck. Domingo ordered and the boy came back with crisp hot bread and a steaming *café con leche* which he placed before the old man.

Domingo studied the crustiness of the bread and how it had been cut on the bias so that it pointed itself like an edible dagger. He held the *café con leche* under his nose to enjoy its smell. When he had exercised his senses thus, he allowed the first sip. Then he dipped the knife edge of the bread into the *café* briefly so he could feel the roughness of the crust in his mouth and suck on the butter and *café con leche*. Domingo ate this way very slowly, sometimes closing his eyes for several moments at a time. His belly became contented and happy. When he had done, he used his fingers to pick up the flakes which had fallen from the bread and drank a paper cup of water filled with ice, clear as bits of glass. America was a wonderful country.

"The bill, please," he said to the boy. The boy slid a scribbled check across the countertop. Domingo reached into his trousers pocket and withdrew only a piece of lint. He tried the other pocket. Nothing. A prickling sensation touched him. He tried the first pocket again, the right one, knowing he'd placed the coins there. He felt high and low, and when his finger ran along the bottom seam of the pocket it poked through the hole from whence his money had escaped. He looked up. The boy watched him coolly, his arms folded across his chest as if he expected the old man to cheat him. Embarrassment crushed inwardly on Domingo like an iron band around his chest.

"I seem to have lost my money," he mumbled. "Please. I would speak with the manager." Domingo could barely look the boy in the eye for the other's contempt now showed openly. Without speaking he disappeared into the kitchen. Domingo trembled inside.

In a moment a large man with an amiable face and thick black hair and a mustache emerged. Domingo took him to be the father of the boy.

"What is the problem, *Señor?*" he asked not unkindly.

Domingo had already gotten to his feet. He turned his pocket out for the man to see.

"My money. I have lost my money. My name is Domingo and with your permission I shall return and pay you this afternoon."

But the other seemed not to hear his explanation. Rather, the large man cocked his head slightly and studied Domingo's face. "Domingo, you say, Señor?" The old man nodded. "Domingo, who has only just arrived here and is the father of Caridad Morales?"

"Yes."

The big man walked out from behind the counter, wiping his hands on his apron and never taking his eyes from Domingo. "You are Domingo Vasques."

"I am." The old man was quite perplexed.

The manager was upon him now, seizing his hand in both his own, holding it warmly, reverently. "You owe me nothing, *Señor*. You are known in this community. It was said that you'd escaped. It is we who are in your debt. I have heard my own father and others speak your name many times." He turned to the kitchen. "Pepe. Pepe! Come out here at once." The boy emerged. "Come here, come here, boy. Shake the hand of Domingo Vasques." The boy did so, his face still vacant, his grasp limp. "If in your life nothing else of significance ever occurs, remember that once you met a man of honor."

Then the father escorted Domingo to the door, his arm protectively about the old man's shoulders.

In a confusion Domingo said, "You are kind in your words, *Señor*. But I am an ordinary man. And this afternoon I shall return with your money as I said."

The other patted his arm and laughed greatly as if Domingo were making a jest. "Yes. Yes, only please return this evening instead. Bring Caridad and Jorge and the children so that I may present a grand meal to you to celebrate your return. *Adios, Señor* Vasques. *Adios*, and don't forget your promise to return."

And then Domingo was alone on the street, dazed, confused, almost unsure in which direction the school lay. It felt as if the blood had drained itself from his head. Perhaps I should not have eaten so much. He looked up at the sky, blindingly bright, merciless, until the wing of a great black bird obscured it entirely. Domingo never felt himself fall to the sidewalk.

When the old man saw again, it was the face of Caridad. Someone had put a cold towel on his forehead. The café manager and his son hovered behind his daughter, worried, and beyond them strangers Domingo did not know. A siren echoed in the distance.

"Caridad."

"Papi. Be still."

"Listen, Caridad. You must help me."

"Oh yes, Papi." She wept freely. "Where is your pain?"

"There is no pain, child," he heard himself rasp. She bent close to hear. "Help me this way: You must pay the manager of the café half a dollar. And something for his son."

Caridad looked at him as if he'd gone mad, but when Domingo pushed himself up on his elbows to make her understand, she cried: "Yes. Yes. Of course, Papi," and gently forced him to lie still once more. One of her tears fell on his cheek like a drop of dew. He fixed her face in his mind and placed his hand over hers, holding it tightly to his chest.

Domingo closed his eyes then and would not reopen them. He heard no more voices or sounds from the street. But it was all right, he knew. If one had one's honor, if one had earned another's love, what was there in God's kingdom to fear?

Licensed to Sell Spirits

Aneka Janeene Roberts-Griffith

If you have ears then you will hear Vonetta Abraham's voice. She is quarrelling five houses away. Metal pans are clanging, hitting each other as they are being pelted to the floor. She is breaking everything that can be broken. She is doing this you will hear her say to fix her broken marriage.

If you have eyes then you would have seen Franklin Abraham leaving his house. He was walking towards Monkey's Beer Garden. Once there he will order a Carib. He will not expect it to be cold because Monkey's beers never are anymore. Gradually the sound of his wife's voice will recede.

I can see and I can hear all these things perhaps more clearly than you can now because there are days when I quarrel louder than Vonetta; my husband is out there drinking with Franklin. Me, I curse everybody's mother, especially Monkey's. I can tell you that Vonetta will continue to quarrel an hour longer to save face. Her threats of leaving will become threats of not cooking till an eventual "See if I have anything else to tell you, Mr. Franklin. I wash my hands."

Then there will be silence until maybe someone takes a spoon to one of those bottles lying in the mud at the beer garden. A drunk will begin to sing. The words won't make any sense to us but there will be laughter from the other drunks who understand.

The beer garden sits fittingly in the middle of our street. It really should be called "the beer shed." It is comprised of two galvanize walls topped by a wooden roof. Customers sit on crudely built wooden benches, leaning gingerly on the galvanize for back support. Their feet eventually sink into the muddy ground. From what I can tell no one ever seems to notice the smell of the pigs in the pen directly behind or the consistent cackling of the chickens and ducks. The mooing of Monkey's cows never drowns out voices engaged in heated debate.

This is a small, remote village, so when the garden just opened it was very exciting. We hardly ever saw a car here, but with the garden came the weekly ice, soft drink and beer trucks. In the beginning, on Saturdays, an ice cream truck would bring jollies, pennacools and coconut ice cream for the kids. Couples would go over in the evenings for "something cold," leaving their children seated behind homework notebooks with strong admonitions about expected behaviour in their absence. Neighbour would call out to neighbour to find out if they were going across, and to let them know, "Well there we is eh!" Everybody was friend then.

The shed seemed much bigger. Perhaps it was because there were metal chairs then and newly built and varnished wooden benches. Twenty people could fit comfortably any time. The muddy ground was layered with gravel to make the surface more pleasant to walk on. The beer garden was a treat, especially for us housewives who hardly get out of the house. It may have been right across the street but it was an opportunity to talk and laugh, and pretend to be socializing with our husbands.

But then Monkey had the prayers. He invited the whole village. It was not surprising because he is a *dougla* and we knew he probably inherited from his Indian father the power to save pennies and turn them into millions. I think everyone was happy to share in Monkey's bounty and I tried my best not to envy his wife Sita in a brilliant yellow shalwar with new jewelled slippers. I had thrown on what my mother used to call "Sunday best," and wondered when my husband would hit on a plan to rescue us from the clutches of poverty. I consoled myself about my shoddy appearance with the fact that I was not Hindu and therefore did not need a new shalwar. I was really just going to eat.

Food was plentiful, the fig leaf plates broad. There is usually only one table and the invited have to eat in shifts. Monkey's yard was not empty until 3:00 a.m. The next day a pick-up truck came for the chairs used at the prayers and took the benches and metal chairs from the beer garden too. By afternoon, Monkey's brother Ram came in another pick-up, bringing the crude replacements that are there today.

Saturday afternoon there were no ice treats for the kids. The traffic to Monkey's beer garden slowed tremendously over the next couple of weeks, until eventually the only trucks that came anymore were the beer trucks. For a while the lime was the same. I tried not to show my displeasure at having to sit on the rickety benches, or drink warm beer with no other alternative. Eventually I got fed up and my husband started going without me. I expected someday soon, he would gracefully stop going too, but that day has never arrived. Instead his visits became more frequent.

I never thought that my husband had tapped into a repressed alcoholic tendency because most other women's husbands were still going too and just as regularly. We were not too alarmed and it became another issue we moaned about over our washing lines or in the market. It was our fate to bear these absentee husbands. "Girl, I don't know what happen to he nuh. When he sick, ah hope Monkey taking care ah he. Ah bet yuh I send he clothes for Sita to wash. I don't know why I bothering to shop for. He does eat? Is only drink. Only drink."

It remained a joke for me until midnight started catching me in bed alone. I could have lived with it until morning showed up muddy footprints on my kitchen floor, a drunk man on the living room floor. My hourly paid husband could not get up on some days and on others came home from work early, doing away with the necessity to our finances of overtime.

While my family grew poorer and I would suppose many others did too, Monkey's prospered. They built a pig pen, then a cow shed and soon they had enough poultry to feed the village again, like they had done at the prayers. While my husband was always absent, of course, Monkey was always at home. Sita sat by his side, giving their customers their change. When the bills got smaller, she counted the "change" instead.

The more pious of the village community obviously chose to deal with the problem using closed bedroom discussions done in violent whispers. Apart from Vonetta, Zarida Parasram better known as "Babes" and myself, no one quarrelled loud enough for the neighbours to hear. However, through my bedroom window, I could see the faces, the same faces that were there every night. Faces that remained, when sometimes pulling on a house dress at 2:00 in the morning, I went out to call my husband.

Vonetta and I met in the market one Wednesday and decided there must be something for us to do. We had a meeting with Babes the next day over midday soap operas. Babes was very anxious and she continually wiped sweat from the moustache above her lip. She blew down the front of her dress, until eventually she unbuttoned it. "This thing have to stop," she said, "my father used to drink just like Harry doing now. Everyday. He used to beat me mudder. Last night Harry try to hit meh. The day he succeed I go cripple he." She looked nostalgic as though remembering the past and her dreams for the future, but prepared nonetheless to put an end to the "sheet" as she called it.

We decided to burn it down. We knew that Monkey had enough money to just rebuild it but it was our hope that he would know it was the act of vengeful wives. Anyway he would know it was someone from the village and he would, in fear, go into another line of business. We did not care if we became the chief suspects, no one could prove a thing.

There was a very thin time margin between when all the men left and 6 o'clock when Sita would be up to feed her chickens. Sneaking out, even if it was at 4:00 a.m., was no problem though. Our husbands slept like logs. The fire was planned for the next Monday night, supposedly the quietest night of the week.

We soaked the whole shed in gasoline. Vonetta is very tall and jumped onto the wooden roof to pour the gasoline there. Then we lit the benches. The sound of the flames blowing in the early morning wind sounded like the cry of a strange animal. I swear when I took my last look back, the fire had taken the form of a woman with hourglass shape and chiselled facial features. She seemed to do a dance just before the cry turned into the normal roar of fire.

Monkey said later in recounting the incident that when the flames began to roar, he looked out the window to see three figure dressed all in black darting into the tall grass across the road. He would have run after them but the shed was dangerously close to his animal pens and he had to secure them.

We buried the evidence of our crime in a prepared hole. I told neither Vonetta nor Babes what I thought I had seen.

But you know that is not the end of the story because Vonetta mouth still going. You would not believe what happened the next day. Around midday two beer trucks appeared in front of Monkey's house. I was not worried. My husband was sure to know I had a hand in the fire and therefore meant business. Whatever Mr. Monkey had planned would never work.

106

Five o'clock brought the largest street procession this village has ever seen. Men, some I had never seen before, were arriving in front of a sign that read, "Fire Sale. Beers half price." They were carrying metal kitchen chairs, wooden dining room chairs, plastic porch chairs and placing them in the ash and debris. I was too dumbfounded to say a word when my husband came in from work, dropped his bag and walked out with my dining room chair. He did not say a word to me either. Just cut me a glance.

The Goodness of It

Nicole Craig

Boom box of sound. White devil on wheels. Striped red. Maxi man comin aboom adoom. . .aboom adoom adooma doom doom. Hear him, adooma dooma doom doom, before you sight him, adooma dooma doom doom, and feel, adooma dooma doom doom, no fear. Adooma D D D, de Cuttyman comin. De Cutty Cutty Cutty Cutty Cuttyman comin. An Cutty is ah dye, ah dye dye dye, Cutty is ah dynamite on wheels. Wild eyed tar baby, slicken greasy, Cutty is ah rudie. Cutty is ah sweetie. Cutty is ah Mac Mac Daddy.

"What happen, yer en go stop fer me?! You en see meh stretch out meh han?!

He watch me. Smiles slick like. Tar baby eyes.

"Come Family."

An I comin wee, I comin and I dragin Claudette wit me. Claudette is ah little sis. Ah little ting. Form two. More whiner than woman, but I really couldn't care. Have eyes jet java black like mamie. Have papa nose an my rude curl up lip. Stupesin stupesin. I grab han an I takin her wit me. My right. Fifteen by age if yer please. She cyah give me no long lip and back answer. I say look here gyal, behave. And we climb up. We up in de centre. We up in de centre an de belly ah de boom box. Up in Cutty maxi, and eyes takin up Claudette and me. Dey scopein out and watchin we.

"Fox! Get up an give de gyal an dem ah seat nah man."

Fox is ah fox in purple. Ah red nigger wit snake oil hips. Squeeze. Slide. Swing out. Oil man's magic makes ah seat for me.

"Yeah family. Right up in front. Yer sittin down right here by me."

And here goes Claudette in proper pleats and here goes me in tight school skirt. In saucy string line. Squeeze. Go real low baby. Tar baby eyes on me. Watchin my. . .boom, adooma doom doom. Seein my. . .and I squeeze, and I fit in.

"Yeah. . .lookin good gyul!"

He move de wheel ter de road but he cyah stop watchin me. One eye on de road, one eye on me. Watchin my stiff collar. My open bold buttons, my powdered chest. Yeah, check me baby check me. He watchin me, he checkin me, an fox checkin out Claudette. Lean paw like into de seat behind she. Lean close close. Breath nasty breath on she. Says she sexy. Says good lookin nice young ting nobody prettier. And she squirm. She tingle. She hot. And I cu my damn eye at he. He ketch de eye and pull up and off my sister. Ketch de eye an pull up off de cradle. Easy. Sly sly slew foot like, he slide ter ah next seat.

So is jus me, Claudette and Cutty up front. Claudette still shock. She in dreamland. But I cyah take she on now cause Cutty an I have ah ting goin. Hand reach up on my knee. Ah hand ter de steerin wheel, ah hand up my knee. Groovin on the up and up. Yeah baby, groove me. Tar baby hand ter thigh ter knee, rubbin me. Smile ter smile. Watch de road, then watch me, and he movin fer higher. But I stop he. Ah jus remember ah ting an it shake me. Shake me till I shake he hand off my knee. Ah remember Mrs. Johnson, that damn mamie ah mine. That big brown machette of ah bad woman. Was jus yesterday. Put ah finger ter my face and curse bout she don't want no belly in she house. Throw meh on ah wall. Put finger ter this face an say Pam, ah goin cut yer ass. Pam, I goin laylay yer tail. Pam, let meh ketch you wit any man an I goin ter bus yer face. An that ting shake me. It shake meh till ah sweat. It shake meh till ah get Cutty hand off meh knee. It shake meh cause Mrs. Johnson is ah wicked woman when she vex. It shake meh cause ah don't know what move she goin ter make on meh if she ketch meh this time. If she find out dat big Friday evenin I drag Claudette up in here. Up in meh maxi man maxi. Headin fer down town Frederick St. fer ah lime. Meh ass won't be mine. So ah shake Cutty han off my knee.

"What happen gyal? Yer fraid ah wah? Or you want some place private?"

"Look , keep yer eye on de road yes man. De only ting I fraid is that yer kill meh wit yer drivein."

Is so I turn an tell him. And is so he stupes. But Claudette watch meh wit ah worry in she eye. She put ah warnin in she eye when she watch meh.

"You go ahead Miss Pam. Play yerself."

" Hush nah gyal. Yer too small ter know nothin bout nothin." I say.

"You feel so!"

Cutty laugh when he hear dat. It sound like ah low sweet gargle in he throat. He pull back he natty head an laugh. He pull back he head an laugh and pull de maxi in ter de Croisee. People bail out and hand Fox they money. And Fox handle de money like ah fox. Quick an light. An we smellin honey. Brown brown roast honey and peanuts. Nex ting ah know Cutty callin cross de road fer four bags. De venda boy bring it an Fox forward him four dollars. Quick and light. Ah bag each fer four ah we, and people bail in ter maxi. An I think bout Mamie. An Cutty land ah kiss on meh before he rev up de engine. Right on meh jawline. An I still thinkin bout Mamie hard enough ter pull back. He stupes again and this time he vex. He put de wheel ter de road an this time he drive it hard. He en even look at me. He en even watch me. An I feel so bad I push up my lip. He en look at meh until he pull de maxi in ter de stan in town.

"Watch nah Pam. Is either yer limein terday or yer ain limein. Cause ah find like yer gettin on real stupid an ting an I ain lucky wid dat."

"Yeah, I limein man. Cutty, I have ter watch it too. Dat Mamie ah mine ain soft ah tall ah tall."

"You fraid she? I doubt dat."

He shake he head. Smile. Wink me dat sweet wink. I feel so much heat wit dat wink. But is like reach we reach. Time ter go. Move it. Smooth. Swing out de seat. Claudette and me. Me and Cutty. Fox takein control ah de maxi. An we comein out de maxi free free. An town is ah mess ah people. Money husstlin.

Traffic shiftin. Everything jammin. Maxi ter maxi. Bottom ter belly. An my man han ter my waist. An Claudette in ah race wit ah double load ah books. Rushin. Hustlin up. Keepin up.

Face ter face. Hand still ter my waist. We on Frederick St. watchin round. Claudette behind we. And I bold. I baaaad. I happenin. I ain fraid ah damn ting. Not in this crowd. Cause all ah dem is meh posse. Every man jack like me. All them school woman. Greeen on green. Blue on blue. Pleated tight fitted women fussin limein in de Friday cool. Hair hot combed. Hair hot forked straight chemical curly. Yeah man, is all ah we.

An is like Africa come ter town too. Wearin red green gold. An look. Africa come wit beads too. Wit rope braids. Is ah limers ting. Is ah tribal ting. Fellas coastin on de Drag. College boys. Senior sec boys. Gapein in front of Burger Boys. Ras. Beads. Grass. Incence. Everyting is ah match. Purple green tangerine, dub is ah ital ting. Dub blastin. People passin. Binghi is de ting. Me, Claudette and Cutty in front ah Town Centre an ting. Claudette leanin up in de back wit de books an ting. An Cutty hand on me hidein in this crowd. He in meh face. Bump ter grind. Lovin sugar lovin. Man nature risein. An yeah, is kiss he kiss meh oui! He say kiss meh nah kiss meh nah gyal. Aaaah baby. Dip inside me. Taste. Sweet sweet. An de music blastin an people passin an Claudette stupesin. An ah baby. Aaaaaah. Aaaaaah. Aaaaaaaaaaah. . .

But wait. . .but wait wait wait. Ah see ah ting. Ah see ah suit. . .Across de road. Suit yellow brown. Bank suit. Prune up lips. Eyes jet java black. Bata flats. Shucks! Bata flats? Mamie! Mamie Mamie Mamie Mamie! Shucks! Is ah Mamie Mamie Mamie!

"Run!!"

And I pelt my body across de pavement. Man I bus it. I scoot. I fly. Claudette take wings behind me and we jus grab bookbag and we fly. We mash toe when we fly. We lick down people when we fly. We lick de shades off ah darkers eye when we fly. We lick and kick de pavement like madness without mercy, an we fly. We reach don't care altitude, wit heavy steps behind we. What is dem heavy steps behind we? Ah heaviness runin bam bam bam behind we. De heaviness grab me. Like ah big rude roughness, heaviness put hand round my wrist. Heaviness wit heavy hand man handlein me. He hoop my woman's waist. He crush my chest, my tenderness of woman's breast.

An I look up an I see Mamie fren. An is whey he come from an is what he doin here I ask myself, an self say chile, he workin de beat. Dat is what he doin here. He workin de beat on de street. He workin de beat on de way back ter de station. Workin de beat an squeezin de life out my belly. An look. Mamie comin through de crowd ah confusion. Step through dem cussin people. Walkin fas comin. Comin. Walkin. An I fightin an strugglin ter make free. But Chris is ah mammoth man. My waist in one hand, Claudette by de collar in he next hand. An he not lettin go an she comin. Oh God she comin! She comin!

"Allyer damn little bitches. Look at allyer nah! Eh? Look at allyer! An if ah laylay allyer tail right here in de road people go say ah bad. People go say I is not ah decent woman. Eh? But look at allyer! Ah decent woman doh raise children like allyer!"

Watch de other side ah she nah. "Mrs. Bank Teller" if yuh please. People doh know de bachannal side ah she. Dah Mrs. Johnson, that big brown machette of ah bad woman. She body vibratin wit vexation. One leg shake shakein. Jelly waist movein, neck groovy groovin ter de soul rhythm ah vexation. Point ah fingr in my direction.

"An you Miss Pam. Yes you! Find yerself here on ah Friday evenin. Eh? When yer should be home. Eh? Eh? You down here on big broad Frederick St. draggin up yer tongue wit some dutty lookin man!! An doh fel ah ain see yer! Meh eye ain short ah tall ah tall. Yer watless lil gyal like yer! De dutty man cyah even give yer ah parrot on ah stick. Eh? Eh? Now tell meh dis ting! After I done sweat nine ter five ter make ah life fer allyer! Eh? After I don give my moher's milk fer allyer eh? Yer go do meh dis ting. Eh? Ain see is best ter bus yer face Miss Pam?"

An man, ah feel bad when she say it. Ah feel bad ter meh heart. It bun meh ter meh heart how she say it. It shame meh ter meh soul where she say it. People listenin. People passin. People walkin. People seein. An ah shame ter meh heart of hearts. Ah shame ter meh death. When Chris leh we go all ah could do is hang meh pull down meh head in shame. An all Claudette could do is cry. She cry an she get one backhan slap in she face. An I stan up dey waitin fer mine. But yer know, all de woman do is watch meh. She watch meh an she eye say whore. Bitch. Dutty gyal. An is like she beat meh. She beat meh witout even touchin meh.

An den I see she mouth movin. It sayin home fer both ah we. But I not listenin because I look into de crowd an I see Cutty. Cutty de Mac Mac Daddy. Cutty wit he han roun ah nex lady. Smile he smile fer she. Winkin he wink. An on top ah my shame find ah new vexation. I want ter cuss. I want ter cry like Claudette. But I hear Chris talkin something bout yer welcome glad ter be there at de time an dat he very glad ter walk we ter de taxi stan, thankyou. An I want ter cry but my eye dry dry. An Claudette cryin fer both ah we. Long long tears. Even in de taxi home. Tears like blood. Like rum. Like rusty rain water. Tears makin ah basin in she breast. An not ah word from Mamie.

Not ah word more. Not ah word more till I wake up next mornin. Wit ah watery pillow of tears. Not cause she shame meh in de road. Maybe meh heart could ah handle dat. Is not dat woh eatin meh. Is dat Cutty was meh man, an meh heart hut meh for what he do. An Mamie see meh an say what yer cryin for yer ain get nothin ter cry bout yet. Look decent she say. Hurry. Get meh skin downstairs. She an papa have ah ting ter discuss wit meh. So ah pull down de pink nightie. Pelt way dem curlers from meh hair. Shower / dress. Do ah fas ting in too tight jeans and t-shirt. Fly down stairs ter see papa in ah vex man pose over sugarless coffee. One bald big eyed Congo man in ah serious grim. Hand ter chin. Hand tappin kitchen table. Waitin. Waitin. Fer who? Me?

"Pam is you behine de curtain?. . .Get in here and sit down fer meh please."

111

Curtain wit coloured stripes plastic parts. And I get in here. Sit slowlike. Tryin fer cool. Tryin fer calm. Tryin fer unworried. An he across from me. He clear his throat. He stare direct.

"Now Pam, listen good. Hear meh. All ah we is decent people in dis house. Yer modder, me, yer sister. Yer modder down by de bank, me pullin bull on meh taxi, an yer sister in she school work. All ah we decent. All ah we decent. All ah we have rules. Rules is how dey does run ah society Pam. . .But you, you think yer doh need no rules in yer life. You think you could jus go an shack up wit man an live like de devil but Pam, leh meh tell yeh right here right now now now!"

An he hit de table wit he han Bam! Bam! Bam! And I look up long enough ter see Mamie by de kitchen curtain. Lip curl upward. Satisfied.

"I is ah God fearin man an I doh want no whores in meh house! Yer hear meh?! Yer hear meh?! Answer meh chile!"

"Yes Papa." An meh eye on de ground.

"Good! Ah glad yer hear meh. Cause yer goin ter get some religion ter set yer straight."

"What?!" I look up fast.

"Ah say yer goin ter get some religion ter set yer straight! An doh ask meh what cause yer modder takein yer ter de Pastor terday. Yer goin ter join bible lessons. Yer goin ter put on ah decent dress! Yer goin ter get some amen rules fer yer life! Year meh?!"

An dat is dat wit Papa. An nex ting I scratchin. I in de toe length cotton dress. Pattern sunny flower yellow. Damn ugly. Damn scratchy. Ain wear de ting since Ole Years but ah leave de house wit it. Wit Claudette bussin back ah laugh. Wit me stupesin and wholein back some tears. Wit Mamie watchin meh cut eye. Eyein meh on de taxi ride, while I holdin back vexation fer Cutty. Fer shame. Fer Papa and he stupid amen rules.

"Look, we nearly reach. Fix yerself fer meh please! Ah doh want ter see no rudeness in de house ah God."

De house ah God. How de hell I reach here? I jus wanted ah little limein. Ah little lovin. Didin't want no churchy churchy ting. No glory be an saints in white decendin. Shoutin amen allilu jah jah, no dusty red road in cocorite, no white brown box buildin full ah proper pentecost ah preachers preachin. Shit. An I vex. An Mamie know I vex as hell an I ain fraid ter show it. I givein attitude. Lip long attitude. Arm double up under chest eye like bull kinda attitude. Wit Mamie nudgein meh, watchin an warnin meh. An we walk in ter preacher's office wit so much attitude.

Preacher Tory say ter call him Pastor. Tall. Thin. Cocoa brown skin. Grey suit like ah undertaker. Nearly lick off meh toe comin in he door. He small office door. Brute brash an carpetless. Wood up desk, an ah woman sittin down next ter him. Preach say this is meh daughter. Fifteen by age if yer please. Hair slick up in one, dark womanish roun face like.

"Mornin sister Pamela, my name is Melissa."

Stretch out she han an smile her smile fer me. Sweet roun face smile fer me. And I shake her han ladylike.

"Mornin." I tell her. "Call meh Pam."

An we settle on that. But I still too vex ter take she on. I too vex ter take on preacher Tory talkin bout God see it fit ter have us here Allilujah jah. An dat I goin ter join de choir. Dat Melissa could teach me bible studies. An then dat Mamie ah mine. Dat big brown machette of ah bad woman talkin bout I need prayers. An I jus stupes. One long long stupes. And dat was dat. Who tell me ter do dat? Dat Mamie ah mine raise up from she chair. She raise up she han ter slap meh. Big brown han reachin fer meh. Right deh in de house ah God, right deh in Preacher box office.

"Miss Johnson take it easy!" I hear Melissa sayin.

An Preacher Tory is ah tall thin middle man, holdin back de wrath ah Mamie han.

"No need fer punishment in here Mrs. Johnson. God go work things out. Jus hold yer peace sister, let de Lord fight yer battles."

An I duck. I creep out she way cold sweatin. An jet java black eyes jus watchin meh. Jus wantin ter kill meh. She calm she self, but she dem eyes want ter murder meh. Eyes deep dirty an straight starein. Body vibratin.

"Little gyal, if yer cyah behave yerself in here, yer goin ter get outside an wait fer meh!"

An I make ah move fer de door an I see Melissa comin wit me.

"Pa I waitin outside wit de sister till she ready ter go."

An Preacher shake he head. An is outside we outside. Outside dis box buildin of ah church. Outside dis red red dusty road in Cocorite. Stiff standin. Scratchin. Waitin. An Melissa walking out in front of me. Watchin blue blue sky. Watchin blood red road. An my eye followin she. Roun roun mango like from back ter breast. Dress prim an proper. Turn roun ter stare me.

"Gyal you lookin damn vex." She say.

An I shock wit de words from she mouth.

"Doh watch meh so nah man. Yer gettin on like ah now drop from heaven."

"But ay ay, yer is de preacher daughter." Ah turn an tell she.

An she laugh ah loose gyal laugh. She laugh ah low loose laugh. Bend. Low low ter belly. Laugh ah loose gyal laugh. She turn an tell me.

"Gyal you an me is de same damn ting yes, an yer have ter realize dat." Ah say "How yer mean?"

"Well I sure your problem is de same ting. Parents problem. Man problem. Freedom problem. All kind ah damn problem."

"How you so sure I have any man problem?"

"I jus have ter watch yer, is like yer have de whole world on yer shoulder."

"Well yer right gyal." I tell she.

"My man pick up wit some other woman an meh father tell meh ah have

113

ter find my skin down here, an gyal, is like meh mother want ter kill meh same time."

An she smile she smile. Shake she head. Shift dat roun woman body. She say, "See what ah mean? Is bleddy jail we livin in. If it ain God then is parents rulin yer business. If it ain them then is yer man dat messin up yer mind. I doh know what kind ah life dey go leave fer people ter live?"

An when she say it is den ah begin ter understand. Ah livin in jail. Wall ter wall. Box ter barrier. Bolt ter bolt. Ah livin in jail. Ah livin in J-A-I-L jail. Is Mamie. Is Papa. Is Cutty. Is God. Is wall, ter wall, ter wall. But then it have Melissa, Preacher man daughter. Stranger. An de woman understan, dat we livin in jail.

"Yes gyal, yer right." Ah tell she.

"Ah damn right oui. An is dead we go dead if we doh stick together."

An me an dat gyal stick together. Close close together. Long after ah leave dat box buildin fer de first time. We stick together shoutin allilu jah jah all through choir rehearsals. Through communions. Through preachins. Through an through baptisms an bible readins. Have my Mamie sayin is such ah good good ting. Ah good ting ah get some amen rules fer meh life. All dem man I stop seein. All de church tings I doin. And tellin Papa bout bible lessons in my room every Friday evenin.

Yeah, dis Friday evenin is bible lessons in my room wit Melissa. My pretty pink room, wit long lacey curtains. Wit sunset light sailin in. Door shut up against de whole worl. Not ah soul dare disturb de fellowship. Of sister ter sister. Daughter ter daughter. Sweet sweet communion waydown. In Egypt land. In depth of places. By dem holy holy drinkin fountains, by holy holy, Nile water.

An downstairs I hear Mamie mout runin. Buffin up Claudette. I hearin her voice driftin up ter my room.

"I doh know what happin ter you? Yer behavin jus like yer sister used to behave. Wotless an runin down ah set ah man. Eh? What yer need is some religion. Yer need ter talk ter yer sister."

An upstairs in my room when Melissa and I hear dat we smile. Lip fer lip. Smile fer smile.

"See how de gyal reformin she life? An doh push up yer mout fer meh yer know."

An Melissa and I in bible lessons deep deep. Way down.

"...What? I doh want ter hear dat, I doh care if she in bible lessons. Yer goin ter talk ter she an yer goin ter set yerself straight right right now!"

An when I hear dat I look up. I open my eye an watch Melissa. An she watch me back big eyed. An nex ting footsteps. Footsteps comin. Outside. Footsteps. Up de steps. An mercy. Lord have mercy! I scramblin Melissa scramblin. Mamie comin. Somebody comin! My mind, my pretty pink room spinin. Door openin. Door openin. Jet Java black eyes screamin. At me. At Melissa. Preacher's daughter. Breast ter butt naked. Bedded. Clothes in hand too late fer scramblin. Fer decency. I look up at Mamie. An she mout drop open. An tears in Claudette eye. Cry cry cry. Tears fall an make ah wet brown basin, in she breast.

114

The Swelling of the Womb/the Forging of a Writer

Opal Palmer Adisa

How it is possible I cannot say, but of this I am certain: I have been more productive as a writer since becoming a mother. Perhaps both are connected to maturity and becoming my own person: giving birth to my first daughter at thirty and in the process giving birth to myself, claiming more the calling of writer; determining more to write—no longer questioning why would anyone want to hear my stories, instead knowing that my stories were food that many craved:

> when the first life
> kicked inside my stomach
>
> i fed her words
>
> suspected she would know me best
> through the alphabet of language
>
> stories were what
> i had to bequeath her

I started to focus more aggressively on publishing the summer I became pregnant with my first child. I don't remember which one came first: whether my writing goals opened my womb or the blossoming of my womb bolstered my resolve to procure critical recognition as a writer. What I know now is that both are intimately connected. I need to be engaged in both writing and mothering to give meaning and order to my life, to help shape who I am and why I am who and what I am.

> ever so often
> a line or word
> i have been seeking for a poem
> comes in the middle
> of making sandwiches
> for my children's lunch
>
> i grasp hold of it
> in between spreading mayonnaise
> on slices of bread
>
> i chant it to memory
> like my children's repeated cry of
> *mommie mommie mommie*

ensuring that their demands
will be granted

sandwiches sealed
in bags
potent phrases
locked into my memory

I am writing all the time, everywhere, and the older I get, and the busier I am with the constant, time-consuming demands of child rearing and nurturing, the more urgent are the stories and louder are the voices of characters clamoring inside my head. Sometimes my children must pull me into the moment to focus on their demands. My youngest daughter, Teju, loves to sit and draw while I am at the computer. She often tells me I need her to help me write because, "I'm a writer too, you know," she says assuredly. Her being has provided me with a lexicon of stories, memories dulcet and deep. I marvel that I would not have known them without having her. My son, Jawara, middle child, loves the stories I tell; he too admires and is drawn to the griot tradition. When he was a baby and still suckling, I often breast fed him while writing, one hand on the computer, or rocked him in my lap, my arms and fingers stretching to reach the key-board. My oldest, Shola, respects me as a writer yet in her own way demands that I respect the choices she makes as an individual, separate from me. She has often said, "Don't except me to be a good writer just because you are." No argument there, yet she serves as the impetus, the first to draw for me the connection between my swelling womb and the rhythm of idiom. My three children are funnels through which words, liquid-sweet as cane-juice, absorbent and nutritious as bread-fruit, pungent as stinking-toe and soothing as bay-rum keep flowing, joining other words into an endless epic.

The same boastful arrogance I nurse about being the mother of these three incredible children is not unlike the pomposity with which I hand my poems and stories to readers. But all is not blissful joy or indulgence. There are times that I resent my children's demands, that I always have to be attending to some task or the other for them, *with them*, that keeps me from writing all that's stored inside my head. Sometimes I get aggravated that they never appear satisfied, that I can never do enough for them, that they sap all my energy and believe and act as if my only function is to please them, take care of their needs, attend to their whims. I lost my identity, I became Shola's mom, Jawara's mom, Teju's mom. Opal was over-looked, brushed aside, dismissed. The writing is the same way, perhaps even more demanding than the spoiled-brats I am raising. How can I begin to explain the countless days when my children are in school and the day is so glorious I want to hang out in the park, or just stroll around window-shopping, but the writing tugs at me, shuts me inside, refusing to even release me so that I arrive late to pick up my children who reproach me for being late. Damn if I do; damn if I don't. I often feel like the defenseless child in this trio: Me in the middle, my children to my right, my writing to my left, a tug-o-war that draws, both refusing to release me.

So I rush back home in between dropping children off to their respective extra-curricular lessons and try to pick up on the pulse of the writing, quickly. I am thankfully surprised at how easily I manage this these days. I rework a few sentences, catching some awkward phrases, misspelled words, complete another paragraph, then I must run again, making sure I have saved everything, to pick up children. In between cooking, returning telephone calls, helping with homework, I produce a few more phrases, even paragraphs, despite children playing outside in the yard, running in and out every few minutes to get a snack or other toys, slamming the door every time, barging into my office to complain about who pushes who, who isn't being fair, who fell and has a bruise and even though I have told them repeatedly not to interrupt me short of death and gushing blood, they never seem to remember. Any and all matters are urgent with them.

Then invariably, after I have solved their major crises, they want to type their names in the middle of my story or poem, and I have discovered it's best to let them, rather than spend wasted minutes arguing with each other about why they shouldn't interrupt me further; the delete key comes in handy. Also, I am looking into buying ear-plugs as my pre-teen daughter's music blares, speakers vibrating. I can't hear myself think. What was the idea flowing through my mind? That writers need quiet space is an ideal I sometimes glimpse.

My writing has become incredibly resilient, seems to understand that often it holds no claim to time, certainly not uninterrupted time, that it must be willing to snatch bits and pieces of this precious commodity in and around children, must be able to carry on several conversations at once, and yet maintain a flow. Its rhythm is just one of the many discordant meters in my household. An example: one of my children is ill, and I have to stay home with him. I often seize that opportunity to do work, but inevitably he wants me to lie down with him. If I decline, then I will only get some peace if I allow him to come into my office and lie on the floor on a blanket. I have found that by sharing my writing space with my son, he is less jealous or needy. As long as I meet his need, to be close, I am allowed time to work. Because I am close, he readily falls asleep and I can work without feeling guilty that I am neglecting a sick child.

However, proximity doesn't always solve the problem. Sometimes these two very different, yet similar children of mine (biological and writing) compete with each other, and vociferously vie for my attention. Although I try to leave time on the weekends just to hang out with my children, sometimes a story, article or a poem possesses me, and every opportunity I have, I must run to it, not unlike a breast-feeding mother whose breasts are on the verge of being engorged. But my other children are waiting, not too patiently either, for me to take them to the park or some place and I am glued to my computer. Often a battle of wills ensues: me demanding that children wait, give me fifteen minutes without interrupting then I will be done and we can go, and the writing whispering, no, I am not going to let you go today, not without blood. And before you know it, an hour has passed, my children are loudly denouncing me as a mean mommie, and are now creating a deliberate, determined racket, and the writing still refuses to let me go. Usually no one wins in that situation: torn between my loyalties as a mother and my commitment to my writing, I end up resenting and wanting to be free of both:

> not true
> that motherhood is choosing
> not true
> that this poetry is my choice
>
> they come at me
> as metal to magnet
>
> their forces
> a dam overflowing
> its boundaries
> insisting on consuming
> or destroying
>
> they have my full
> attention

The only way I, a single-mother of three children who demand lots of my attention, have been able to continue to be productive is to accept that I am a mother of four children, writing being the fourth child, an indulgent baby-of-the-family. And because I pride myself on being a good mother, giving each child undivided attention, I find that I am then less in conflict about which child to attend to when. However, while I have often said that writing comes last, I now know this to be untrue. In many ways writing always comes first because I am always thinking about it. My mind is forever engaged in pre-writing or writing even when I am not at the computer so that when I do have fifteen minutes or two hours to sit undisturbed, the writing flows because all along I have been writing. I no longer limit myself by thinking: "It makes no sense to sit down to write because I will be interrupted" or "I only have fifteen minutes." Sometimes that's all the time I need to find a word that has been eluding me, or to write the sentence that will make the piece all hang together. It's no different from stopping inbetween slicing up vegetables to read my youngest a short book, listening to my oldest read her essay ("Look at me when I am reading," she demands) from giving her feedback or praising my middle child about his art work or some other fantastic tale that he is spinning. What's important is that whatever snatches of time are at hand, to use them actively, to give the moment your all. I believe I have gotten my three children to buy into my writing, to understand what it means to the quality of their life: how much more relaxing and enjoyable a household we have if Mommie is the writer she wants to be than if Mommie is a frustrated would-be writer. Perhaps because all my children have deep artistic interests—Shola is a singer and actress, Jawara is an illustrator and painter and Teju is a storyteller/fashion designer—and they are older now, (12 ½, 7 ½ and 5 ½), they are more willing to grant me my art.

I truly love being a mother. I greatly love being a writer. That doesn't mean sometimes I don't desire a break from both or lament these so-called gifts. However, what I truly love about both is the discovery of self and others that being a mother and writer affords. If, like me, you are not obsessed with any preconceived notions about motherhood or being a certain kind of mother and you are not afraid to discard previous notions about suitable writing subjects or even genre, then you are open and free to enter some fabulous spaces, to have big fun, to be able to laugh at your and other's silliness, to appreciate each moment, to sing your own songs, and sing them loudly, even if you are off-key, because you have no investment other than to be as truthful and as feeling as you can be at any given moment.

The correlation between my writing and my mothering is that because of my children I experience and often relive childhood memories that lay buried, some euphoric and contagious and others painful and banishing. But because I want my children to avoid some of my pitfalls, I don't shy away from the painful, no more than I abandon all of myself in the joyous. I allow myself to experience both, and then my writer self takes over and applies analysis or brooding to the experience which often results in an insightful and lucid piece of writing.

> the pain is always new
> no matter how many times before
> they fell and scraped the skin
> off their knees
>
> the truth of the story
> is yet another star
> never too much
> in a luminous sky
>
> i mix the pain
> blending in the truth
> and the taste
> sweeps me up
> wraps me in its aroma

As with raising children which always suggests immediacy, and being up on situations in which your children are involved, my writing has taken on that same level of tension and edge. I worry less now about when a piece of work is polished, ready to be shared, and more about how it will feed another's soul. Let's face it: sometimes my children embarrass me in public and I want to hide and

119

deny any affiliation with them. At such times I ask myself: Is it just my imagination? Didn't I teach them how to behave—manners, acts of politeness? Similarly, there are times I write things that are shocking even to me, that would be considered vulgar in the context of my middle-class, Jamaican upbringing. Yet I obviously needed to write and say those things. Well, until I had a child, who one day decided to lie down in the middle of the side-walk at a major intersection because I refused her some treat, I did not share certain poems and prose pieces because of the subject matter and or language. And the worst thing a writer can do is to impose self-censorship. The very nature of writing, I argue, demands non-conventionality, at least on some level. It calls for the ability to abandon fear, to wrestle with it constantly so that it doesn't overpower you; to not be afraid to travel down untravelled roads or to be open to see those things you missed if you are retaking the same route. The fact is I love my children, even when they are being abominable. They are spoiled because I spoiled them, and wouldn't have them any other way. I am gratified that yearly I find them more amazing, more enthralling. Sometimes they are inappropriate, but then so is my writing because it shocks people, makes some feel uncomfortable, causes others to be too reflective and indicts a few. They are demanding. Need I say ditto? Some times the most surprising and wise things come from my children's mouths.

Over a three-year period I wrote a novel, *It Begins With Tears*, and in it some of the most unexplainable things appear in print. I love my writing now in a way where before I was always critical and dissatisfied with it. It is not perfect, such a cliché, but I believe it is always honest and open. More importantly, it always strives to say what it means, and is willing to face the consequences. It is forever running, falling down, getting bruised, getting up and going again. Sometimes it gets tired and falls out. Bathed in dirt and sweat, it stumbles to bed; other times it's all prim, a love affair with the mirror, hair just so, clothes coordinated, shadow dancing with its image, conceited, self-absorption is its disposition. Because of rearing three very different children, as a writer I am more accepting of the range and breath of my work, the phases and mood swings, the obsessive demands and the periods of release—withdrawal. I no longer worry or think that each work requires equal time or attention. I make sure I am always there for it, ready to praise, advise, listen, probe, explore. I have disbanded with a definitive plan.

Mostly I go with the flow, accept where the writing is taking me, allow my children to be who they are, guiding without imposing my will on them, not forcing the writing to support my basic values or endorse a particular way of life; accepting, being open, knowing that I have a lot to learn and must be receptive to being taught.

> the moment
> i stop dreaming
> the world comes
> crashing down on me

all i own
is the space that surrounds me
my hand cannot stop
the clock
but my mind
can change
the taste of water

my children run
heedless to the edge
of the mountain
i chant the poem
to break their fall

words bow in respect
i juggle them in relief

I cannot begin to record how much I have learned from my children in these almost thirteen years that I have been a mother. Being a mother has taught me how to be a more effective writer, how to be more loving and gentle with my writing, how to coax and soothe it, how to let it flow. Consequently, I am more comfortable about being a writer and I have been more prolific. Sometimes while breast-feeding my son at the computer, ideas would flow, not in one great urgent rush like some poems, but in a steady and even pace, and although I could only use one hand to record my ideas, I usually managed. By the time I had my last child, I had figured out how to use pillows to hold her in place, thereby freeing both hands, somewhat awkwardly, to type while she nursed. Breast-feeding became a creative, fulfilling time. Rocking my children to sleep was a reflective time; it allowed me to develop and see characters more clearly, to explore a plot. However, if a poem or line of a poem came, I would invariable lose some of it, unable to retain it all in my head. But I also learned to trust the instinct and the feel of it. I discovered that the poem would return; my babies always smiled at me when I nursed and rocked them, so too would the poem, not like before, but every bit as precious, as searing. Through rasing children I learned not to always chase down the muse, to trust her abiding presence, to participate in her desire for pranks and antic. It never amazes me how untiring a child is in dropping a toy for you to retrieve, or how determined and self-righteous a two year old is declaring "mine" to whatever catches their fancy; how possessive my children are in thinking they own me, that I have no right to privacy or a life outside of their own reality, so they come into my bed, forcing me to balance dangerously at the edge, barge into the bathroom when I am engaged in the most private act, pull me in stores to direct me to their wants. In other words, take over and absorb my entire life. My writing never stays home or takes a vacation; it has been known to intrude itself during an orgasm as easily as when I am mopping the floor, attending to a laceration on one of my children or watering my garden. My poetic eyes and mind are always present, seizing every moment, whetting my appetite, soliciting and enticing my attention.

As with my children, I have been rearing my writing, guiding it from its tentative crawl, to its dashing sprint. I am grooming it to be responsible, to be concerned with social issues, to be a conduit and a healer. My work is as serious and life-encompassing as is my heart; it is the other beat. It is fully integrated into my everyday life, yet it serves an entry into the public domain. As a writer, I am not shy or introverted. The spotlight suits me, I make it my clothes. I am intrigued and fascinated that others, complete strangers, often, will actually leave their cozy homes to come out and hear me. That is having a certain power that not everyone can boast of. Yet I wouldn't dream of taking this for granted. In many ways I have to be more careful in public than I am at home with my children and the rough drafts of my poems and stories. My children know I am not perfect, that I am more prone to shout and snap at them when confronted with a deadline. They know that usually a deadline means after dinner when they are snugly tucked in bed, I will hurry to my computer, and my addiction will be momentarily relieved, until the next assignment or story engrosses me.

My power as a woman is connected to my mothering, not simply because that's the role through which our patriarchal society chooses to empower me, but rather because the very act of giving birth is empowering. I have always felt invincible when I was pregnant, even with my huge girth almost blocking my vision. After completing a poem or a story I grow wings; I am satisfied, light as a feather, I soar. The feelings are different, yet similar; they intersect, complement and thrive off each other. When I am no longer recognized as a mother, I gain entry, and sometimes if I am lucky, acceptance as a writer. My poetry opens doors that I alone cannot open; my poetry paves the way for my children. I am raising my children to be mannerly and polite, to question everything, to not limit themselves or allow others to restrict them. I am rasing children who will be critical thinkers, who will have a sense of history, who understand that each of us progress on the backs of those who walked before us. Hopefully, I am rasing compassionate and passionate children who enjoy life and aren't afraid to live it. Because I insist that my writing has a life off the page, I labor over it, breathe history into it, lace it with joyous moments, and lots of hope. Its language must be clear, precise and uncompromising; it must ooze passion.

My writing is meant to be functional, healing art, its beauty not separate from its usage—impact. While I can pretend to be a passive participant, a conduit for both my children and my writing, this would be less than accurate. I actively sought both; I have wanted to be a mother from as far back as I can remember and I have been writing since about that time, when I was eight or nine years old. I desired both: mothering and writing. I am striving to be good at both. It is through my writing that I offer healing to a world encased in pain. I believe in this medium as a vehicle for transformation. Words, poems, stories are the medicine, injection and balm I offer those who grapple with illnesses. Stories are also the wisdom I feed my children, to help them cross the bridges I know they must cross, to help them to get up after they have fallen, to let them know that the songs they sing were voiced by others who came before them. I see my writing and the mothering of these three children as my faith in and gift to a brighter more harmonious future. My writing is part of a circle in which my children and I are joined, fingers clasped in fingers, hearts dancing to the music of love. My writing like my children are priceless gifts that will always be with me, today and for the rest of my life. I stand back and watch them acting silly and fooling around.

> sometimes it's a coy dance
> who will pursue whom
>
> the three of us
> locked in lust and guilt
> attraction and insouciance
>
> love aggravation
>
> we prance about
> then decide on a pack
>
> communal sharing
>
> it is never easy
> but my warrior self
> is bountiful and replenishing
>
> mother of minds
> guardian of language
>
> perhaps thief
> is more appropriate
> exposed   naming
>
> i twirl in the center
> they must abide by me
> follow my shadow
>
> mouths taste vernacular
> i rejoice the marriage
>
> this interminable
> love-affair with immortality. . .

LIBERATED

Marvin E. Williams

Cast of Characters:	Soursop
	Manjack
	Jojo (Soursop's wife)
	Josie (Jojo's sister)

| *Year:* | Late 1970s |

PART ONE

Scene One

[Soursop's modest house with bedroom, living room, and kitchenette exposed. Two wicker chairs sit in front of the house; out back, off the kitchenette, a washboard on a standing crate serves as a seat. Saturday, foreday. Soursop and Jojo sleep. Several cock crows pierce the silence. Soursop begins to stir. Dogs bark. Soursop eases out of bed. The barking picks up as Manjack, dressed in overalls and whistling "Barna Jam," comes to the front of the house and hollers.]

Manjack: Soursop, you ready or what? *[He picks up his whistling.]*

Soursop: *[Soursop grabs the overalls off the chair and, moving like a thief, tiptoes to the window. Whispers.]* Cut out that blasted noise. I coming, man. *[He cat burglars back across the room, kicking one then another object. Pauses, checks Jojo who appears agitated by the commotion. Meanwhile, Manjack bangs on the side of the house with a club, and shouts.]*

Manjack: Man, you ain't ready yet? The fish them gon stop running soon.

Soursop: *[To himself.]* Lawd, these bachelor ain't got no heart atall. You think I could tell he what problem his noise could cause? No. He gon just laugh like the idiot he is. But let Jojo wake up, nuh. It gon be "Soursop, take mey to Woolworth to buy a girdle for Mespel wedding." Since Mespel wedding to that long-tall Hess man from Aruba announce Jojo got mey running a limousine service for Mespel. Harassing mey head. Lawd, help mey when her sister from Tobago come to visit we next month. *[He rushes to get dressed, hopping on one foot as he tries to get into his clothes. Manjack starts drumming again, and singing "Barna Jam." Dogs bark and howl to Manjack's song.]*

Jojo:	*[Jojo rolls over and groans. Jojo, still asleep, speaks.]* Soursop, oney.
Soursop:	*[Bending toward his wife.]* Sweetheart, you call mey? *[Jojo smiles but doesn't answer. Soursop takes a deep breath.]* Good, she only talking in her sleep. *[He picks up a bucket with fishing gear out of the kitchenette and moves swiftly out the house to confront Manjack who is really into his song now.]*
Manjack:	"Small barna, big barna, young barna, old barna, barna in-between. . ." *[Throughout this scene the men ready their gear—stretching the lines, winding them on their spools, checking bait, etc.]*
Soursop:	*[He jerks club from Manjack.]* Manjack, your head good or what?
Manjack:	It good like what.
Soursop:	I ain't joking, you know.
Manjack:	Yes, I know you ain't Joe King. You is Soursop James, former resident of 37 Pondbush now urban renew out Barren Spot.
Soursop:	Keep it up.
Manjack:	I just in a good mood, man, a singing mood. What wrong with that, eh?
Soursop:	I don't like your choice of song, but nothing ain't wrong with singing. If tis that you was doing.
Manjack:	What wrong with the song I was singing? *Barna Jam*, what a mashup.
Soursop:	Another mashup of woman.
Manjack:	What you talking bout? Barna, big one, is culture, heritage, sweet genes. What wrong with celebrating something so exquisite, so. . .so we?
Soursop:	Nothing you would understand. *[Manjack starts to sing again.]* Look, if you gotto sing you can't wait til the sun come up, man? And you must do it so loud?
Manjack:	Calypso supposed to be sing loud.
Soursop:	But you can't at least sing a calypso what all these dog round the place ain't know enough to howl along with?
Manjack:	They howling in tune, eh? This song so pure every dog know it.
Soursop:	Pure assishness. Pun intended.
Manjack:	What shit you talking bout? These dog is island dog, man. They got calypso in they blood. Listen to this—
Soursop:	Knock it off before you start, you hear me. Knock it off right now before me and you fall out over stupidness.
Manjack:	What wrong with you, Soursop? Since when you ain't like to hear calypso?
Soursop:	Nothing ain't wrong with me. Calypso should be left to calypsonians. And maybe not even to them.
Manjack:	But you yourself say I gotta heapa potential to make calypso.
Soursop:	I was drunk when I say that. Look, tis wake up you trying to

125

	wake up mey wife and the rest of the neighborhood, nuh?
Manjack:	You ain't worry bout no neighborhood; you worry bout your wife waking up. She got you under wraps, bwoy. You need to get liberated, man. Dog and all howl for theirs and get it.
Soursop:	If you is any indication, tis dogs what making all the noise, keeping man back.
Manjack:	Only man who dey under manners, heavy manners from woman, keeping man back.
Soursop:	Let we go, you hear. Tis you who say you want to go catch fish, you know. If you stay here and keep hitting them wrong note you dey calling calypso and wake up Jojo, we ain't going fishing. At least not me.
Manjack:	You ain't tired let that woman boss you round, man?
Soursop:	Tain't a matter of she bossing me; tis just that she want mey to help her do some things today and I really ain't dey in the mood for it. But if she catch mey, of course, mey mood have to undergo a radical change.
Manjack:	*[Sucks teeth.]* You is a man or a mouse?
Soursop:	When you married the two of them is the same thing.
Manjack:	I believe in what Sparrow say. *[Sings.]* "Be ah man and not ah mouse; put some pepper in she souse; show that louse who is boss in the house." *[Speaks.]* Bam, braga dam! That's calypso.
Soursop:	That's calypso for bachelor to hear. Besides, I ain't got Papa Jack problem. Tis a jack rabbit I be.
Manjack:	Man, you damn well know what I mean. The thing is, married or not, no woman ain't bossing me. I gon wear the pants not the panty in my house.
Soursop:	A panty is a pants too, you know.
Manjack:	Stop talk shit.
Soursop:	Besides, woman does wear heapa pants nowadays. And they ain't got to be designer models neither. Tain't like long ago. You ain't notice? I mean, even pom-pom shorts ain't just exposing backside.
Manjack:	I know what you mean. A gang of woman showing they ass for true. *[Pause.]* And I notice that it have a pack of man- mouse, present company inclusive, who ain't like the man them from long ago. Evolution assbackwards. My father, man, that was man. Marmy was mey mother name and when he say "Marmy, jump," Mammy hit the trampoline. I gon carry on that tradition.
Soursop:	Tis you and your kind who got the woman shelter doing more business than they want. And the violence what you exposing is only a front for weak man who can't face the truth. Man always been mouse when it come to woman. We. . .they. . .allyu

	does only play rat when allyu round other man. Tain't nothing new. You know the difference? Long ago woman used to laugh behind man back and call he mouse; nowadays they does call we heapa pack rat mouse to our face. Wise up.
Manjack:	No woman could ever call me a mouse. Tis this damn American television what corrupting woman down here. Let any woman who think as the world turns it turn for she come play young and restless with me and I gon send her straight to our general hospital. Charles Harwood. Trust me, I would blue-black her eye them. Tis ah liberated man I be.
Soursop:	Manjack, you ain't tired chat shit? No woman ain't gon call you a man if you hit her. Not with any sensitivity or conviction anyway. What kinda man feel he could find manhood in beating up woman? No woman ain't gon call you a man unless you is mouse enough to let her be a complete human.
Manjack:	What that bullshit supposed to mean?
Soursop:	It mean that a real man won't hit he woman; a real man would liberate heself from treating his woman like she inferior, like she's meat, like she's a frigging punching bag for his craziness or his frustration or his insecurity or his excuse.
Manjack:	Soursop, since you start playing scholar in your old age, reading book left and right, and messing round with them nursery rhyme you does call poetry, you talking pure shit.
Soursop:	Let we go, man. We only making nar, I only knocking my head against a wall—you—and the sun coming up in another hour or so. *[They gather up the fishing gear which they have sorted and begin to exit. Manjack stops and faces Soursop.]*
Manjack:	Them rastaman got the right idea, bwoy. Woman is to procreate and cook food from ground provision. Not give backchat and orders. No siree. A woman is supposed to support her man and see that he happy in the sight of Jah. If I wasn't so old I woulda been a rastaman.
Soursop:	If you wasn't ah old jackass you woulda been ah young jackass.
Manjack:	Soursop, you really brainwash for true. What you trying to prove? That you is the original sensitive man, Captain Considerate?
Soursop:	Oh Christ! All right, Captain Crunch, have it your way.
Manjack:	Sometimes I does have to stop and wonder if you is the same sweet Soursop who used to be a proper gable around this island with woman falling all over you and you only saying "Get up and have pride in yourself" while you steady thiefing they pride and more. . .
Soursop:	*[Getting vexed]* Look, man, everybody responsible for they own

127

	pride. Anyway, I outta that now. I grow up. Why you don't join me?
Manjack:	No thanks but no thanks. *[Shakes head in wonderment.]* I does really have to stop and wonder sometimes for true. What happen to you, Sop? Jojo make you sour, no?
Soursop:	Jojo help me to correct mey errors.
Manjack:	No woman could correct my error them. Carve that in stone.
Soursop:	Yes. You is a serious cave man for true. A macho-saur. *[Manjack sucks his teeth and Soursop grins as they exit.]*

Scene Two

[Two hours later. Lights come up to suggest daybreak. Jojo, still in bed, stretches, feels for Soursop, discovers he has already risen. Sits up and calls for him several times. Puts on bathrobe over her slip and goes into living room then kitchenette.]

Jojo:	He think he slick. Sneaking out in the dark like a local thief. Knowing full well I want he to drop me Sunny Isles. I give he fair warning yesterday. Wait til that sweet mouse come home nibbling round mey body for cheese. *[She smiles and puts on kettle for tea as lights come up full. Leaves for living room where she presses on a cassette tape. Soso's song whose lyrics go "Some man like a woman with a big bottom, plenty hips," etc., comes on. Taken by the music, she starts to wind, checks herself, and flips tape off. Sucks teeth.]* This damn tape must be Manjack own. I tired of man treating woman like slabs of corn pork. *[Grins and winds a little, hearing the song she has turned off.]* The music sweet though. *[Flips back on the music and begins trashing back as she sings along.]* Oh Lawd! *[Flips off tape again, shakes head, grins.]* What we need is some more woman calypsonian to tell them man about theyself. Shatter they illusion about they prowess in and outta bed. Bedroom bully, the dub man call heself. Ha! That's the problem in a nutshell. Too much bullies and not enough lovers. Role models for young boys who shamelessly making love to they gun. *[Sings.]* "Woman want man who could use they lips as well as they move they hips." *[Speaks.]* Better than they move they hips. *[Laughs.]* Lawd, forgive mey for speaking the truth so early in the morning. *[Returns to the kitchenette. There are several raps on front door before she goes to answer it. Josie is there with seven pieces of luggage; Jojo stands in momentary shock.]* Lawd, Josie. What you doing here now? *[Rushes forward and hugs her. Pushes her to arm's length to get a good look while Josie grins widely.]* Girl, you look too good. When you come? How

come you didn't warn me? How everybody? *[Notices luggage.]* What you doing with all them suitcase? You plan to stay? Where you gon stay?

Josie: *[Laughs.]* Stop, stop, sis. Ketch you breath. Yes, I plan to stay in truth. I figger I could stay with allyu until I get something. Girl, you look good youself. Marriage suit you.

Jojo: Soursop ain't gon be ready for this, you know. He ain't like these kinda surprise.

Josie: From all the glowing things you write tell me about the mister, I not worry. What happen? You don't have you touch again? *[She smiles so Jojo laughs.]*

Jojo: You fast, you know.

Josie: *[Smile widens.]* Man is like ah lump of putty in ah artistic woman hand. Is easy to shape them. You don't need no heapa imagination.

Jojo: Keep talking loud like that let them hear you. I say let sleeping dogs lie with they myths for a blanket. *[They laugh.]* So, if man so easy to mold then how come you ain't got one at hand?

Josie: Is because not enough putty to shape them I steady bouncing up. They too gritty like sand or gravel or something. *[They laugh.]* Like you not going and invite me in you house, I see.

Jojo: Lawd, forgive mey. I just so shock to see you. Come, man. *[They gather up the luggage and go in, put stuff away and move to the kitchenette where Jojo serves tea.]*

Josie: So, how you sweet Soursop?

Jojo: Growing sweeter with age.

Josie: Mind he get overripe and spoil.

Jojo: I say growing sweeter not riper. Sweeter—heaven alone know how—in bed.

Josie: Like you bragging.

Jojo: Bare facts, girl. *[They laugh.]*

Josie: I had was to ask you about his friend. What he name again?

Jojo: Manjack. The wantobe calypsonian who can't even carry a tune.

Josie: Well, if he could carry me, my music go tune he up.

Jojo: Stop it. You too fresh with yourself. You ain't self meet the man yet.

Josie: Calypsonian, eh. Is what he does do? How he is? Sweet?

Jojo: He all right—although he feel he is macho man in print. He all-time braying like a jackass. He way behind the times. A dinosaur in polyester pants.

Josie: What you mean exactly? The man can't be that bad again.

Jojo: You should hear the man. He always singing loud about putting woman in they place when the truth is the only woman he ever

	had for any time in he place was he mother who dead the other day from natural causes. God bless her soul. But if you hear he talk you would think he was a real saga bwoy or something who got woman hand-over-fist and got them train good-good like them white people dog what does eat steak for dinner and even got they own bed and thing.
Josie:	Be serious no, girl. So he never get married?
Jojo:	For about thirty-five seconds to a woman who was looking for her papers. But I ain't want to get into that debacle. *[Pauses, reflects.]* The thing is, he good-looking and everything and he got a good foreman job with Public Works and plenty woman like he. Yet when I stop to think bout it, I never see he with no special woman. Maybe he attitude frighten them.
Josie:	Pure grandcharge, I bet. He still don't have a woman?
Jojo:	Cool your heels, no man. Cool out, you just come.
Josie:	My heels cooling so long now that they chill. In fact, they chilly. And not just me heels either. Don't even talk about just come. Answer me question.
Jojo:	Like I say, I don't see he with nobody special. I don't see he with nobody atall. Except Soursop. He always running off somewhere with mey husband. Sometimes I does wonder if one of these good days they gon elope.
Josie:	Hmm, hmm. I see. I don't think I go need a lot of putty for this one.
Jojo:	Stop it. He might surprise you, give you a run for your money.
Josie:	I does do aerobics. I in shape. I hope he have stamina.
Jojo:	Let's go in the living room and get comfortable. We have tons of catching up to do.

Scene Three

[They move into the living room, sit, and mime an involved conversation as lights go bright to indicate midday then fade to dark for several beats. They come back up bright with the women in the kitchen snacking. Shortly, Soursop and Manjack enter with gear and a bucket of fish. They pause in the yard sorting things as Jojo, hearing them, alerts Josie to their presence and goes outside with hands on hips.]

Soursop:	*[Almost to himself though Manjack, who's laughing at Jojo's combative posture, hears]* Oh Gawd, Jojo, not now. Not in front this assbird. *[Jojo smiles now, relaxes.]*
Manjack:	Don't let that smile fool you, bwoy; tis licks coming.
Soursop:	Mean't worry bout licks because Jojo ain't into hitting me. But

	I have a feeling that curse like rain waiting in her smile although it clear not cloudy.
Jojo:	*[Moves jauntily towards men; Manjack moves aside where most of his comments here will serve as counterpoint and critique.]* Soursop, darling, how much fish allyu catch?
Manjack:	That question sound fishy, bwoy. Watch out.
Soursop:	Bout. . .bout ten yellowtail snap. . .snapper. Nothing else wasn't bit. . .biting and you love yellowtail anyway.
Manjack:	*[Coughs pointedly.]* Since when you start to stam. . .stammer?
Jojo:	Let me see them, nuh.
Soursop:	They ain't too big, you know, Jojo.
Manjack:	*[Sings.]* Tis big-big bamboo you want.
Jojo:	Oh Lawd! They lovely yes. How much is ours?
Manjack:	Something is rotten in the state of affairs.
Soursop:	All. Since Manjack eating here everyday like he is a supplementary breadwinner.
Manjack:	Tis big-big bamboo you need.
Jojo:	I gon clean them and cook them up right away. When you wash off and get settle, come help mey turn the fungy.
Manjack:	*[Sings.]* Move leh mey get mey share, she licking Soursop without ah care.
Jojo:	*[Walking away, remembers Manjack and stops.]* Eh-eh. Manjack, I forget you been there. How you do, man?
Manjack:	I can't complain, Jojo. I can't complain atall. I dey good. I dey good and free as a bird.
Soursop:	*[Aside.]* Ah assbird.
Jojo:	Well, it good that you so free because it have somebody inside I want you to meet. Soursop, I want you to meet her too.
Manjack:	Tis only when a man tired everybody does want he to meet people when they know full well that a tired man don't make good company. And besides that a man would rather not be introduce to no woman when he got on this heapa old clothes and stink ah fish. And maybe you could see clear to tell your company that I gon meet her later seeing as how I indispose at the moment. *[Pauses and fidgets.]* And I hope she enjoy her visit whoever she is and if she still around for awhile then perhaps maybe I might drop by and say hello although she shouldn't take that as a promise because I is a busy man who ain't like idleness and got heapa thing to do to keep meyself occupy fruitfully. *[Begins to leave.]*
Soursop:	Manjack, you know you ain't got a damn thing to do. And what stupidness you talking about the clothes you got on too old for introductions? Only old clothes you does wear.

131

Jojo: Stop your stupidness, Manjack. She really want to meet you. And she understand you been fishing so that ain't no problem. Bring he in, Soursop. I going to tend to the fish. *[She leaves.]*

Soursop: *[After a few beats, starts in but notices Manjack hanging back.]* You ain't coming?

Manjack: Man, you can't wait? A man just trying to cool out and you acting like a Russian. You should pay more attention to the old saying them. You never hear "Don't rush the brush, you might get daub"? I ain't like people rush me, you know; it does get me well ignorant, you see me yah.

Soursop: What you fraid of? Stop stalling, nuh man.

Manjack: Fraida, fraida? Who you calling Stalling? Tis you is the Russian, not me. Just for that I got a good mind to leave you yah and go straight to my own yard. Everybody too damn hurry these fast-food nowadays. That's the problem with this world. Everybody running like wild ants and ain't have no particular place to go. Shit now, you can't wait?

Soursop: I sorry, man. I see how ignorant it does get you for true.

Manjack: That's supposed to be funny?

Soursop: Look, man, let we go in. I sure the woman is Jojo sister.

Manjack: What make you so sure?

Soursop: SusChrist, man. It make a difference who she be?

Manjack: No, ain't make no difference. But still.

Soursop: I know Jojo would of tell me something about meyself for running out the house this morning. If she wasn't trying to get on mey good side.

Manjack: All woman too slick. What her sister name?

Soursop: Josie. She from Tobago.

Manjack: Tobago? I didn't know Jojo was from Tobago. She don't have no accent or nothing.

Soursop: Yes, man. But she been here from small. I see a lot of pictures of Josie and she pretty too bad. *[Manjack perks up visibly.]* It hard to believe she only two years younger than Jojo.

Manjack: You best not let Jojo hear you saying that. She would probably give Mighty Mouse, i.e. you, a proper cutassing.

Soursop: *[Sucks teeth.]* You coming or what?

Manjack: I coming, man, I coming. Bwoy, you more Russian than dead Khrushchev.

Soursop: You look like you want to stand out here until you dead like Khrushchev. *[They move inside to the living room, Manjack stuffing his shirt in his pants, smoothing back hair, etc. They pause.]*

Manjack: So, how I look?

Soursop: Like the jackass you is. *[Manjack attempts to bolt; Soursop grabs*

	him.] Take it easy, man. The woman ain't plan to judge you like you is in some kinda beauty contest. Like you was a stud. . .or gelding on a farm.
Manjack:	You talking shit because you married and ain't have nothing to worry about. Why you don't just shut up and let me get meyself presentable. *[Manjack continues his grooming while Soursop goes further in and notices the luggage. He staggers from their number.]*
Soursop:	But what is this atall? *[Manjack joins him.]*
Manjack:	It look like a family of awesome proportions visiting you, man. *[Chuckles.]*
Soursop:	*[Scratches head.]* Jojo ain't tell me that Josie planning to stay for more than a week. She ain't tell me no such thing. *[A refreshed Josie enters.]* Jo. . .jo.
Manjack:	*[Smitten.]* Let we fire some rum. *[Josie smiles throughout.]*
Soursop:	Josie—I recognize you from your picture them—Josie, I is Soursop. And this is mey old friend Manjack.
Manjack:	Old is just a figure of speech, of course. *[Pulls stomach in as Josie laughs.]*
Josie:	*[Extends hand.]* Glad to meet you at last, Soursop. *[Soursop pulls her in and kisses her on cheeks.]* Jojo write tell me so much good things about you. You sound like you is a very good man. *[Soursop grins foolishly; Manjack sucks teeth.]* Manjack, I happy to meet you.
Manjack:	*[Moves forward, arms open for hug.]* You ain't happier than me. *[Josie steps back from his reach.]* I mean, I glad to meet you too. *[Josie enjoys his embarrassment; he turns to Soursop.]* Why you don't get the damn rum!
Soursop:	Take it easy, man. Take it easy. *[Manjack nervously wrings hands, etc.]* So Josie, you look good, man. How long you planning to stay with we? I give you a week before you start bawling for Tobago.
Josie:	*[Goes seductively to couch, sits.]* I come to stay for good. If everything work out.
Soursop:	*[Rushes toward her.]* Come to stay for good?
Manjack:	All of a sudden wax stopping up your ear.
Soursop:	You stay outta this. So, where you working and where you plan to stay?
Manjack:	Don't tell me you plan to pitch the woman out in the street.
Soursop:	If you ain't want me pitch you out this house then you better hush the frig up.
Manjack:	Temper, temper.
Josie:	*[Smiling]* I here on a Kasha Hotel bond and Jojo say that you would happy to let me stay here until I find some place.

133

Soursop:	*[Paces.]* Jojo say so, eh. She say so, eh. A architect can't fit two mampee in yah with we.
Josie:	*[Stands, croons.]* Jojo all time boasting how you so considerate, kind, caring. But she ain't start to tell me how handsome you is.
Soursop:	*[Grins.]* Heh-heh. Heh-heh. Of course you could stay with we till you get on your foot. *[Josie gives him a warm hug and "dances" slowly away into the bedroom as the men look on hypnotized.]*
Manjack:	*[Recovers; then with an affected voice and slight bow]* Your wimpship, for once your wimping out pleases me.
Soursop:	Kiss my ass. *[Paces as Manjack laughs.]* Jojo ain't ah bad woman and she usually don't take advantage of me, but lately I notice that she abusing mey good nature. *[Pause.]* I need to make a stand on this issue because ain't no way in the world Josie could fit in this lil piece of house with we.
Manjack:	But you so considerate, kind, caring, and handsome.
Soursop:	Cut the shit.
Manjack:	Face facts: your fate is to wilt under the ploys of woman. Take your ordain pressure quietly and dish out liquor like a good bwoy.
Soursop:	Wait here. We gon see about that. *[Storms out to the back of the house where Jojo is preparing the fish. Josie returns to the living room and sits across from Manjack.]* Jojo, how come you ain't tell me that your sister was coming here to stay? I thought we used to communicate.
Jojo:	*[Turns swiftly.]* What? You frighten me, man. What you say?
Soursop:	I say, since when you going doing thing behind my back?
Jojo:	Honey, what you talking bout? What thing I do behind your back?
Soursop:	Invite your sister to stay here when you know we ain't have room to sneeze as it tis already.
Jojo:	Soursop, I was as surprise as you when Josie come out that taxi and start stalking the house with that mound ton of luggage. But since she was already here, what I coulda do except make what little space we have here available to her? She is mey sister, Soursop.
Soursop:	It ain't make no sense trying to argue with you. *[Starts to leave but turns back.]* I see a pattern developing lately where you making promise left and right for me. That ain't fair atall, and I want you to know firsthand that I ain't gon stand for it.
Jojo:	*[Stands.]* Soursop, honey. Soursop.
Soursop:	I mean, tis fifteen years we married now and this is ah hell of ah time to start acting the fool with me. Taking me for granted. I ain't know what get into you other than age, but you better start

	cleaning up your act posthaste because I—
Jojo:	*[In stitches]* Oh, Lawd, Soursop. I ain't mean to laugh. *[Laughs.]* Oh Lawd, mey belly.
Soursop:	What the hell you laughing for? You hear me say anything funny?
Jojo:	Yes! *[Riotous laughter]* Sorry, honey. *[Chuckles.]* Sorry, man. Forgive me.
Soursop:	*[Laughs uneasily.]* I is the one who should say sorry. I had sound like ah idiot, eh?
Jojo:	*[Laughter.]* Yes!
Soursop:	You ain't have to agree with me so strong, man. I love you.
Jojo:	Even though only age get in me since we together? *[They laugh and embrace.]* I more than love you. Give me ah lil kiss, man. *[They kiss.]* Ummm. Thank you.
Soursop:	*[Disengages.]* But how we gon manage this thing, man, Jojo?
Jojo:	Don't worry, honey, we gon manage. I gon tell you the game plan later. Go entertain your guest them. *[Chuckles.]* Let me finish cleaning these fish yah.
Soursop:	You want a rum and something? I fixing one for Manjack. Oh, I forget Josie. She does drink?
Jojo:	Anything but liquor. Give her some of the passion fruit from the icebox. And yes, honey, you could make me ah drink. Rum and water. And make sure it strong.
Soursop:	Gimme ah minute. *[Goes to kitchenette speaking to himself]* How ah man gon fight against a woman like that, eh? Pure assishness to try. She too fair, logical, and loving, man. *[While he gets drinks, Manjack gets up and through an elaborate but amateurish ploy makes his way over to Josie and sits. Soursop takes Jojo her drink and pauses on his way back to listen to Manjack who reclines as he speaks.]*
Manjack:	Yes, man, it have place like dirt here where ah woman as nice looking as you could lime. And, in fact, I would be happy too bad to take you out on the town being as how I does frequent all the spots and know all the real good band them. *[Soursop stifles a snicker.]*
Josie:	How come you not married, Manjack?
Manjack:	Eh?
Josie:	Why you not married yet with ah island full of no doubt available women?
Manjack:	Oh, that. It have so much confusing fish in the sea and I meticulous and selective and choosy. That's why I ain't bite no bait yet. But I ready to bite anytime I find the right fish. *[Looks her over tellingly.]* And if you want to go out sometime soon let me know because I could see right now that you like to lime and mean't no

135

	less than the same way. *[Soursop stifles another laugh.]*
Josie:	Well, I would like to see the place in truth.
Manjack:	Let me take charge.
Josie:	Only for awhile.
Manjack:	*[Entranced, distracted]* Eh?
Josie:	Nothing just yet. *[Soursop enters with drinks.]*
Soursop:	See rum yah! Let we go back to the trough.
Manjack:	*[Stands.]* You come back so quick?
Soursop:	It only quick because, you dirty dog you, you been having fun. *[Manjack grabs bottle off the tray along with a glass; pours and offers drink to Josie.]* Eh-eh, who elect you mine host?
Josie:	Thanks, but I don't want no drink right now *[Soursop laughs; Manjack glares at him before he downs drink.]*
Manjack:	What you braying like ah jackass for? *[Pours himself another and downs it.]*
Soursop:	*[Takes bottle and pours himself one.]* All jackass does recognize they own species.
Manjack:	*[Reaches for bottle.]* What you imprisoning the rum like some warden for?
Josie:	*[Almost rising]* You don't have enough of that rum, Manjack?
Manjack:	*[Laughs.]* You hear she, Sop? Tis man I name. This lil bit of rum we drinking can't nearly get me high much less drunk. *[Staggers, regains balance and grabs bottle away; staggers slightly as he moves to join Josie who promptly gets up.]*
Josie:	Excuse me. I go help Jojo with the fish. *[Leaves with a walk that enchants Manjack; Soursop sits with his drink.]*
Manjack:	*[Still staring at the space Josie has passed through]* She nice, eh? You say she is two years younger than Jojo?
Soursop:	Yes.
Manjack:	Bwoy, she ain't look a minute over twenty-five. And she solid-solid and pretty. Lawd, Sparrow right for true bout Tobago woman. *[Sings.]* "Nice and round like a butterball." *[Speaks.]* Sop, talk the truth. You think she like mey?
Soursop:	She crazy about you, man. You can't see how she eyeing you and eating up your stale rap?
Manjack:	Nothing ain't stale bout my rap, you hear. As a matter of fact it kinda fresh. You ain't see how she been blushing? But you right for true, you know. She was eating up mey words like ah gamadizer. You think she would go out with mey tonight to the quadrille they having down by the Hall? *[Pours drink for both of them; Soursop takes the bottle and rests it on the coffee table.]*
Soursop:	You have to ask her that, man. Don't ask me. *[Takes a sip.]* And, furthermore, you sure you sober enough to carry anybody

any place?

Manjack:	*[Stands.]* I sober like ah top. *[Staggers.]*
Soursop:	And you staggering like one what tired spin too.
Manjack:	Who staggering? *[Staggers.]* Soursop, you know I tired drink you under that old table you have in your kitchen. Stop talk shit and pour rum, man.
Soursop:	*[Picks up bottle.]* Josie ain't look like she too like the fact that you dey drinking so much, you know.
Manjack:	Watch mey, I is ah liberated man. Tain't her damn business how much rum I drink. *[Pushes glass out to Soursop.]* Fling Cruzan, man.
Soursop:	*[Begins to pour.]* Tis your funeral.
Manjack:	*[Pulls away; liquor spills.]* You really think she worry bout how much I drinking?
Soursop:	Watch what foolishness you make. You drinking rum or what?
Manjack:	I just ask a simple question, man. You ain't gotto go on so. *[Sits.]* She had just look ah lil upset when you think about it.
Soursop:	If you is "ah liberated man" you ain't have to worry your head over what Josie think about you drinking. *[Gets up and begins to clean up spill.]*
Manjack:	You right. Cut loose rum in mey cup. *[Offers then pulls back glass.]* But wait, man. She had look kinda funny when we was drinking for true. I gon drink ah lil bit after we eat dinner.
Soursop:	You staying for dinner then?
Manjack:	You deaf or what? You think I give you my fish them for joke?
Soursop:	You is joke enough. You want to hear music?
Manjack:	Play ah old Sparrow. In fact play "Tobago Girl." Let we honor our guest.
Soursop:	*[Going towards tape player]* I didn't know you had ah guest. Not ah bad touch though. *[Sometime during their conversation Jojo and Josie moved inside, Jojo to cook, Josie to the bedroom. Now, as music plays, Manjack, going to bathroom, bumps into Josie who's coming out. Stops and mimes speech. Josie blushes then signals yes with a smile. She joins Jojo and Manjack continues off stage. He returns shortly, dancing to the music. After several beats, Soursop turns the music down.]* It look like something sweet you, man. *[Manjack continues to dance.]* Remember what they say: "What sweet in goat mouth sour in he backside." *[Turns music off and Manjack sits.]*
Manjack:	She say she gon go to the dance with me. Stale rap? You think I does play, nuh?
Soursop:	*[Laughs.]* It look like Josie don't play neither.
Manjack:	What?
Soursop:	*[Produces deck of cards.]* I say let we play some rummy let me spank

137

	you. *[Clears table and deals, and the men settle into their game.]*
Jojo:	*[Stirring pot]* So what you think about our friend?
Josie:	Who? Manjack?
Jojo:	No, the jumbie sitting there by you. Who else?
Josie:	He all right. But he does drink one set of rum.
Jojo: today	Not really, you know. I don't know who he trying to impress with his drinking. He only all right?
Josie:	I just meet the man. What you expect?
Jojo:	I ain't expect nothing. Excuse mey, but I thought I see diamonds in your eyes.
Josie:	*[Laughs.]* I don't know bout that, but he interesting yes. Another thing bothering me though. It look like you right about his ideas about woman in truth.
Jojo:	Don't pay that too much mind. Manjack is ah shy man. All that talk is to cover up he shyness.
Josie:	I don't know again, girl. Like he want ah dog not ah woman. *[Pause.]* He ask me to go out with he tonight.
Jojo:	So what you gon do?
Josie:	I going.
Jojo:	What about his funny ideas?
Josie:	I concern but I not worry. I giving him plenty rope to hang himself. *[They laugh as lights fade.]*

PART TWO

Scene One

[Six weeks later. It is dusk, and a well-dressed Manjack paces in front of Soursop's house and grooms himself as he waits for Josie. Pulls afro comb out of his back pocket, raises it to his head but changes his mind. Pats already flawless hair instead. Brushes imaginary speck off pants, straightens tie. Adopts a soldier's posture as he paces. Whistles a love tune. Mimes asking a lady to dance, taking her hand, and leading her in a ballroom dance as he hums. Eventually Josie comes out dressed brilliantly. They give each other a brief kiss, hook arms, and leave smiling as lights dim and go out.]

Scene Two

[Minutes later. Lights come on after a few beats. Jojo and Soursop are having dinner in the kitchenette.]

Soursop:	The love bird them fly the coop again, I notice.
Jojo:	Dinner and dance, mey child. The fourth time this week. I self didn't know it had so much music on this island.
Soursop:	The music dey in they head. Wait til it stop. Or at least change tempo.
Jojo:	Still, Josie very happy and I feel good for her. And I think Manjack want to married her.
Soursop:	At least he want the new marriage—to shack up with her til it last. Every time he come over here he pulling me aside and asking questions what ain't so subtle.
Jojo:	Like what?
Soursop:	*[Stands, and in Manjack's voice]* This house ain't too small for all allyu? Allyu must be butting up in one another can't done.
Jojo:	You joking. I didn't know he was doing it with you too.
Soursop:	How the crab hole treating allyu since I been yah last time?
Jojo:	*[Laughs and stands in the spirit of the mockery.]* Sardine in ah can got more room than allyu.
Soursop:	If ah mosquito fly in this house it gon be severely overcrowded.
Jojo:	Ah callaloo pot got less confusion than this house.
Soursop:	I can't even stretch when I dey here. I fraid I slap one allyu.
Jojo:	*[Laughter becomes reflection; she sits.]* Honey, traffic heavy in the house for true, you know.
Soursop:	*[Rejoining Jojo at table]* I know, but tain't none ah Manjack damn scheming business. Besides, I get use to Josie being here.
Jojo:	Me too, you know.
Soursop:	She add something what been missing.
Jojo:	*[Sharply]* What?
Soursop:	Ahh, ahh, nothing in particular. Company. Craziness. I don't know.
Jojo:	You don't know, eh? You think I don't see you scoping out backside?
Soursop:	*[Laughs uneasily.]* Behave yourself, Jojo.
Jojo:	Maybe that's my problem. I alltime behaving. Tis take you taking me for granted.
Soursop:	I love you, Jojo. My eyes, bad as they is, are for you only.
Jojo:	Words. Borrowed ones at that.
Soursop:	If something fit perfect, why change it? So when Manjack start

139

up he slickness. . .

Jojo: You don't start yours. You ain't getting off so easy.

Soursop: So when Manjack start up with "My house got room knocking dog in stark contrast to this doghouse," I does stop he cold. I does tell he married the woman else she staying right here in the sardine-can-crab-hole-dog-house.

Jojo: But, Soursop, you can't speak for Josie.

Soursop: I know that. I just calling Manjack bluff. I know she good for he and I know he want to married her, but for some strange reason he dey dancing in place, holding strain when it come to marriage.

Jojo: Well, I know Josie love he and I think Manjack is ah change man.

Soursop: In ah kinda way, yes. He is a sharp bwoy overnight. He sell he old truck and buy ah brand new Mustang as becomes his new incorporated status. Crusing round town with Josie tight-tight up under he arm like she is sweat. . .or deodorant.

Jojo: *[Laughs.]* Ah deodorant what making he sweat. And the way he tack down day-in-day-out. Sharp bwoy! I self ain't mind being home-up under he. Clinging on like Secret Ultra Dry. *[They laugh.]*

Soursop: The thing is, me ain't self know he had so much clothes. This man been my friend for donkey years and I didn't know that he was ah closet gable.

Jojo: Ah real saga bwoy. And check the style. *[Stands, mimicks.]* Evening. I'm here to call on Miss Josie. Ah English butler can't touch he.

Soursop: Pure pappyshow. Yes, Manjack change for true. He more assish than ever. He more clownish than ever. But in ah way he ain't really change atall.

Jojo: How you mean?

Soursop: Weeks now he liming with Josie and he still talking big about how woman must follow his program else he ain't want no part of them. And I ah lil surprise because I didn't think ah woman like Josie would allow such ah attitude. But I notice she going along with the program and looking like she happy with it.

Jojo: Who could explain love, eh? Manjack really showing her ah good time for true. Everyday after work he coming like ah hurricane, sweeping Josie up and taking her out for dinner and dance. When last we been out, Soursop?

Soursop: Oh Gawd, Sweets. Don't start that. Don't let them pretend teenagers influence your good senses.

Jojo: Why youth got to be squander on young people who ain't want it, hurrying to be older than they years? Why we have to stand up stupid-stupid like two tree and let age, like ah nest of woodlice, eat we away?

Soursop: *[Reaches out to her with a smile; Jojo rejects gesture.]* Until your sister come yah I was the only woodlice you used to worry bout. And I had ah open invitation to all your limb them.

Jojo: I was sleeping. Tis like comfort drug me and put me in ah kinda coma. But Josie—and Manjack too, the two of them—act like ah antidote what wake me up. *[Pauses, goes around table to face him directly.]* Soursop, I wouldn't trade you for any man. . .

Soursop: Only for ah Manjack.

Jojo: I serious. I wouldn't trade you for anybody. But you ain't everything, honey.

Soursop: I gon have to talk serious with Manjack. Tell he what shh. . .what stupidness he cause.

Jojo: He ain't cause no stupidness. . .or no shit neither. What he do is give we ah model if we want to take it. Honey, don't lie, you ain't miss the excitement?

Soursop: *[Holds and caresses her.]* You know I ain't lying when I say you is major excitement, more than enough excitement for me.

Jojo: *[Breaks away.]* Don't sweet talk me, man. I serious.

Soursop: I dead serious too. It ain't working?

Jojo: No. Watch, honey, you know you ain't got to do nothing special to turn me on. Just sit down and look stupid-stupid and I want you. But what I talking bout different. And you know it. So stop playing the ass.

Soursop: *[Dreamily]* The Vibratones at Eve's Garden, Tarco and Milo tearing up Plantation. Archie and his bwoys mashing up Vickey's and the Hideaway. Them dey was days. Booke and Bailey, Baga and Edgy. Archie and the solo sax and Wesley and the cylobox. *[Sings.]* "In St. Thomas at the Hideaway everybody was trashing back." *[They trash back and Jojo sings chorus.]*

Jojo: "Archie buck them up."

Soursop: "Don't go by Saint Cee if you ain't feel okay."

Jojo: *[Really dancing now]* "Archie buck mey up!"

Soursop: "Tis then Mattie Gru get up and start to break away."

Jojo: "Archie buck mey up!"

Soursop: "Tinny ling, tinny lay."

Jojo: "Buck mey up."

Soursop: "Yeaaah."

Jojo: "Archie buck them up."

Soursop: "Ah seh Archie fling mey down."

Jojo: "And Archie bruk mey up."

Soursop: *[Speaks.]* Oh Christ! Music in your tailpart. *[They struggle to catch breath.]* Jojo, sweetheart, I really miss it, want it, need it in the

141

	heart of mey soul case.
Jojo:	Meain't know bout you, but I gon take ah shower and get ready.
Soursop:	Ready for what?
Jojo:	I want you with mey, Soursop. But if you ain't coming, don't wait up because I going. And going, and go. . .
Soursop:	Go start the shower. I coming. *[Sinks into chair and sighs as Jojo leaves, singing. Lights fade to black.]*

Scene Three

[A week later. The men sit outside on chairs with glasses and their stubborn bottle between them. Jojo in kitchenette cooking.]

Manjack:	Josie is ah woman, bwoy. She sweet too bad. And she know how to make ah man happy without forgetting her place. When I say jump, she flying. When I say sit, tis lying down she lying. When I say shut up, she does ask til when. When I say I is man, she does say I is men. Oh Gawd, I should write that down. Yes, man, she is ah perfect woman for mey. What you think, Sop?
Soursop:	I think she very nice, but I don't believe she's the kind of woman who would stand for all this bossing around you talking bout.
Manjack:	Your problem is that you like to spoil woman. Watch how Jojo does have her own way. Even got you liming when you ain't want to lime, bucking up when you bruking down. I is ah liberated man, bwoy. Josie know that and she respect herself when it come to me. What that book you show me the other day name? *The New Improved Man*? *[Sucks teeth.]* This old. . .this mature man ain't need no improving. Them book don't teach you nothing but how to be ah good manmouse (no hyphen). When it come to you "henpecked" is putting it mildly. You better throw away them book and liberate yourself.
Soursop:	I is as liberated as I want to get. Don't worry bout me.
Manjack:	Meain't worry bout you; I sorry for you. Yes, bwoy. Josie is the kinda woman ah man should married if he want to live happy, in peace.
Soursop:	Go on and married her then.
Manjack:	A man should think serious about marriage before he jump in it. I mean, watch what it do to you. Atlas turn to alas.
Soursop:	It obvious you seriously ready to married Josie. What frightening you? You ain't got to pretend with me.
Manjack:	*[Springs to feet.]* Stop chat shit, no. Who frighten? Josie really got some funny ideas, bwoy.

Soursop: Hello.

Manjack: Acting like she is ah liberated woman and she must have equality. Bull junk like that. Going against nature.

Soursop: *[Shaken by the thought, sits.]* Going against nurture, you mean.

Manjack: Going against culture and tradition.

Soursop: I don't know what culture and what tradition you talking bout. What about the African system of reciprocity or, to bring it down to your level, sharing?

Manjack: Sharing what?

Soursop: Responsibilities, man. And power. And stature.

Manjack: Ah recent myth concocted by nationalist looking for woman converts and lil wife; ah makeup history by so-called woman libbers and they sympathizers, you inclusive.

Soursop: Our African-Caribbean warrior and rebel queen them is myth? Nzinga, Nita, Nanny, Queen Mary; them woman you calling just makeup history?

Manjack: Exceptions to the rule. That's why people of your ilk does keep so much noise behind they name. What they do frighten allyu precisely because it unusual.

Soursop: Keep that up and you gon lose Josie, you know. From what I could see she is more like one of them rebel queen than some meek queenie.

Manjack: Lose her? Stop talking assishness like that, no man. You trying to frighten me?

Soursop: I trying to tell you that you better ease up before you drive Josie away. Look, you love the woman, right?

Manjack: Yes. I love her bad. More than air. More than water. More than food.

Soursop: So why you can't leave the woman alone let her be ah woman, ah person?

Manjack: *[Leaps to feet.]* Because love ain't mean surrender, you hear me. Love ain't mean dishing out your manhood to some woman, no matter how beautiful she is. I is ah man, you hear me. And I gon continue to be one. *[Manjack storms off as Josie enters kitchenette from bedroom. She is near tears.]*

Josie: I love the man but he is ah real ass.

Jojo: Honey, what happen?

Josie: I thought I could of change him, but is no use. He won't change again.

Jojo: But allyu seem so happy, like everything working out.

Josie: We happy. I happy. But I unhappy too. Is because this man is ah mule in truth.

Jojo: What happen? What he do?

143

Josie: Is what and what that man not say. He pick me up from work yesterday and we drive out to the beach. I say eh-eh, this sweet man full of surprises. And he sweet, Jojo. I can't lie. *[Dreamily]* Sugarcakes I does call him every now and then when. . .

Jojo: But?

Josie: But the ass, without leave or license, start one set of verbal abuse. Threatening to slap me in me tail if I don't give he what belong to him.

Jojo: What you take from he?

Josie: Nothing. The man accuse me of thiefing. . .trying to thief his manhood.

Jojo: His manhood?

Josie: He say I is one of them kinda woman who feel she have to be boss, who feel she have to run things, and he ain't in that with me, and ah barrage of nonsense so.

Jojo: *[Cups her sister's face.]* He hit you?

Josie: And you not bailing me out? That man. . .no man could put his hand on me. Is suicide he would be committing. I really can't understand some men, you know. I mean, what he fraid of? How I being meself going and reduce he? Tell me.

Jojo: Tis ah sickness, ah sickness I know you could cure.

Josie: I doubt it. When you mix horse with jackass you go get mule. Manjack stubborn like hell and nobody go change that.

Jojo: But he love you, Josie. Tis just fraid he fraid to commit to marriage. That's why he hiding behind that macrone-ass macho talk. But, trust mey, he ain't really mean none of it.

Josie: Well, is ah good job he do convincing me. I sold but I not for sale.

Jojo: Well, he think he mean it, but he ain't ready to face the truth, see the light yet. Which remind me, he see or had delight yet?

Josie: Everytime we hug up tight-tight and start ah slow grind, delight does shine in he eye and them. But no, not yet. *[They laugh.]*

Jojo: No wonder he steady sniffing around you and panting with he tongue darn near beating he chest. I give the poor man less than ah month before he surrender. Or collapse. You wicked you know, girl.

Josie: I ain't that type of woman. *[Jojo glares.]* In Manjack case I ain't that type of woman. And it killing me. Is doubts, serious doubts I have that I could hold out longer than him. I long past ready.

Jojo: He gon come running. . .I mean crawling with ah ring directly, man. Don't worry.

Josie: I not worry bout that. I expect it. Is what it go commit me to that bothering me. Cause no amount of love go make me surrender my independence, myself. I live too free. . .

Jojo:	And lonely.
Josie:	It had loneliness, yes. A whole set. But I live too free too long to accept that man nonsense. Is against my nature. Against all nature. Ah frigging death in life.
Jojo:	Amen. *[Darkness.]*

Scene Four

[Afternoon two weeks later. A car pulls up to Soursop's house. Josie, dressed in a sexy negligee, goes to window and sees an agitated Manjack approaching. She hurries into living room to couch. Sits and pretends to read. Manjack raps; gets no answer; raps again. Calls.]

Manjack:	Josie. Jo! *[Josie sucks teeth, shifts position away from his call, flips pages idly.]* Josie! Come nuh, woman. I know you in there. Soursop them tell me you home. Josie! Sweet stuffing, come nuh.
Josie:	Nobody home.
Manjack:	I guess tis ah jumbie talking to me then.
Josie:	Yes. Ah jumbie. A nobody. The nobody jumbie you want me to be.
Manjack:	Stop playing, nuh man. I need to see you.
Josie:	How you going and see Nobody again?
Manjack:	Woman, open the blasted door! I ain't come here to play.
Josie:	No. You come to play-play.
Manjack:	Don't make me break down this damn door. I ain't playing like I mad, you know.
Josie:	I agree. You really mad in truth.
Manjack:	*[Struggles to calm himself.]* Watch, what going on, love? What this all about?
Josie:	Certainly not love.
Manjack:	What?
Josie:	You hear what I say.
Manjack:	I gotto talk to you, doh-doh.
Josie:	*[Stifles a laugh. Rights her anger.]* We talking.
Manjack:	Not like this, for godsake, love bread. You hear what shit you have me talking? I begging you, let me in.
Josie:	*[Flings magazine down, jumps up, takes a deep breath, and goes to window.]* Manjack, what you want with me, eh?
Manjack:	I want to say sorry.
Josie:	There. You said it. Good day. *[Closes curtains.]*
Manjack:	*[Falls to knees.]* I begging you, sugar dumplin, let me in.
Josie:	*[Opens curtains.]* I let you in and you acting the ass. So stay out;

	stay away from me; go back to your caveman fantasies.
Manjack:	I caving in, Josie. My heart caving in without you. Tis three whole days now I ain't see you. I can't take much more of this. Come to your senses.
Josie:	I do that three days ago when you make to slap me in me tail. I leaving you to spare your life.
Manjack:	*[Springs to feet.]* I didn't hit you. I can't hit no woman! Woman, I say I sorry.
Josie:	I'm afraid I agree with you.
Manjack:	Tis ah ass you playing me for? I ain't begging no more. I demanding. I giving you five seconds to open this frigging door, then I kicking the rass of it in. I counting: One, two, three—
Josie:	*[Opens door but stands in doorway.]* Nobody going and blame me for contributing to the delinquency of a psychotic. The door open. Now what?
Manjack:	Now we gon talk serious. *[Gets an eyefull of her dress.]* You put on that piece of thing to tease me, eh?
Josie:	I have no idea what you talking about. I was preparing to take a nap before you decide to start World War III.
Manjack:	You wicked, you know. You know I was coming.
Josie:	You giving yourself undue credit.
Manjack:	You prepare for me, eh? You make arrangement to torture me.
Josie:	*[Sucks teeth.]* Manjack, what the France you want?
Manjack:	*[Lusting over; pushes door open, and grabs her.]* I want what they say them French man like. For starters. *[Tries to kiss her.]*
Josie:	*[Pushes him away roughly.]* Take control of yourself, man. You mad or what?
Manjack:	*[Moves in as she edges back.]* Yes, I mad. Mad for you. And I taking control. Now. I taking what belong to me! *[Pounces on her and wrestles her to floor.]*
Josie:	*[Struggles.]* Police! Police!
Manjack:	*[Pins her solidly.]* A jury of my peers ain't gon give me wrong. In fact, they gon ask me how I hold out so long.
Josie:	*[Struggles up to a half-sitting position.]* Manjack, you going and do ah thing like this to me in truth? And in people house?
Manjack:	*[Relaxes hold.]* Don't confuse me. We gotto do it now. I bursting at the seams. *[Pushes her back down.]*
Josie:	You think is you one bursting at the seams? My seams got so much run in it that it shredding.
Manjack:	Then what we waiting for?
Josie:	A more romantic moment. When everything perfect. Your house. Candle lights, soft music, me at mey best, giving like you never get, making you bawl.

Manjack: *[Snaps out of the spell spun by her reverie.]* Tricks.
Josie: No, tricks. I serious. *[She gives a sexy wiggle.]*
Manjack: Oh Godddd.
Josie: What you bawling for? *[Wiggles slower, longer.]* Call me name.
Manjack: Sweet Godddd.
Josie: Remember it well. *[Throws him off her; springs to her feet; Manjack massages his hurt back.]* Let us get ah thing or two straight. This body is mine, not yours. Not no man. Now get up and get the hell out of here. And don't come back until you bring champagne. *[She storms into bedroom and Manjack crawls out the house, nearly bumping into Soursop and Jojo who enter with some packages.]*
Jojo: Manjack, you all right?
Manjack: I fine. I just drop something.
Jojo: So you say. *[She goes in.]*
Soursop: *[Laughs.]* I see you adopt the posture of a liberated man.
Manjack: *[Groans, rubs back and knees.]* Stop chat shit and help me up, nuh man.
Soursop: *[Rests down packages and helps Manjack into a chair.]* Josie fling you down with the gauntlet, nuh?
Manjack: Mock mey pain.
Soursop: Hold on a minute, man. Let me get some rum.
Manjack: Good. Make yourself useful instead of grinning like ah ass. *[Soursop laughs as he retrieves packages and takes them into the house, returns with rum and glasses to a still aching Manjack.]* Dish out rum, no man. What happen? Jojo rationing you again? *[Takes glass from Soursop who laughs and pours. Manjack takes a big swallow. Ponders the glass.]* Soursop, you know me good, right?
Soursop: Right. *[Sits and refills Manjack's glass.]*
Manjack: You think I is marrieding material?
Soursop: *[Takes a swallow.]* No.
Manjack: I don't know why I does bother to ask you anything, you know. You ain't tired joke?
Soursop: You ain't tired ask me shit?
Manjack: You more experience in these kinda thing than me, so what big thing it tis if I ask you ah few things, eh?
Soursop: I just sick and tired of your indecision. If you love the woman, married her. She looking forward to it because she fall in love with ah cunomuno like you. But if you don't want marriage—and heaven know you need it like ah baby need milk—then leave her alone. But stop asking me all kinda bullshit, okay?
Manjack: Okay, man, okay. But what you think bout marriage in general?
Soursop: Oh Christ. I think tis ah institution your membership would disgrace.

147

Manjack: *[After a long, nervous swallow]* I want you to be mey best man. *[Grins foolishly.]*

Soursop: *[Stands, offers hand.]* Praise the Lawd. When is the big day?

Manjack: In three weeks. I pop the question outside her job today. I even bruise up mey knee playing romantic. Tis the first weekend in June. Josie tired hint that she had always want to be ah June bride. You think I making the right decision?

Soursop: Manjack, bwoy, I just glad you make ah decision period. But all-yu work everything out? About your man-woman thing, I mean.

Manjack: That settle long time. I is man and the mold fling way.

Soursop: So you say.

Manjack: And mean. I done got the ring them and thing, everything square away with the church and so, and I keeping the reception at my place. You think it big enough? Of course it big enough. But what you think?

Soursop: *[Laughing]* I think everything gon be all right, man. Let's go out and celebrate. Fire big rum. Ah bachelor party of two. *[Manjack continues to sit, worried.]* You could still use ah lil taste, right?

Manjack: *[Stands slowly.]* I could use ah big-ass taste, if you really want to know the truth. This wedding business is ah hell of ah thing. You think it too late to call it off? I mean, I only tell two-three people so far. And I only tell them I might get married 4 pm on Saturday June 3rd. Moravian Church in West. Reception to follow immediately with Blinky them cafooning music at my house. Unless things fall through.

Soursop: *[Sympathetic.]* Stop talk shit, man. Let we go get drunk. It might be your last chance before Josie fling down the gauntlet.

Manjack: You think I is you, no.?

Soursop: I forget. You is ah liberated man. *[Laughs.]*

Manjack: You going drinking or you have to go ask permission first? *[Hugs Manjack around shoulders.]* Let we go, man. *[Hollers to Jojo as they leave.]* Jojo, we going by the club for awhile. *[Manjack is smug as she answers; they exit and lights fade.]*

Scene Five

[Late afternoon four weeks later. Soursop and Jojo sit in the living room, Soursop reading a newspaper, Jojo reading a novel. Jojo puts her book away and goes to the front window. She looks longingly outside, shakes her head in the negative, and returns to the living room. She goes to the stereo, briefly scans the tape collection, selects "Pikey's Waltz" and puts it into the machine but does not play it. She turns to Soursop.]

Jojo:	I really miss Josie. I know you must miss Manjack.
Soursop:	*[Without looking up from his paper]* The sea does miss water? The desert does miss dirt?
Jojo:	You ain't tired lie?
Soursop:	*[Laughing]* Of course I miss he. . .and, at the risk of getting on your jealous side, I miss Josie too. *[They laugh.]* The honeymoon must be sweet them. Tain't one week they say they was going for? Tis bout twelve days they gone now.
Jojo:	So I see you been counting too. Since they wedding I can't get this waltz out my head. *[She puts the song on and dances for a few seconds while Soursop buries himself in the paper.]* Don't bother hide. Come waltz with mey, man.
Soursop:	*[Almost under his breath]* SusChrist, man. Manjack harassing me even in absentia. *[He gets up and, with a wide grin, joins Jojo and they dance for about twenty or so seconds with music up. Music falls but stays on as they continue.]* You remember how we tear this waltz up at the wedding?
Jojo:	Why you think I can't get it out mey head? *[They laugh.]* What ah Manjack. You had see he when they was repeating the wedding vows?
Soursop:	*[He disengages from Jojo and mimicks.]* I don't do. Don't. I mean do.
Jojo:	And the man hand them been trembling so much. *[Demonstrates]* I don't know how he get the ring on Josie finger.
Soursop:	Poor feller. He darn near stab up her finger to put on the thing.
Jojo:	But Josie dress was beautiful though. And they really had look good together. *[Soursop nods his agreement.]* And the reception was a real fete. Manjack ain't play like he could throw ah party. The man full of surprises.
Soursop:	Roast goat and rum for spite. I smuggle out ah half case of scotch with the champagne we been drinking like royalty for darn near two weeks now. The scotch dey out in the car. You want some?
Jojo:	No, but I gon take some of the champagne. *[Soursop goes to kitchenette and gets champagne and glasses while Jojo picks back up her dance.]*
Soursop:	*[Pours the liquor.]* You had notice how Manjack was thirsty-thirsty to join the fellers at the trough but Josie won't let he?
Jojo:	*[Takes glass.]* No, man. I was too busy boogieing, roasting ah time. Trashing back and backing trash talk with trash. *[They laugh and clink glasses.]*
Soursop:	Well, everytime Manjack make ah note toward the trough, Josie buckle her arm in his and drag he close. And though she pulling he hard nobody ain't notice because she steady smiling up in the guest them face meanwhile and saying "Glad allyu come." She

	had method, you check?
Jojo:	That's my sister. *[They kiss glasses and drink.]*
Soursop:	*[Returning to his seat with the champagne]* She only release he when it was time to leave for the honeymoon.
Jojo:	*[Sits on Soursop's lap; wistfully]* Old San Juan. Honey, when last we take ah trip? I longing for ah second honeymoon.
Soursop:	*[Stands, pulls her up.]* Well, this house so empty and quiet, it come like we have ah "no disturb" sign on our front door. Let we go to the honeymoon suite. It calling. *[Lifts her towards bedroom as Manjack approaches the house and bangs on the door.]*
Manjack:	Soursop, why you got this place batten down like you expecting hurricane? Open the damn door.
Soursop:	Shit. The bedroom calling, but Manjack calling harder. *[He puts her down and they hurry to answer the door.]*
Jojo:	Manjack, allyu back! Where Josie?
Manjack:	No hello, sir dog. Just where Josie. And people under the impression allyu is my friend. *[He walks past the couple into the living room. They trail behind him.]*
Soursop:	The honeymoon certainly ain't cut your shit. How things, man? *[The men hug.]*
Jojo:	Not to break up this lovefeast, but where Josie? Home?
Manjack:	Yes, the queen has claimed the throne in my castle. Her majesty say she will grace your doormat later as she has a ton-load of man mess to clear from her palace. I took the opportunity to haul ass. *[They all laugh as the men sit.]*
Jojo:	So how was the honeymoon?
Manjack:	Josie say it's over.
Jojo:	Be serious, nuh, man. How it went?
Manjack:	The story waits to be told.
Jojo:	I wasting my time here. I going by mey sister. Knock allyu self out. *[She picks up purse and keys and leaves.]*
Manjack:	Where the rum?
Soursop:	We been drinking champagne.
Manjack:	Repeating for the near deaf: Where the rum?
Soursop:	*[Laughing as he goes into kitchenette for a bottle of rum]* Okay, brother, rum coming up.
Manjack:	*[Stands, paces. Soursop returns and pours two shots. Manjack downs his quickly, takes the bottle from Soursop, and pours out an even larger portion for himself. He takes a healthy swallow as Soursop, intrigued, retires to his seat to observe an increasingly agitated Manjack.]* To steady mey nerves.
Soursop:	That last shot make a bull bassidy.
Manjack:	*[Suddenly stops pacing and sits next to Soursop.]* Oh Lawd, Soursop,

	Josie sweet but she change already, man. She change too bad. SusChrist, man. I particularly ask you bout married life and your ass only been there making joke and acting ignorant.
Soursop:	*[Amused.]* The honeymoon was a big success then. *[Manjack sucks his teeth.]* Hold on, man. Cool your heels. Cool out. What you talking about?
Manjack:	I talking bout the fact that Josie blackmail mey love; the fact that Josie lie down next to mey in that hotel in Old San Juan, playing that bitch Lysistrata, and won't let me touch her until I agree to all kinda assishness.
Soursop:	So she make you understand Greek. *[Laughs.]*
Manjack:	You laughing like ah idiot, but this thing serious. Woman too damn devious you see them there. She had mey at her mercy but she wasn't merciful at all. She lie down naked in ah black see-through negligee, acting sexy-sexy, purring like ah cyat but when I meow back she won't let me touch her. She won't let me touch her although I been swearing mey love for her and begging her, sweetheart, to please return to her senses.
Soursop:	*[Enjoying this]* So what she make you agree to? *[Gives him drink which he gulps down.]*
Manjack:	She say like she is some bigtime judge or somebody, that from now henceforth I was to treat her civil and not presume that I could boss her around because tis woman she name and she ain't plan to put up with that kinda oldtime nonsense. Then she stop to purr and snarl.
Soursop:	*[Laughs.]* Have another drink, man. Stop talking shit.
Manjack:	Laugh. *[Takes bottle, puts it to his lips, and slugs.]* The woman purr, meow, and snarl. Then she say she is my pussycat and my behavior gon determine what kind of cyat I gon get. She say furthermore if I ever dare try anything like bossing she around she gon show me drill sargeant.
Soursop:	*[Snapping heels together.]* Tention!
Manjack:	Keep piassing. She say she got as much right as any man, and the fact of the matter is she ain't approve of her husband drinking rum like it was water. *[Swigs, grimaces, wipes mouth and gives Soursop the bottle.]*
Soursop:	Watch your rass, bwoy.
Manjack:	*[Waves it off.]* Moreover, if I think I gon be liming every minute with you I lie and all kinda shit like that she make me agree to.
Soursop:	Then the real purring start.
Manjack:	To hell with you. Tis your damn wife what put all this lime in her head and make her sour. And although she still sweet like what, she lil more bitter than I expect.

Soursop: A match made in heaven.

Manjack: But the worse thing she plan to do. . .Sop, I can't tell you why.
[Laughs sheepishly.] The worse thing she have plan for mey is ah
pet name. MOUSIE. That crazy woman want to call mey
"Mousie" in public. You see mey predicament?

Soursop: What predicament? *[Sings as lights fade and Manjack glares.]* "Be
ah mouse to be ah man; let the woman stand hand in hand; only
ah damn jackass don't understand."

Special Section:
Poems by Célie Diaquoi Deslandes
Translated from the French by Peter Constantine

Introduction

The Haitian poet Célie Diaquoi Deslandes was born in the seaside town of Gonaïves in northwestern Haiti in 1907 and lived in the capital, Port-au-Prince, where she ran a prestigious cultural and literary club.

Célie Diaquoi Deslandes became one of the most prominent women poets in Haiti. In the 1950s she worked with the literary magazine *La voix des femmes* (*The Voice of the Women*). She used universal themes, but also evoked the ritual rhythm and imagery of Haiti. Much of her work, like "Desperation," was outspokenly political, but in a poignantly personal way. In the 1960s she published three highly acclaimed collections of poetry: *Chants du coeur* (*Songs of the Heart*), *Arpent d'amour* (*An Acre of Love*), and *Crépuscule aux cils d'or* (*Twilight on Golden Eyelashes*).

Célie Diaquoi Deslandes was featured in the 1980 anthology *La poesie feminine Haitienne* (*Haitian Women's Poetry*), along with other important women poets, such as Cléante Desgraves Valcin, Marie-Thérèse Colimon, and Jacqueline Wiener. Célie Diaquoi Deslandes gained a following in France as well as in Haiti, and her poetry was included in the French anthology *Poesie vivante d'Haiti* (*Living Poetry of Haiti*) published in Paris by Lettres Nouvelles in 1978.

Little is known about her after the 1980s, and her current whereabouts remain a mystery. All efforts were made to contact the copyright holders, but to no avail. Any information would be appreciated.

Peter Constantine

Feast of the Dead

Mother Nature is sad.
She weeps for her dead.
The sky is dark.
And the sun thrusts
Timidly
Its yellow rays
Onto the gnarled mountains.
The trees drenched in rain
lean their branches
down to the ground.
Mother Earth is impassive.
In her entrails
She jealously guards
All she has snatched
from life.

Desperation

I

Today
Is the Feast of the Dead.
I put on my finery.
I go out.
I shall laugh, have fun.

II

Today
Is the Feast of the Dead
I shall head to the movies
While others go to the cemetery.

III

Today
Is the Feast of the Dead.
I am jealous of those mothers
Who will pray by the graves
Of their children.

IV

Today
Is the Feast of the Dead.
My heart bleeds.
I do not know
Where my child's remains lie.

V

Today
Is the Feast of the Dead.
I no longer have tears
I have cried too much
In days that are gone,
Seeking the tomb
Of my child.

Tenderness

Sit by me
on the swing;
Listen to that nocturne of Chopin
It is intoxicating.

Let me place my head
upon your knees
so I can appreciate
this delicious music
that inspires dreams.

Célie Diaquoi Deslandes

The cool breeze teases us.
A moon beam
plays near us
in the foliage.
Tonight, you have the beauty
of a Greek statue.

"We are all Contributing to Life": A Chat with Louise Bennett (1992)

Lilieth Lejo Bailey

Louise Bennett, a Jamaican folk poet and performer, has been instrumental in giving "voice" to the intellectual and cultural identities of the Jamaican peasantry. In using her art to record the life of ordinary Jamaicans, Louse Bennett has been recognized as the foremost West Indian female to employ the Creole idiom for promoting the acceptance of a diasporic wisdom embedded in the Jamaican poetic tradition.

Born in 1919 in Kingston, Jamaica, to a widowed dressmaker, Bennett's artistic learnings, creativity, and love for performance were nurtured by her mother and grandmother. Bennett recalls that as early as age seven, she delighted in telling stories and performing for play-mates and family members.

Unlike poets Una Marson (1905-1965) and Claude McKay (1898-1948) who experimented with the Jamaican Creole, *all* of Bennett's works (1943 to present) are written and performed in the Jamaican vernacular. Despite vehement criticisms from the upper classes and their concerted efforts to sentence her works to a marginalized position in the emerging Jamaican literary canon, Bennett has continued to use folk language to express the experience of the ordinary Jamaican. She is indeed a revolutionary who uses Jamaican Creole as a fundamental tool for bringing respect and literary recognition to Jamaica's national language.

"Miss Lou," as Bennett is affectionately called, has been writing, performing, and publishing for over forty years, but recognition only came in the 1970s. For her contributions to the preservation and development of Jamaican culture, she has received numerous awards, including the Order of Jamaica in 1974. Today, she is known as the "Honorable Louise Bennett."

There are clear distinctions in the development of Bennett, the artist. Her works can be divided up into four distinct categories: pre-World War II, post-World War II, pre-Independence, and post-Independence. Because many of her works are commentaries on everyday events, the topicality of much of Bennett's earlier poems received biting criticisms from several critics. To these criticisms, Bennett responded with the pen and the voice, as if to insist "important things can be said in the native language."

Examination of Bennett's works brings to light successes in the development of national pride. Indeed, she has challenged the position that the national language is inferior to standard English because both, she contends, are derivative of other languages. The respectability that English enjoys, she believes, ought to be afforded the native Jamaican tongue. The capacity for rational choice, social responsibility, and demand for respectability in a class-conscious, racially ambiguous society, finds Miss Lou giving voice and chiseling out a space for the everyday Jamaican folk.

LB: I noticed that in most of your works, you haven't addressed very much one thing that is a certainty in life, and I think it's a very colorful aspect of the Jamaican lifestyle—our treatment of death.

MISS LOU: I used to start off most of my lecture demonstrations with the Dinkie Minnie which was a function held to cheer up the family of the dead person or to banish grief.

LB: Like a Nine-Night?

MISS LOU: But the Dinkie is not a Nine-Night. The Dinkie is eight nights after the death. From the first night to the eighth. The Ninth Night is a more religious ceremony. The Dinkie Minnie is to keep the family from grieving. And the number eight is definitely significant.

LB: From the African cosmology.

MISS LOU: Yes, from the African tradition. I have talked about this all over the place. I can remember talking about it in Britain once, years ago. There was this lawyer who said he came to London years ago as a law student. He said to me, "I have become so British and have begun to look at things through the British eyes." You know the stiff upper lip and what-not.

And he said, "I used to think that when you go to a funeral, it is such a sad thing and all that." And I said, "In our tradition, we danced." He said that he used to think that was primitive. He had this terrible thing about being primitive.

And there I was talking about the Dinkie [during the lecture in London] and telling them about the jollity. You laugh your loudest; nothing sad must happen at a Dinkie.

You find that in a lot of our folk songs, where the tune of the song might be sad, the mood is happy. Because it's a Dinkie. The whole Dinkie mood is happy. I always cite songs like "Linstead Market": "Carry mi ackee go a Linstead Market / Not a quattie wut sell." It is a sad thing, you know. But instead of singing it in a doleful mood, you sing it happily.

LB: So even though you're dealing with serious subjects. . .

MISS LOU: Yes, you can think about the Dinkie as a creative center because a lot of our folk songs come from the tradition of the Dinkie. Things like "Judy Drownded" and "Herrin' an' Jerk Pork." The important thing is that whatever the songs, they were topical at the time. Whatever was topical, they would make a song on it, eh.

LB: They are doing that still.

MISS LOU: Yes, the Dinkie goes on, man. The Dinkie really goes on. There can be a time in the Dinkie when you feel sad. If the people notice that there is somebody who is grieving within, and not dancing it off, not moving it off, not bawling it off, word would go around, "Boy, we don't mek her cry yet, you know. She no cry at all yet, you know. We haffi mek her bawl."

Most of these things are done in circles, in a ring. Everybody would hold hands, including the grieving person. If it's a woman grieving for her husband or if it is a man grieving for his wife or if it's a parent grieving for a child, that person would be in the circle and hold hands, and in the center of the circle they would put. . .If it is a woman and a child, in the center they would put a woman and a child. And if a child had died, a child in the circle would lie down, as if he were dead. And the crowd would just circle. . .everybody start to sing this doleful song:

Bawl 'oman bawl, yuh baby dead
Bawl 'oman bawl, yuh baby dead
Bawl 'oman bawl, yuh baby dead
Bawl 'oman bawl, yuh baby dead
Bawl 'oman bawl.

And they keep up that tune until you hear this scream. The person who was grieving inside screams! And the minute she screams, you know, they hold her. They know she's gone. And they start something that is stronger, a more frivolous beat to get her moving, moving.

So I talked a lot about Dinkie at this lecture demonstration in London, and this fellow came to me and he said, "You know, I experienced that. I came to this country and for years, I never went back home." Then his father died. And the day he heard that his father died, he was so sad. And everything came down on him. And he talked about the number of times he could have really gone back to look at them. And all the things they did for him. And he felt it.

And when he got at the airport [in Jamaica], his three brothers came to meet him, and they took him home. And on the way home, near home, he heard the music and the drums. All the time he was grieving inside, you know. And then he said to himself, "My father is dead, and they're dancing." But he never said a word; he just sat down inside the house.

And the brothers came in and said to him, "Come and dance." And he said, "No. I am not dancing. How can I dance? My father is dead." And the brothers said, "Yes, your father is dead. Come."

They grabbed him, man, and they took him out to the drums. And then he started to move. And the next thing, he was really dancing. And he got into the mood, until he suddenly realized what was happening. He felt so much better after the dance. And he said, "What a great therapy that I had, and yet I never realized how good it is." He said he saw everything in perspective after that.

LB:　　　　Would you say that your work functions to connect people with their past? Do you have that in mind when you are writing or performing?

MISS LOU:　(*Laughs.*) No. My main thing is to get people to respect the language. I was thinking mostly of Jamaicans. One night I sat in a theatre waiting to go on and in the darkness, I heard two male voices—but I never knew who they were—and I heard one say, "What yuh tink 'bout Miss Lou?"

LB: How early was that? When you just started?

MISS LOU: Yes, it was within the first year or so of my really performing. And the other one said, "She is all right man, but she limit herself, man. She limiting herself. She won't get any show but in Jamaica. She can't go no further but Port Royal with that."

You know, this is the way they were talking. And I said to myself, that if I can get Jamaicans to understand what I mean, that's all I want.

But, Jamaicans are all over the world—those men forgot. We export our people, and we like to travel. We are adventurous. That's the type of people we are. And because of that, I have been to every country you can think of. But my main thing was to make people respect their language.

LB: You seem to be so unlike people of your time who aspired to become so British. Yet you were one person who saw the value of using our language—the value of our culture which, looking back, is remarkable. What would you attribute this insight to?

MISS LOU: I believe it's my early connections with the language, with the people. My mother was a dressmaker. She sewed for every type of person, from the fish lady, the coal lady, to the governor lady. Everybody was a lady. My mother lived in town (Kingston) for about 17 years of her life, but she was always a country girl. Eleven years of her life she spent in St. Mary. And St. Mary is one of the parishes that maintains a lot of the traditions, the African customs, and so on. My grandmother, my mother's mother, used to tell me "nancy stories," especially at bedtime. It was almost like a lullaby to me, singing the songs and the Anancy stories and all that.

All types of people would come into my mother's sewing room. And gal, people would talk. And sometimes you would hear somebody bus out "Cooyah!"

LB: What I'm trying to get at, Miss Lou, is what is the one thing that you'd put your finger on, if possible, that allowed you to see value in this?

MISS LOU: You would have to tell me that. You would have to figure that out from when I talk to you.

The thing is, I never had a feeling of inferiority. Praise God. When people say, "She have bad hair, and dat one have good hair," my mother always said, "There is no such thing as bad hair or good hair. It's just different types." So I said to myself, the talk is not bad either. How can everything be bad about our people. These are the people that I know and love.

You know, you read about the whites a lot in school. We were never taught much Jamaican geography, not much Jamaican history. We were singing English folk songs; we were doing the English dances. I was doing Scottish waltzes before I knew how to do "Come Mek Mi Hol' Yuh Han'." The teachers discouraged our folk dances. So, I always asked myself how it could be bad.

LB: It seems to me your mother's view of the world and her values were passed on to you.

MISS LOU: She passed that on to me. Yes. The way in which people treated each other. We were all friends. You know, I was remembering. (*Laughs.*) I'll tell you the joke about this teacher.

These teachers were teaching us obedience, and there was this poem "Casa Blanca": "The boy stood on the burning deck. . ." Oh, child, we went through that. And the teacher told us, "The boy obeyed his father," and all of that.

So I went home in the evening now, and I walked into the sewing room. Everybody used to call me Miss Bibs. They said, "Well, now Miss Bibs, wha happen today? I answered, "I learned about obedience." And it sweet mi now for hear mi to di people dem, "The boy stood on the burning deck." And I went on with this thing, man. And when I finished it, I said: "You see that, the teacher said, the boy obeyed his father. He even died." Hear a little old woman, "She a wait fi somebody clap her. Poor ting. Him time did come." (*Laughs.*)

LB: Had nothing to do with obedience.

MISS LOU: Had nothing to do with obedience, for "him time did come." It struck me, you know. "Him time did come."

LB: So it seems to me that the feedback you got from these people reinforced what you valued, and gave you more of an insight into life.

MISS LOU: Yes, a great deal of insight into life. Well, I tell you now. As you see, I like to tell stories. Suh mi use to do yuh know. An' mi use to try it out on de people in de sewing room same way, yuh know. Go een man, and tell dem story and ting. And I found that I had the gift of laughter.

Anyhow, I used to go and try out my little things, and tell them jokes, and tell them stories.

Then now, there was a little boy. He was between four and five. He was my mother's good friend. It was almost like she adopted this little boy, man. That was in the days when we didn't have radio and television and those sorts of things. So in the nights we would have little concerts. At the concerts we put on shows about all the things we learnt at school. You know, about good faeries and bad faeries, about sleeping beauty and all dem sort a something.

So now, wih come home, an' wih trying out our ting. And I would plan the story, man. I would be the good faerie, and I would come in, and I'd say to him, "Boysie, you are lost, you see. And I'm going to show you the way home." Boysie, said "Yeah. All right."

I said, "Boysie," (We would call him Bwaysie, because if you call him Boysie, he would say, "Bwaysie"). When we were practicing man, I'd say to him, "Bwaysie, man. When I come on, you see, you must look like yuh wandering, and yuh laas. And yuh must sey, "Time to go home." And yuh mus' bawl man. Hear him, "Yes, mi wih bawl." And hear me now, "When I come on, I'm going to say, (*with proper Jamaican English*) "What is the matter little boy?" And you are to say, "I lost my way in the woods." Hear Bwaysie, "All right."

Suh di play start. Suh hear mi now, "What is the matter little boy?" Hear bwaysie, (*with flat Jamaican tone*) "Mi laas mi way ina di hood." (*Laughs.*) And I

161

said to him, "Come on, man, you're not to say "mi lass. . .You must say 'I lost my way in the woods.'" So Bwaysie say, "All right. Mi wih sey it. Mi wih sey di right ting." Now I begged him, "Go on, go up back and do it right."

Well, Missis, the night of the play, we came on. Boysie bawling, and I said, "What is the matter little boy?" Hear Boysie, "Mi laas mi way ina di hood!" Lawd! It look like mi haffi go come off and gwan back. The concert done, you know. (*Laughs.*)

People used to call him "Course Material." Let me just give you this little joke. The first day he went to school, he came home, and my mother said, "Boysie, wha' happen at school today?" Hear Boysie, "Di teacher call out, and di teach seh, 'Boysie Allen'? An' a woodn' ansa. An di teacher seh, 'Boysie Allen,' and a woodn' ansa. An' di teacher call out, 'Course Material!' an' a sey 'present.'" Well, that is just to show you the kind of humor of this child. And I was in contact with all of this.

And it was a thing, that Boysie decided one time that he wanted to write a letter to his Godfather, so that he could spend Christmas. Him seh to everybody, "boy a wan' write a letter to Godfather." And dem seh, "Weh Bwaysie wan' write letter fah?" And I said, "Come Bwaysie, mi wih write it." "Bibs, yuh wih write it fi mi, Bibs?" I said, "Yes, man. Come." So mi get the pencil, and him seh, "Putti down same way like weh mi seh, yuh know. Putti down same way like weh mi seh. Yuh putti down same way?" I said, "Yes man." So, I took the pencil and Boysie said, "Dear Godfather. . ."

And listen nuh, I wrote the thing same way Boysie tell mi, yuh know. The Godfather came down when he got the letter, dying with laughter. When they got the letter they said, "You know, the only person who would have written this letter is Bibs." Boysie dictated the letter, and I was the only person who would write the letter as Boysie speaks.

So you see now, I had this thing that I wanted to write stories. So I wrote. I was writing about the sun and the moon. I wrote all sorts of things in the standard language, of course. You had to write in that language. Until one day, I went on the tram car. I was about 13, between 13 and 14. I was going out to the movies. And I dressed up, not in school uniform. It was a matinee, and this was a country tram. They call it the country tram because the four back benches were reserved for the country people, the people who were bringing food to Kingston in their baskets and all that, you know. They couldn't sit up front with their basket and thing because they might tear somebody stockings, and so on. I didn't realize how strongly they felt until that evening. The tram car had stopped, and I just headed to one of the back benches.

I was a child then, you know. When I say a child, I wasn't yet 14. But I must have been looking well because after mi Granny dead, she blow good breeze pon mi. (*Laughs.*) So anyhow, I walked toward one of the empty benches in the back, and one woman said to the other one "Pred out yuhself, one dress 'oman a come. Spred out gal." And she just spred out, and cover di whole a de

162

seat. Pred out, and yuh want to see di apron." (*Laughs.*)

At that stage, I said, this is the language I must write in. Nobody was really taking much notice of what these people are saying. The lady is saying, "If you can sit up front, why come 'round here?"

LB: You have the freedom of movement, while they don't.

MISS LOU: Yes, yes.

LB: So at that moment you saw the beauty. . .

MISS LOU: Yes, yes, I knew that this is the language. Because I didn't have anything against it. In fact, I respected the language. That's why I could write for Boysie. When he said he wanted to write the letter same way as how him talk, I did it.

LB: How old were you then?

MISS LOU: When I was writing Boysie's letter? Nearly 10. But at that stage I thought, "Boysie want the letter write how him talk, and I said O.K." So anyhow, when the matinee over, I went home and I wrote about it:

> Spred out yuself de Liza
> One dress 'oman a look like sey
> She see de likke space
> Side a wi
> And wan' poke herself in deh
> . . . .
> Pred out gal, she deh come
> No Mah, no space in yah atall
> Weh mek yuh fool so Liza
> Pred out yuhself nuh gal

And my dear child, I went to school and tried it out. Cho! And dey seh, "Louise, man. . .wih like it man." (*Laughs.*)

So I started to listen more and to write. And to write in the language. . .write about all the things that the people were saying. And so I said, "This is what I shall do."

And I tell you, nobody else was doing it—writing in the language. Well, of course, I met with a lot of opposition.

LB: How did you handle that? This was really radical then.

MISS LOU: When I left school, before I went to high school, I was writing that way. It started with my mother's friends first. You know those friends. They would say, "The child should turn nurse or teacher or something. Why you can spend money on a child and have her a write like this?"

My mother said, "She tell yuh she wan' turn nurse? She tell yuh she wan' turn teacher? She seh she want to write."

My mother looked at me, and she said, "Bibs, if you can write as well as I can sew, you will be a success." (*Laughs.*)

She was wonderful, truly wonderful. And she said, "I will look after yuh, yaah." As simple as that. And it happened the same way. She just left me free to write. So I owe a whole lot to that spirit of my mother.

So I started to write in newspapers now. I was very happy to know that people were actually reading my articles because we were never taught to read the language. The response I got from the country asking for me to come down and judge drama competitions and judge speech competitions. They would be reciting the verses, and I would go down to the country. And the drama! And that was the main reason I went to drama school. I did a formal course in drama. I got a scholarship.

LB: I'm sure you got a lot of opposition from the "proper" people in society, for "corrupting the language," if I may use your words. I'm just wondering where did you get that strength to maintain your position?

MISS LOU: Because I believed this thing must be respected. Let me tell you now. I had a great aunt—my grandmother's sister—who used to come to my birthday; my birthday was a Saturday. . .and she would travel. In those days it wasn't easy, you know. And she would come to my birthday party in a buggy. And what happen?

Aunt Hilda was a strong Marcus Garvey person. She was a nurse by profession, and she was a Marcus Garvey nurse. There were always these Marcus Garvey marches. And they would sing, "Ethiopia, the land of the savior / March on, march on to victory / Let Africa be free." So, this sort of thing, and this talk of black dignity affected me. But there was the fusion of European and African tendencies. But, as I say in my verses, the African was the strongest of the cultural patterns.

LB: I can see that you had strong role models who seem to be all women.

MISS LOU: My father died when I was seven.

LB: Any uncles?

MISS LOU: Well, my mother had two brothers, but they lived in America. Once when I was about 17 or so, one of them visited us in Jamaica. But there was a sort of uncle-cousin who used to come to visit us, and there were other country cousins who would come. But the dominant influences in my family were my mother, my grandmother, and Aunt Hilda.

LB: Did you have a yearning for a male figure?

MISS LOU: Not really, because they were there. All the people came around—all our family. My mother had six uncles. And my great uncles used to visit. We used to visit Uncle Tom; my mother used to love him. I spent quite a lot of time during my holidays at Uncle Tom's house.

And I had a beautiful piece of furniture, a table. And I remember Uncle Tom telling me, "You see that table, Bibs. I hand-carved it myself. And if you like it, I will leave it for you."

I had it in my drawing room [in Jamaica] until I sold the house. That is one of the pieces of furniture that. . .because how would I travel with all that?

LB: You seem very sad about that.

MISS LOU: Yes, yes. Because umm. . .You thought that you would spend the rest of you life with. . .

LB: The things that are familiar and mean a lot to you?

MISS LOU: Up to today I was talking to somebody about my mother's dresser. A real old-time one, a vanity dresser. It had three mirrors. A down center mirror and two side mirrors. It was mahogany. And I used to love to go and sit in front of it. One day mi dear chile, mi decide mi going to sew. I was never taught to sew. But ah watch, you know. What dey call "ketch a peep." Yuh have a lot of Jamaicans, you know. Dey just wan' fi ketch a peep after something, and dem gone.

Anyhow, mi dear missis, here am I now. My mother bought this piece of cloth, and she promised to make dis dress fi mi. But she, you know she was busy; she had to sew to make her living. But when you're young you don't have all that understanding. She said, "Bibs, I think you have sufficient clothes. . .you don't need to get a new dress now. I need to finish these other dresses and so on."

I said, "I can do it. I can make a dress."

By that time, I must have been about 14. So weh yuh tink now? Mi tek di claat and cut. . .(*Laughs.*) She doan seh a ting to me. And I get on, and ah sew and sew. An' a put on di ting. An' in front a dat same mirror, you know. An' a go out. I was going to Gildry. I was a Gildry girl because I was a Presbyterian. I liked it. I liked Gildry.

Anyhow, yuh want to see me. An den a jus' felt a presence behind me. And I knew. And I just heard, clip, clip, clip, clip. My mother with her scissors, and she just clip the dress right up, yuh know. Mi seh, she jus' clip it up! She jus' cut it off a mi, yuh know.

Mi seh, "Lawd, yuh cut up mi dress!" She sey, "Bibs, I make my living from my sewing, and I wouldn't like you to go out to the street and anybody think that I made that. Bibs, you'd be shaming your mother."

LB: Your mother sounds very much like Aunty Roachie.

MISS LOU: Well, Aunty Roachie is really public opinion. What other people think. But it's not anyone exactly. Sometimes it's like her. I'm not lying to you.

Anyhow, that's what we had in Jamaica. These strong women. A whole lot of mothers and grandmothers who were strong.

LB: Miss Lou, could we turn this conversation a little bit to some modern issues, especially things that women are looking at now. Although your works reflect what's in society, I see that in pieces like "Cuss Cuss," "Kas-Kas" and others, you seem to be reinforcing the stereotypes that women are nagging, gossipy wretches.

MISS LOU: I wouldn't say they were nagging. They are not afraid to speak if they feel that a thing is not right. Because a lot of times, you know, in Jamaica, it is the woman who really carries the burden of the family, mostly.

I have a male cousin who used to talk a lot. I'm not sure where he is now. I stayed with him in Barbados. He is a businessman. But you know what he said to me one day? He said, "You know what I miss now-a-days, Bibs?" The old aunty—the old woman who you could always go to." He said, "In my family, there was always an aunty this, or a cousin that, that you could always go to and talk to. And you know when they finish talking, you would always feel as if you got something of value. You got that emotionally and materially too."

"Yes, man, they always can give you a smalls. When you need a little help, you could go to an uncle or so, and they let you know how life hard. But if you go to a little old aunt or so, she would say, 'you have to pay me back,' but she always have tie up in some little place, a little money. She would say, 'This is all I have, but help yuhself, and remember, yuh have to give me back.'" He said he had that experience throughout his life.

LB: So, even though you say that you may not believe all the stereotypes about women, do you think that your art is somewhat constrained by what you know to be true and what is actually reflected in the culture?

MISS LOU: I'm not quite sure what you mean.

LB: I'm just wondering, as an artist, do you find that sometimes you want to be so true to the art that you adjust or decide to edit certain things out?

MISS LOU: Do you know "Jamaica Oman?" (*Recites poem.*)
Jamaica oman cunny, sah!
Is how dem jinnal so?
Look how long dem liberated
An de man dem never know!

Look how long Jamaica oman
—Modder, sister, wife, sweetheart—
Outa road an eena yard deh pon
A dominate her part!

From Maroon Nanny teck her body
Bounce bullet back pon man,
To when nowadays gal-pickney tun
Spellin-Bee champion.

From de grass root to de hill-top,
In profession, skill an trade
Jamaica oman teck her time
Dah mount an meck de grade.

Some backa man a push, some side-a
Man a hole him han,
Some a lick sense eena man head,
Some a guide him pon him plan!

Neck an neck an foot an foot wid man
She buckle hole her own;
While man a call her 'so-so rib'
Oman a tun backbone!

An long before Oman Lib bruck out
Over foreign lan
Jamaica female wasa work
Her liberated plan!

Jamaica oman know she strong,
She know she tallawah,
But she no want her pickney-dem
Fi start call her 'Puppa'.

So de cunny Jamma oman
Gwan like pants-suit is a style,
An Jamaica man no know she wear
De trousiz all de while!

So Jamaica oman coaxin
Fambly budget from explode
A so Jamaica man a sing
'Oman a heaby load!'

But de cunny Jamma oman
Ban her belly, bite her tongue,
Ketch water, put pot pon fire
An jus dig her toe a grung.

For 'Oman luck deh a dungle',
Some rooted more dan some,
But as long as fowl a scratch dungle heap
Oman luck mus come!

Lickle by lickle man start praise her,
Day by day de praise a grow;
So him praise her, so it sweet her,
For she wonder if him know.

LB:	In other words, that's the answer to my question?
MISS LOU:	(*Laughs.*)
LB:	So what you are saying is that you don't really contribute to the

view that the woman should not be liberated from the kitchen, for as your Aunty Roachie says, "They have been liberated a long time."

MISS LOU: Long time. Long time. Oh God.

LB: To take care of the home is not necessarily a way of limiting the woman?

MISS LOU: That's right. You see, women stand up for their rights too, you know. If she doesn't, it is because where she is, she has a stronger role to play there.

LB: So even though you are reflecting what's in the society, you're still portraying the stereotypical woman—being stuck in the home, in the kitchen. As a person who champions women's rights, how would you comment on that?

MISS LOU: They are very, very important roles, darling. I don't care whether they want to stereotype them or not. That little woman you see, catch water, put pot pon fire, and dig her toe a ground. She is not a fool, for what she is doing is very, very important. She has her part to play.

You see, the thing is, I cannot feel that anybody's profession or skill, or whatever, is superior to the other. We are all contributing to life. Whatever you have to contribute, if you do it well, then it is important. For you must remember now, when everybody was saying that I should "turn nurse or teacher," my mother said to me, "If you can write as well as I can sew, you'll be a success."

Some people like to disparage certain types of jobs and certain types of things, but the whole lot of the "backitive" we have had in life is from those people who are doing what they call menial work.

My Aunty Roachie says that "no work is menial. You have menial people. If you're doing bad work, then you're menial."

LB: Miss Lou, you have seen a lot of political changes in Jamaica.

MISS LOU: No badda get mi in a nuh politics now, you know.

LB: I can't help it. I'm Jamaican. But, I'm just wondering—did the political movements influence your art? If so, how?

MISS LOU: We are very fortunate in Jamaica in that the two leading parties are both culturally supportive. I have never found any sort of opposition when it comes to the culture.

Even though there were a lot of people who wrote to the newspapers and said that Jamaicans would never be able to talk properly again because of me, I had a lot of support from the different governments. I feel we are culturally emancipated, or we are on the road to being so because our children are now singing their songs in the schools. During our festivals, the children are using Jamaican art forms, and they are writing too. A lot of people are now feeling that they can express themselves in their language.

LB: Yes, they can say something that's worthwhile in their language. I know nothing happens in a vacuum, and I'm now looking at the early stages of your art. For example, when Jamaica became independent, you wrote several pieces like "Govanah," etc. Was there any special kind of lesson that you wanted to leave with your audience?

MISS LOU: Well, these were more than just passing comments. The new governor and wife were my good friends. If you listen to "New Govanah," you will notice that the last lines are, "A wonda if him coulda stay, him woulda stay wid wih."

LB: Did you hope—or was it your goal—for people to use your works as motivation for political action?

MISS LOU: I don't know. But I have always felt that politics is a very necessary evil. It is necessary, but you must have some type of control. I have known people who go into politics with all the good intentions, but when they are actually in office, it's a different thing.

LB: Now could we talk a bit about the Jamaican spirit? We call it the Jamaican pride, and sometimes we scold ourselves for having this "false pride," but I believe this "false pride" is being read in a negative way. It is rather the Jamaican spirit. There is something about it that is distinctive.

MISS LOU: Well, a lot of us came from the Ashanti. They were warrior men and women. Out of slavery, came that Nanny, for example.

A lot of people don't believe in Nanny, but, I tell you, there was such a woman. She was the sister of Cudjoe who was then the leader. And all the wars that Cudjoe was fighting, you never heard about Cudjoe fighting war until after Nanny Town was burnt. You see, Nanny was behind most of it. She was a strength; they have more legends and more stories, and you can hear this in the people's expression.

Anyhow, I have a great respect for that sort of strength. Our people still have that in Jamaica. Our people never sat down under slavery. If you follow the history in Jamaica, there were so many slave rebellions that they didn't know what to do. And because of that strength—and you see it all around—we have that spirit of leadership that is seen even in the poorest person.

LB: What would you say to some critic's comments that some of your pieces reflect the European view that broad noses are ugly? I'm thinking particularly about "Cuss Cuss" in which you seem to make fun of a young girl's nose.

MISS LOU: Listen, you know the visual—how we make the word sound like what it looks like? It is not disparaging. It is something you look pon, an' yuh seh a ting. Hear a woman tell anadda one, "Yuh fava bite an' spit out!" When you bite something, and you spit it out, it's not looking so good.

LB: I hear you saying that the descriptions are not necessarily applications of views outside the culture. These terms are simply metaphors.

MISS LOU: That's right. It has nothing to do with European views. We had a time in Jamaica, when there were certain people who told their children that they have to "raise their color," but you will find that I make fun of that type of thinking. So, you'll find "Colour Bar." You'll find "Pass fi White." You'll find

"White Pickney."

LB: So, before people read European ideologies into your work, they should read your work as an entire body rather than judging from isolated pieces?

MISS LOU: Oh, Lord, yes. That's the same reason I wrote "Back to Africa" and all that. Jamaica has years and years of African consciousness with Marcus Garvey and all his supporters. I have written plays and things that reflect the lives, the tradition of the people.

LB: Thank you so much, Miss Lou. Ah doan wan' fi wear yuh out."

MISS LOU: (*Laughs.*)

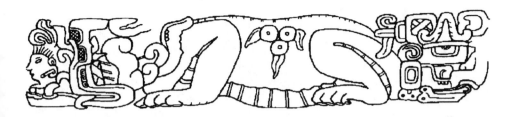

Special Section:
Poetry and Fiction from Belize

Introduction

For many years, Radio Belize's slogan was "the Caribbean beat in the heart of Central America," and this, perhaps, is a good place to start in trying to understand Belizean culture and literature. This new nation, independent only since 1981 and with a population of slightly more than 200,000, has struggled with its cultural identity both because of its long colonial history and its position somewhere between Latin America and the Caribbean. The literature of Belize, however, is generally grouped with that of the Anglophone Caribbean since the majority of its writers are working in English with bits of Spanish and Creole adding local color.

The history of literary publication in Belize is quite brief and it has only been during the past fifty years that much of anything has been published and certainly only since the early 1980s that the works of local authors have become more widely available and have begun to make their way into the curriculum of Belizean schools as well. Cubola Productions of Benque Viejo has been the driving force in Belize, and recently Angelus Press has emerged. It is important to note that a number of expatriates—those from other countries living in Belize and Belizeans living abroad—have played a significant role in the development of Belizean literature. For example, Zee Edgell and Mary Parham, presented in this section, now live in the United States.

In this short introduction to the literature of Belize I will briefly look at four genres: novels, plays, short stories, and poetry.

Belize is best known internationally for the work of novelist Zee Edgell. Three of her works have been published by Heinemann as part of the Caribbean Writers Series: *Beka Lamb* (1982), *In Times Like These* (1991), and *The Festival of San Joaquin* (1997). *Beka Lamb* was the winner of the Fawcett Prize in 1982, is on the CXC list, and is widely regarded as the most important work of Belizean literature yet written. This deceptively simple novel is a wonderful introduction to culture, history and literature of Belize. Several other novels have been published within Belize, the most noteworthy of which is Glenn Godfrey's *Sinner's Bossanova* (1987), a work which begins with a great deal of promise but never quite lives up to its potential.

The writing and production of plays has enjoyed some success in Belize, especially as the result of a National Arts Festival which took place annually from 1953-1980. Important figures from the wider Caribbean, such as Errol Hill and Rex Nettleford, were involved in the Festival as consultants and judges and encouraged Belizean playwriting. Most of the plays produced for the Festival have been lost, but some are still available in the national archives, and six of them were published in the second volume of the Belizean Writers Series entitled *Ping Wing Juk Me: Six Belizean Plays* (1996).

Short stories have enjoyed perhaps the widest success in Belize, in no small measure because the country has produced a number of very good short story writers including Leo Bradley, Evan Hyde, Colville Young, and Zoila Ellis. An early anthology, *Among My Souvenirs*, was the first collection published in Belize, and recently the first volume of the Belizean Writers Series has reprinted some of those early stories along with more recent works in *Snapshots of Belize: An Anthology of Short Fiction* (1995). In addition, two single-author collections, Zoila Ellis's *On Heroes, Lizards, and Passion* (1988), (reviewed in this volume), and Colville Young's *Pataki Full* (1991) have been adopted by many schools and have enjoyed some commercial success.

The poetic tradition is strong in Belize; however, as one would expect, the production has been very uneven. Early collections published by the government tended toward patriotic works and effusive ramblings about the beauty of the land, but those early poems have given way to a more measured tone perhaps best exemplified by the collection *Shots from the Heart* (1991) by three young Belizeans, Yasser Musa, Kiren Shoman, and Simone Waight. The recently published third volume of the Belizean Writers Series, *Of Words: An Anthology of Belizean Poetry* (1997), brings together the important poems from Belize written over the past forty years.

While young and uneven, the literature of Belize is showing signs of maturing, and efforts to bring the works of local authors into the schools of Belize show some promise in not only increasing a sense of identity in the people of Belize, but also in inspiring budding authors to take up the pen and write.

Michael D. Phillips

The Many Lives of Zee Edgell

Irma McClaurin

If one believes in reincarnation, then Zee Edgell, internationally renowned Belizean novelist, has lived several lives: as a journalist, director of women's affairs in Belize, wife of a development professional, mother, sister, daughter, and always, a writer. At first appearance, a somewhat reticent person, Edgell is much more complex than what may be immediately visible. The same can be said of her novels as well. While at the heart of each are conventional literary themes—coming of age in *Beka Lamb* (Heinemann, 1982), culture change and personal transitions in *In Times Like These* (Heinemann, 1991), and a woman's attempt to overcome her past in her newest work, *The Festival of San Joaquin* (Heinemann, 1997)—they are all fraught with complexities and layers. Richard F. Patteson insightfully observes in his critical essay on Edgell's work that "like Olive Senior, Caryl Phillips, and a number of other third wave West Indian writers, Edgell has made fiction a vehicle for the retrieval of subsumed and submerged elements of Caribbean consciousness" (52).

It is these submersions that Zee Edgell retrieves to form the main narrative, and numerous subtexts, of *Beka Lamb,* her first novel chronicling the journey of a young Creole Belizean girl through the difficult waters of puberty toward adulthood. Paralleling this personal coming-of-age story is one of a country growing out of its colonial status as British Honduras into the independent nation of Belize.

Another buried strand that Edgell excavates is that of Belizean women's active participation in the country's political struggle for self-rule. Most of the social histories written about Belize describe the country's political development through the action of men, inscribing the quest for self-rule as a male-centered narrative.[1] Inspired by her grandmother and other strong women she encountered growing up, Edgell succeeds in creating "a record of the Belize she remembered that would include women's contributions to the nationalist and independence movements, as well as to the entire process of decolonization" (McClaurin, *Americas* 40). As she observed in the same interview:

> I think more women than men were in the streets supporting the
> early leaders. They contributed money and labor. But apart from
> very token acknowledgment of their contributions, the women were
> not part of the   dialogue. They weren't part of the discourse. (40)

Thus, it is through the character of Granny Ivy, fashioned after Edgell's own grandmother, that we come to recognize and appreciate the centrality of Belizean women to the country's struggle for independence. It should be clear that the fiction of Zee Edgell derives not only from personal memories, but a mixture of historical facts copiously researched and the writer's imagination.

In Times Like These also contains this blend of historical facts, fiction, and memory. Whereas Edgell's first novel was concerned with an emerging

nationalism, her second work takes place on the verge of self-rule. The contradictions and tensions of values, ethics, and political visions are brought to our
attention through the female protagonist who has just returned from living
abroad in London and Africa, and assumes the position of director of the newly
formed Women's Desk, in a politically charged atmosphere. Edgell, "relying
upon newspapers, archival sources, firsthand accounts from Belizeans and her
own experiences as the head of the Women's Desk and later as the first director
of the Department of Women's Affairs, "weaves a story of how women and a
nation struggle toward independence" (McClaurin, *Americas* 41). As is true in
Beka Lamb, certain elements in the novel resonate with Edgell's own life: her
studies in England, her travels to Afghanistan and Somalia, her return home, and
her position as head of the first Women's Desk, and some years later, under a
different political party, the first director of the Department of Women's Affairs.

In this novel, as the newly independent nation of Belize struggles with
both the euphoria and problems of independence, the travails of women are
prominently featured. Each becomes a metaphor for the other. On the one hand,
Belizean women, embodied in Pavana, a single mother who refuses to name the
father of her children until she is ready, struggle with the excitement and
problems produced by a rising consciousness that supports independence and
challenges colonial notions of morality and values; on the other, Belize is a
country struggling towards independence in the face of threats to its sovereignty
from external enemies like Guatemala and internally faced with civil disorder and
political corruption and decisions that wreak havoc in the personal lives of its
sons and daughters. As critic Richard F. Patteson notes, "*In Times Like These*
exposes the extent to which power dynamics underlie, direct, and sometimes
poison personal relationships" (McClaurin, *Americas* 69). The vicissitudes of life
and human nature, the mysteries of the future, the nexus between the personal
and the political, and the unpredictability of human responses and actions are
themes woven throughout Zee Edgell's novels.

Her latest work, *The Festival of San Joaquin*, embodies all of these themes
but also reflects the writer's personal desire to document Belizean cultures in her
work. Says Edgell, "I have this great longing to see on the bookshelf a novel from
each culture—to preserve them" (McClaurin, *Americas* 43). With *Beka Lamb* and
In Times Like These, the Creole experience has been preserved. *The Festival of San
Joaquin* draws us into the parlors, verandahs, and huts of Belize's Mestizo population. Notwithstanding Edgell's caveat, "It is not possible to capture an entire
culture in one novel, or even, perhaps, with ten," she does see *Festival* as "a partial
realization of my hopes for the future" (as she wrote in a letter.) Stylistically, this
latest novel displays other important differences from Edgell's earlier works as she
herself claimed in the same letter: "I think *Festival* is different. . .in several
significant ways. It is written in the first person, in scenes rather than in chapters;
I also use the present tense as well as the past. I am also writing from the point-
of-view of a Mestiza. I found it much easier to write about the characters [in this

novel] using the first person."

What is most striking, however, about *The Festival of San Joaquin* is its explicit subject matter of domestic violence and the impact and consequences this has on all involved. In taking on this topic, Edgell slides gracefully into the role of social commentator. The protagonist of her novel is a poor Mestiza woman with simple desires who finds herself in a very complex situation as a victim of domestic violence and her lover's murderer. The novel highlights the increasing prominence of domestic violence crimes in the pages of Belize newspapers while also presenting readers with numerous and layered moral questions: How should victims of domestic violence respond? And what is the role of the state in protecting all those who are impacted by such acts of violence? Luz Marina loses custody of her children and becomes a pariah in her own community. She struggles to remain connected and sane as people isolate and judge her. While Belize operates under an ethos of ethnic and social tolerance, class differences and ethnic conflicts are part of the country's social fabric; and Edgell places these issues before us in compelling ways. When asked why she chose this particular topic, Edgell responded in a letter: "The story chose me rather than the other way around. I heard and read about a similar story many years ago. The characters of Luz Marina and Doña Catalina never abandoned me for an instant. We became great friends, as we visited daily trying to make some sense out of our experiences and our pain. The more I wrote the more I realized how many other Luz Marinas and Doña Catalinas were buried in my subconscious." Memory, history, and the pathos and joy of human life are central elements in the writings of Zee Edgell. As a self-appointed custodian of Belize's diverse cultures, she has given us insights into the Creole and Mestizo worlds.

The future portends well for Edgell who does not shy away from new challenges. She speaks of her plans: "I am hoping to write about the Garifuna, another very complex culture. Their story is one that has always gripped my imagination. I am also at work on a group of short stories." Such are the many and varied directions that shape the life (lives) of Zee Edgell.

Note

[1]Compare Nigel O. Bolland, 1977, 1986, 1988 and Assad Shoman, 1987.

Works Cited

McClaurin, Irma. "A Writer's Life, A Country's Transition." Interview with Zee Edgell. *Americas.* 1994: 46 (4): 38-43.
Patteson, Richard F. "Zee Edgell: The Belize Chronicles." *Caribbean Passages: A Critical Perspective on New Fiction from the West Indies.* Boulder & London: Lynne Rienner Publishers. 1998.

Irma McClaurin

For Further Reading:

Bolland, Nigel O. *The Formation of a Colonial Society: Belize, from Conquest to Crown Colony*. Baltimore: John Hopkins University Press, 1977.
___. *Belize: A New Nation in Central America*. Boulder and London: Westview Press, 1988.
___. *Colonialism and Resistance in Belize: Essays in Historical Sociology*. Belize City: Cubola Productions, Iser and SPEAR, 1988.
Henderson, Peta and Houghton, Ann Bryn, eds. *Rising Up: Life Stories of Belizean Women*. Toronto: Sister Vision, 1993.
Kerns, Virginia. *Women and the Ancestors: Black Carib Kinship and Ritual*. Urbana: University of Illinois Press, 1983.
McClaurin, Irma. *Women and the Culture of Gender in Belize, Central America*. Ph. D. Dissertation, University of Massachusetts, Amherst, 1993. (Unpublished)
___. "Women's Groups in Belize, Central America: The Quest for Female Autonomy." *Gender and Race through Education and Political Activism: the Legacy of Sylvia Helen Forman*. D. Shenk, ed. Washington, D.C.: Association of American Anthropologists and the Association for Feminist Anthropologists, 1995.
Shoman, Assad. *Party Politics in Belize*. Belize: Cubola Productions, 1987.

My Uncle Theophilus

Zee Edgell

The day after the ex-servicemen's riots, my Uncle Theophilus and I made our way through the streets of Belize City. Groups of people were gathered on Albert Street, littered with glass from shattered, looted shop windows. Uncle Theo, recently returned to British Honduras from Egypt at the end of the World War I, had no sympathy for the British merchants. He believed they were hand in glove with the government.

"Let them feel what people like us are up against," Uncle Theo said, his voice hoarse, his eyes bloodshot, a ferocious scowl on his broad face. There was no sign of his dimpled smile today, no sparkle in his brown eyes. My Uncle Theo was now at war against the British.

As we paused at a corner near Regent Street, I straightened the felt hat that was askew on his head before slipping my hand into the elbow which he held up for me. Uncle Theo was over six feet tall, a broad shouldered man and strong, not afraid, he said, "of a single soul, high or low."

We waited for an old black man, driving a slowpoke mule and cart toward others parked near a sad looking coconut tree in the middle of the dusty road. A white official on a brown horse trotted by, in a flash of glinting brass and polished leather, on his way to the government buildings close to the sea. "Force is the only thing the British seem to understand," Uncle Theo was saying. "Petitions are ignored."

It was hard to believe that a little over two weeks ago, in early July, the houses, stores, and government buildings had been draped in red, white and blue banners and buntings. The Union Jack flew everywhere to welcome home our boys who, the newspapers said, had all done so well, which did not surprise anybody. We had expected no less.

Aunt Adele and I, at the time, loyal, patriotic, and British to the backbone, plunged into the spirit of the celebrations. After the soldiers landed, we followed Uncle Theo's contingent as they marched to Government House at the far end of town. There, on the spacious lawn, facing the Caribbean Sea, we watched the review of the ex-servicemen by the new governor. The men were served a meal and given some money.

Standing with Aunt Adele, just days ago, waiting for Uncle Theo outside the gates of Government House, I couldn't wait to tell him that the year before a flagpole had fallen from a burning storefront hitting the last governor on his head. He had died, perhaps in an upstairs room of the huge white house towering above the ex-servicemen scattered about the grounds. During the same terrible fire, the courthouse in the center of town had also burnt to the ground.

When Uncle Theo finally emerged from the gates of Government House, Aunt Adele and I rushed towards him, shouting his name. He had the biggest smile on his face as he hugged and kissed us. But as we began the long walk home,

I was at first surprised, then very disappointed, to see that my Uncle Theo, glad though he said he was to see us, did not seem at all moved by this public display of love and gratitude.

"I don't know why they are making such a fuss now," he said, gesturing at the buntings and flags fluttering on brightly decorated houses, stores and government buildings. "The British didn't want any niggers fighting alongside their white soldiers. Over there in Egypt, I was what I am here in Belize City, a common labourer without eyes to see, ears to hear or any feelings."

Uncle Theo slipped his hand into a pocket of his trousers and took out ten dollars he'd received at Government House. He held the money out to Aunt Adele. "I was fooled by that recruitment officer," Uncle Theo said, "taken in. And now the rumor is that our pay will be late, if we get it at all."

Aunt Adele looked taken aback. She tried to keep up her smile, but her plump, good-natured face saddened underneath the wide brim of her stiff straw hat, decorated, like my own, with red, white and blue streamers. She removed her silver-rimmed eyeglasses, polishing them with a scented handkerchief. Aunt Adele was known as one of the best seamstresses in town. She had stuck to her sewing and embroidery, supporting herself and me, all the while Uncle Theo was "at war, covering himself with glory," as she told any customer waiting for a fitting in our tiny parlour.

"But, Theo, I can't take your ten dollars," Aunt Adele said, shaking her head, her bosom heaving with surprise and distress. "The governor gave it to you as a token of his intention to pay the rest. It's on account. And you're all to get special treatment."

"I don't have any faith in the governor's word, Adele, not where money is concerned, and not after the way they shamed us overseas, not only us, but black fellows from all over. The governor must have had a good laugh today at all you good Belize people lining the road and waving the Union Jack."

Uncle Theo's words made Aunt Adele and me feel strangely guilty. Unwittingly, we seemed to have taken part in a British conspiracy to hurt my Uncle Theo and the other ex-servicemen. At that moment, glancing at Aunt Adele, I could tell that she was feeling, like I did, as though foreign oceans still separated us from Uncle Theo who had seen new worlds, who now carried them in his head, and who was glowering at us as if we were the enemy.

But then Aunt Adele uttered a little cry, opening her arms wide to him. There in Duck Lane, with the neighbors tilting their jalousies, Uncle Theo stumbled into her embrace, burying his face into her shoulders. We turned into our gate, the two of them leaning one against the other, and my bringing up the rear carrying Aunt Adele's handbag, Uncle Theo's cap, and the flags under which my Uncle Theo had been dishonoured overseas.

I was thinking so hard about my Uncle Theo's return home, only thirteen days before, that I was startled when he gave a little chuckle, "Funny to think, Daphne, that we are fighting at home when we spent the last two years labouring far away on a water transport system."

"Funny in truth, Uncle Theo," I said, though, I wasn't sorry that he had spent the war with a shovel in his hand, rather than dying, in all likelihood, at the front. My Uncle Theo, though, had dreamed, perhaps, of honours floating, like feathers to his hat, or like plumes that flew from the governor's helmet.

I looked in amazement at the angry, determined faces of the men and women around us. Everything seemed upside down. Occasionally I saw a policeman or a member of the volunteer army. According to Uncle Theo, even the police and the volunteers were behind the ex-servicemen. Belize City had suddenly become almost like a strange place to me. I felt like returning home immediately to Aunt Adele, but Uncle Theo and I had important visits to make that afternoon.

Despite the threat of further rioting after dark by the ex-servicemen and thousands of supporters, of more arrests to be made, and warships in our seas, or soon to be, Uncle Theo was going, as he did everyday, to try to see James Brindle, Esq., about his rights. Mr. Brindle had been the government official who recruited Uncle Theo into the army. He was also a share-holder in a department store which, Uncle Theo said, "was guilty of profiteering on the backs of poor, suffering people," like Aunt Adele and me who, through our ignorance of the outside world, bought, at exorbitant prices, flouncings, ribbons, and threads, which sold for little or nothing in England.

I was going, as I had to do each month, to ask Papa McGilroy for money to pay the fees for my two year diploma course. Uncle Theo called my father, "a force-ripe white man," because Uncle Theo said he had it on good authority that although my father looked white, and lived like white, his mother had been a light brown woman like me. Uncle Theo and Aunt Adele hated my father because he had not married my mother, "a perfect lady, proud, and too good for the likes of him," Aunt Adele said. My mother died in an influenza epidemic which had raged through the town when I was a little girl.

But according to Aunt Adele, it wasn't the flu alone that had killed my mother. She had become pregnant again for my father, and she had refused nourishment, prefering to die rather than to face the shame and heartbreak, or so Aunt Adele said. I didn't quite believe that my mother would choose to die, knowing she was leaving me behind. Often I dreamt about my mother. She steps out from the photograph we keep on a small shelf in my bedroom. Mama is dressed in a floor length white dress, with long sleeves. A fancy straw hat, ridiculously small, is perched on top of her crown of braids. Her face is heart-shaped, her eyes big, round and bright. In the dream, my mother seems to be talking with me, but I rarely remembered what we spoke about. I woke up sometimes, on the bed which had been hers, thinking that she was warning me about my father.

Aunt Adele did not earn enough money for expenses like school fees and books. These had to be begged for, at scheduled afternoon visits to my father, when he was in town, usually near month's end.

Papa McGilroy was thin, almost skinny, tall, with pale blue eyes and a sharp nose. Almost bald, his remaining reddish brown hair was turning white. His hands and face were sunburned from travelling by river boats up and down the country on special assignments for the government. Uncle Theo said he wouldn't be surprised if Papa McGilroy was put in charge of one of the districts, at some future date. "The British are raising up Creoles like him," Uncle Theo said.

Unmarried, my father lived in a two-storied white house, with green shutters, near the Foreshore. "Sit down, sit down," he would say, his voice brisk, pointing to one of the high-backed mahogany chairs, darkened by polish and age. The last time I was there, he looked at the clock on the wall and said, "After five already. I suppose you've had your tea?"

"Yes," I said, although I hadn't. Aunt Adele and I usually worked until dark. Then I lit the kerosene lamp, carrying it through the back door, along a short walkway to the kitchen, built away from the house in case of fire.

"Bring her a glass of lemonade," my father sometimes said to his servant. "Or would you prefer some tea?" "Lemonade," I said. The freshly made drink would be sweetened with imported white sugar; Aunt Adele and I used brown sugar at home. I knew I made my father uncomfortable, so I never stayed longer then necessary. My mother is so much a part of me, like a secret twin, that I can never smile in his presence, or make him smile. He is glad, I think, that I use my mother's maiden name, and that his name is not on my birth certificate. I was registered by my Uncle Theo. Not many people know I am Peter McGilroy's daughter, and Aunt Adele cautioned me against unnecessarily advertising the fact. "All assistance may be lost, if you do," she often said.

We were nearing Mr. Brindle's office now, and Uncle Theo was still talking to me about his experiences during the war. He didn't seem able to stop. "The British Tommies hated to hear us sing, "Rule Britannia," if you can believe that, Daphne."

"No, Uncle Theo," I said, and in all honesty I couldn't. Britain was our mother country and I sang, "God Save The King," and "Rule Britannia" here in Belize any old time, even when I was washing dishes, if I couldn't think of anything else I wanted to sing.

"And listen to this one, Daphne. We couldn't go to the Tommies Club anywhere out there just like we can't go to the Golf Club here in Belize City. They drove us away like dogs."

To distract his attention, and because the things he was saying were upsetting to me, I said, "Big July and no rain, eh Uncle Theo?" But he didn't even seem to hear the question. I was praying for it to rain that night so that the rioters would stay at home. The elastic band holding my hat in place felt tight at the base of my skull. My white cotton dress, freshly starched and ironed that morning, was already drooping around my ankles. I tilted Aunt Adele's black umbrella to the west shielding my face from the sun, always too hot, too bright on

July afternoons. Uncle Theo was saying, "I don't hesitate to tell Brindle about our treatment overseas, so the last two days he's been refusing to see me. But I'll catch him today, even if I have to stay outside his gate until morning."

"Promise me that you won't stay out late again tonight, Uncle Theo, please." I said. Earlier that morning he had returned home just as light was breaking through the coconut trees to the rear of our kitchen. The front of his shirt had been covered with blood. He swore me to secrecy and then I watched him cut up the shirt and burn the pieces in the coals of the firehearth. The kettle of water I was boiling, to make a pot of tea for Aunt Adele, steamed into his face, but he didn't seem to feel it.

"Promise me, Uncle Theo," I said again, "or I'll tell Aunt Adele that you were in the riots, and that we should expect the police at any time now."

"I don't believe you would do that, Daphne. Would you?" My Uncle Theo looked genuinely shocked and hurt.

"You just try me, Uncle Theo," I said. "Aunt Adele doesn't approve of all this rioting and breaking up shop windows and what not."

"Adele is out of step, Daphne, behind the times. But I thought you and I were in league."

"Only so far, Uncle Theo."

"And that is far enough for a nice young lady like you, Daphne," Uncle Theo said. He was silent for a while, then he said, "In any case, what are you going to do after you get that so-called diploma? Only the lucky few and the well-connected can find work nowadays, or so I've been told. Is that no-good father of yours going to help you when the time comes?"

"Maybe, Uncle Theo," I said, tilting the umbrella forward to shade my face. I was hoping to get a job, someday, as a secretary, or clerk, in the governor's office. On a visit to my father, shortly after my sixteenth birthday in May, he'd said that if all continued to go well, he would consider putting a word in the right ear. But I knew better than to share my secret with Uncle Theo as I had hoped to do in the days before he returned home.

Uncle Theo would laugh me to scorn. He would probably tell me, again, about the time when in the middle of the night, in pouring rain, after a long day's march, the British made the hungry men put up tents in what Uncle Theo thought was a field. In the morning, the soldiers were shocked to find that they had slept in an ancient Egyptian cemetery. To Uncle Theo, all Britishers, and all those who wanted to be British, like my father, in Belize City or abroad, were now one and the same.

We were just about to turn left, into my father's street, when Uncle Theo suddenly stopped, saying to me, "There he is, the very man!" and he started walking away from me down the street, shouting, "Mr. Brindle! Mr. Brindle!" I followed Uncle Theo, frightened that he would get into some kind of trouble. I thought of Aunt Adele waiting for us at home, of my father who would leave for the club if I was late.

I called out to Uncle Theo but he walked faster, and faster, before breaking into a run. He waved his hat in the air trying to catch Mr. Brindle's attention. Up ahead I saw Mr. Brindle on his horse starting to trot past Uncle Theo, ignoring him. Uncle Theo made a swift grab at the horse's bridle, yelling at the top of his voice, "I'll kill all you bloody British!" Mr. Brindle threatened Uncle Theo with his whip but Uncle Theo continued to hang on.

"My God, man, get hold of yourself," Mr. Brindle said, but Uncle Theo wouldn't let go. I saw Mr. Brindle bring the whip down on his hand. Uncle Theo reached up, attempting to drag Mr. Brindle off the horse. Mr. Brindle's huge brown horse reared up high above Uncle Theo and came crashing down with its entire weight on my Uncle Theo. He fell to the ground unconscious, blood trickling from his head. My heart felt as though it was about to burst through my chest. There was a terrible heat in my head and my eyes burned. I couldn't get to my beloved Uncle Theo, who I knew was counting on me to help him. People had gathered, police whistles blew, and Mr. Brindle shouted,

"Arrest that man! He is a dangerous agitator!"

The policeman stared at Mr. Brindle and then down at Uncle Theo, surrounded by men trying to lift him gently onto a passing mule and cart. I pushed my way through the crowd until I was right next to the heaving flanks of Mr. Brindle's trembling horse. Mr. Brindle's face was brick red, narrow, hawkish, his nose hooked, his lips thin. He looked neither frightened nor sorry, merely extremely annoyed. Perhaps, to him, people like us didn't have feelings to be hurt, or bodies and minds to be broken. Was this the kind of person my own father was? Did I have his chilled and chilling blood in my veins? If I did, I was sorry for it, and knew, in the end my mother had been too.

Feeling totally in league with my Uncle Theo, I picked his hat off the street and waved it at Mr. Brindle, shouting with all my might above the noise of the crowd, "First you fooled my poor Uncle Theo, and now you have killed him! I hope you are satisfied. Uncle Theo was right about you thieving, murdering British."

Mr. Brindle looked first at the surly demeanour of the silent men who were removing their shirts and jackets to place underneath my Uncle Theo's bleeding head, and then down at me. His eyes were cold and dark. "He's not dead, but he might have killed me. Do not address me in that fashion again. If you do, I shall have you arrested." He trotted away. I ran in the opposite direction following the mule and cart carrying Uncle Theo to the hospital under arrest for threatening to kill an officer of His Majesty's Government.

My Uncle Theo did not die, but in the hospital he suffered from terrible headaches and sometimes he confused us with people he had seen in Egypt. Aunt Adele and I have never understood how it was done, but during his trial my Uncle Theo was declared insane. He died in the asylum only a year later. A wire cross was found in his throat. The officials told Aunt Adele that my Uncle Theo had committed suicide. But Aunt Adele and I have always believed that my Uncle

Theo had been murdered, one way or another, by agents of the colonial government.

I was glad that I didn't tell my Uncle Theo, on the last afternoon we were alone together, about wanting to work in the governor's office. After Uncle Theo's brutal encounter with Mr. Brindle, I decided not to complete my diploma course, and didn't have to trouble myself to visit my father's house anymore. He doesn't seem to have noticed. Aunt Adele says she admires me for my decision. We are to become business women, she and I, sharing the profits fair and square. I now sew beside Aunt Adele as my mother used to do.

As a result of the riots, the British government has decided to give house lots to the ex-servicemen in an area called Mesopotamia. The streets are to be given names like Tigris, Amara, and Euphrates.

Aunt Adele has decided that I should write a letter to the government about placing her name on the list to get one of the free lots. She is beginning to sound more and more like my Uncle Theo, the dangerous agitator, and I am not far behind.

Return to Punta Gorda, Belize

Irma McClaurin

In the half life
of a sudden rain shower
I listen to the rooster
trumpet the debut of a new day.

Life moves tight and close
on these quiet streets.
Strangers command attention
while neighbors' faces and names
are remembered, catalogued
like familiar roads and cross streets.

Here, in Punta Gorda
a half-ripened moon blushes
behind the dark fingers
of a mahogany tree;

here, in Punta Gorda,
the sheen of your eyes glisten
like twin flecks
of black coral;

here, in Punta Gorda,
your fragrance lingers
like the aftertaste
of sea salt;

and, it is here,
to Punta Gorda,
I shall return someday
to rest in the sanctuary
of your touch—
a gentle seabreeze
that comforts me
in the hollow emptiness of night.

Yorke's House

Irma McClaurin

Peace descends here
like a mosquito net
delicate
over memories
charted through years:
children who sing and dance
the miracles of life.

Knowledge here
is thick
as zerricotte
splintered deep
with rough filaments
of people's stories,
and life's inevitabilities.

In Yorke's house
life's curtains gently part
to welcome
those who care enough
to enter.

School Children Haiku

Irma McClaurin

Fresh daisies huddle
in groups of ten
their dark faces bright
above the crisp whiteness
of school uniforms

My Father Becomes the Ogun

Joey García

The Belizean jungle opened
to a thickness of trunks and vines that tumbled
wildly into braids, like the mane of a horse
chased by *duendes*, opened deeper to the breathy sweat
of darkening matter rustled along edges of hooves,
paws and mouths, unfurled a heat
sweetened by rotting bananas. All this opened

to tutor my father in civilization. At fourteen
he quit the colonizer's Academy for Boys
to apprentice beneath skies of quetzal,
bronze-green and red that floated
through gasps in the jungle's canopy. He studied
three years under that roof, tested by trees
to live with his spirit as tap root
so he could learn the limitations of pain. He learned

while harvesting logs for shipment to England
down the Belize River and out to ships
waiting in the Caribbean Sea. And he was schooled
by mosquitoes and no-see-ums to hear
the singing of blood. For this, he planted
himself six days a week in bush litter,
his pants tucked into work boots as shield
against leaf-cutter ants in Cohune Ridge
whose territory was startled by such feet.
As those feet cleaved to earth
giddy with limestone and life,
my father would settle in with sawteeth
balanced against bark to open a trunk

the way a moment crosscuts the future.
And with his weight matched by another, he pulled
a two-man saw across logwood, across cabbage bark,
tamarind, sapodilla, mahogany. . .Trees with more substance
than the girls his budding arms embraced. The bougainvillea
smiles of girls trailed him into the jungle, just as the honey-
call of their bodies, blooming in Belize's hothouse seasons
invited him back out. After work on Saturdays,

he would fall upon his bed with a splintering
crash, rising hours later to party
with buddies at a Soca Club. He was six-foot tall,
coconut-brown with breath as sweet
as coco milk. In his village of Burrel Boom,
named for logs colliding in the river,
even grandmothers hailed my father,
"Prince of Boom."

                     But no prince would enter
his younger sister's quarters each morning
while roosters still dreamt of light,
patient as she sleepily bound his hands
in strips of old cotton shirts. The weave of the shirts,
broken in river baptisms and tired by sun,
swallowed the blood he sacrificed
at the altar of trees. The fabric was subtle
padding beneath the varnished wood handle
of the saw my father pulled to himself, shoulder muscles tensing,
until he remembered to slacken

for the inevitable pull away. The saw scratched
a hymn to rock the trees to rest, scraping
dusty blessings for the sweat of his nostrils,
brow and forearms. Mantled by wood flesh,
he could hear the confessions of trees, wishes
for afterlife, shapeshifts into other forms.
Mahogany thirsted for anointings, cabbage bark
to prove its grain. Once, a tree marked by loggers
prayed to *duendes* for protection. In his preferred
silence, my father heard

and understood. He hunted the jungle
for termites, kicking their black pots, until
pale bodies bubbled furiously. With cellulose
fingers he scooped and deposited those insects
beneath the tree. The trick fooled the British foreman
but cheated of pounds, he insisted that my father
salvage the timber. The task was refused—

                     No Belizean
dared infuriate *duendes* who in legends levitated
then lowered, axes in their thumbless hands

187

to destroy the neatly-stacked labors of men.
Men like my father who awakened at dusk,
fingers stiff-curled around saws,
palms shelled by dried blood and bodies
that still swayed to the saw's teething rhythm. All this
for a dollar a day, a man's wage paid
for a boy's education.

Note

Ogun is a Yoruba god who is patron of civilization and jungles.

Sea Death: Thoughts While Flying from Belize City to San Pedro

Mary Gómez Parham

God:

this is how I want to die:

blue face to blue sky
between reef and beach.

I've been in the sea
and it has offered me, salt-sweet,
a taste of death.

There I feel death swirl about me;
it spirals in long slimy strings
like amphibians' eggs.
Beasts lurk: scales and silence.
And violence that knows no shame,
rot that trails no stench
and leaves no stain.
You die more cleanly here.

They say that the sea is a symbol of life;
I say no:
the sea is made of unburied death,
dissolved and drifting.
Washed death, sky blue—
the one I want, God.

Pierced

Mary Gómez Parham

For Uncle Dick

The universe was a gentle white dome over us;
I used to believe that we were
sealed tight inside, children in our mother's warm kitchen.

But now a tiny hole has been
pierced in the sweet white dome.
Just a tiny hole, a pin-prick really—
but through it my blood trickles out,
purple-red onto the sterile gauze of infinity.

Slowly his death, and the others,
will fill the smooth white with small scarlet wounds,
wounds that will drip shocking spots
on my polished kitchen floor.

The Emigrant's Lament

Mary Gómez Parham

Space and time are revisited in a
ritual reaching for roots;
sunburned souls grasp at what was
and beg the green of the Caribbean
to take us back, back to that other time
when only the reef was old.

        And we cry out to
this sea, this reef, these sands—
        our mothers—
to wave wands and chant chants
and swirl skirts in a frenzy, sweat, fury,
in a mad dance to bring back the gone
and stop the going.

But sea, reef, sands
stay on while we come and go—
we, our grandmothers, grandsons;
blood-multitudes ever returning,
dragging our years across the white beach,
searching it for bones or newborns.
The beginning pulls and is,
and battered pilgrims return,
laying memories, dreams, questions
at the feet of a warm sphinx-sea
and on the graves of silent ancestors
who do not hear and who,
like our sea-mothers,
have no chants to chant for us.

About Cicadas in August

Mary Gómez Parham

As if the world didn't notice,
had no opinion on the matter,
summer goes.
      No bells toll,
      no curtain falls,
      no drums roll.

Yet there, in the fierce still,
they vibrate and spin, the cicadas,
clinging to August's sweating back
as it gallops into the dark.
Their great eyes see and know,
and frenzied, panting,
they shriek summer's going.
So lately burst from their old brown skins,
they finally know why
their shell-bodies dangle dead from tree trunks
and why their groins now pulsate and press.

The Caribbean Writer

10TH ANNIVERSARY LITERATURE CONFERENCE

CONFERENCE

UNIVERSITY OF THE VIRGIN ISLANDS
ST. CROIX, U.S. VIRGIN ISLANDS
OCTOBER 25-27, 1996
(Revised Program)

Friday, October 25, 1996

2:00 p.m. - 5:00 p.m. - Registration at Florence A. S. Williams Library lobby

Virgin Islands Writers Read
Sponsored by Island National Insurance

Florence A. S. Williams Library, theater (King Street)
3:15 p.m. - 4:45 p.m.

Chair: Ruby Simmonds, University of the Virgin Islands, St. Thomas
"Virgin Words, See How They Grow: The Growth and Development of Virgin Islands Poetry"

Phyllis Briggs-Emanuel	Marty Campbell	Monique Clendinen
Patricia Harkins-Pierre	Aubrey Danielson	Bertica Hendrickson
Carol Henneman	Elaine Jacobs	S.B. Jones-Hendrickson
Lorraine Joseph	Marvin E. Willaims	Tregenza Roach
Lilian Southerland	Winnie "Oyoko" Loving	

Afternoon Tea: 4:45 p.m. - 5:15 p.m.
Florence A. S. Williams Library

****

The President's Reception
6:30 p.m. - 8:00 p.m: *Hotel on the Cay, Christiansted*
(The ferry leaves from the waterfront, near the Fort)

Welcome
Dr. Erika J. Waters
Editor, *The Caribbean Writer*

Dr. Orville E. Kean
President

Dr. Darshan S. Padda
Vice President, Research and Land-Grant Affairs (on sabbatical)

Dr. LaVerne E. Ragster
Acting Vice President, Research and Land-Grant Affairs

Dr. Denis Paul
Vice President, Academic Affairs

First Plenary Session: Caryl Phillips

8:00 p.m. - 9:00 p.m.
Introduction by Mr. Dennis Parker
Chair, Humanities Division

Closing remarks by Dr. Roderick Moorehead
Dean of Instruction and Academic Affairs (St. Croix)

****

Saturday, October 26, 1996

(All sessions to be held at Florence A. S. Williams Library, King Street)

Session 1 - 8:30 a.m. - 10:00 a.m.

a) **Caribbean Diasporic Literature**   *Caribbean Collection (3rd floor)*

Chair: Vincent O. Cooper, University of the Virgin Islands, St. Thomas

> Reinhard W. Sander (University of Puerto Rico, Rio Piedras), "Caryl Phillips: A Crisscrossing of the Diaspora"
> Linda M. Rodríguez Guglielmoni (University of Puerto Rico, Maya-guez), "*Este ojo que me mira/This Eye that Looks at Me*: Power Structures"
> Sandra Pouchet Paquet (University of Miami), "The Thematics of Diaspora and the Intercultural Identity Question"
> John M. Figueroa (Formerly of Open University, U. K.), "Writings on the General Theme of 'Cosmopolitan Pig'" (video)

b) **The Caribbean View of Women**   *Theater (2nd floor)*

Chair: Roberta Knowles, University of the Virgin Islands, St. Croix

> Merle Hodge (University of the West Indies, Trinidad), "Caribbean Family Values and *Beka Lamb*"
> María Elena Alonso (University of Puerto Rico, Rio Piedras), "For the Construction of Identity"
> Phyllis Briggs-Emanuel (Clark Atlanta University), "Rites/Rights of Passage: Growing Up in the Caribbean in Zee Edgell's *Beka Lamb*"
> Elaine Savory (New School for Social Research), "Jean Rhys, the Writing Narrative and the Writing Life"
> Opal Palmer Adisa (California College of Arts & Crafts), "We is More Dan You See - Dried Coconuts or Pomegranates: Caribbean Women Speak"

Coffee break: 10:00 a.m. - 10:30 a.m.

Session 2: 10:30 a.m. - 12:00 p.m.

a) **Caribbean Drama** *Theater (2nd floor)*

Chair: Rosary Harper, University of the Virgin Islands, St. Thomas

> Alwin Bully, "Caribbean Theater Today"
> Joseph L. Mbele (St. Olaf's College), "Existentialist Notions in
> Walcott's The Sea at Dauphin"
> Lowell Fiet (University of Puerto Rico, Rio Piedras), "Impossible and
> Essential: Theorizing Caribbean Theater and Performance"
> David Edgecombe (University of the Virgin Islands, St. Thomas), "A
> Professional Caribbean Theater"

b) **Literary Publishing in the Caribbean** *Caribbean Collection*
(3rd floor)

Chair: Erika J. Waters, University of the Virgin Islands, St. Croix

> E. A. Markham (Sheffield Hallam University), "On Editing the *Penguin
> Book of Caribbean Fiction*"
> William Riggan (University of Oklahoma), "Publishing and Writing in
> the Caribbean: An Outside Reader's Report"
> Howard Fergus (University of the West Indies, Montserrat), "Literary
> Magazines in the Development of a National Literature"

****

Second Plenary Session: Kamau Brathwaite
Theater (2nd floor)
12:00 p.m. - 1:00 p.m.

Lunch - 1:00 p.m. - 2:00 p.m.

Session 3: 2:00 p.m. - 3:30 p.m.

a) **Caribbean Literature in the Classroom K-6** *Theater (2nd floor)*

Chair: Sarah Mahurt, University of the Virgin Islands, St. Croix

> Ashley Bryan, "A Tender Bridge - Caribbean Folktales with African
> Roots that Connect the Past to our Present and Future"
> Darwin Henderson (University of Cincinnati), "Caribbean Children's
> Literature for the Elementary Classroom"
> Phillis Gershator & Willie Wilson (Antilles School, St. Thomas), "A
> Story to Tell"

b) **Caribbean Literature in the Classroom:**   *Caribbean Collection*
   Junior and Senior High School   *(3rd floor)*

Chair: Trevor Parris, University of the Virgin Islands, St. Thomas

> Tracy Thompson-Johnson and Irose Payne-Chalon (Eudora Kean High School, St. Thomas), "Strategies for Teaching Literature"
> Trevor Parris (University of the Virgin Islands, St. Thomas), "Student Products in Caribbean Literature"
> Gayle V. Dancy-Benjamin (Charlotte Amalie High School), "Strategies for Teaching Caribbean Literatures: Focus on Caribbean Poetry"
> Patricia Harkins-Pierre (University of the Virgin Islands, St. Thomas), "The Caribbean Play in the University of the Virgin Islands Classroom and Suggestions for Further Reading"

Coffee break: 3:30 p.m. - 4:00 p.m.
Sponsored by The Division of Student Affairs (St. Croix)

Caribbean Poetry and Fiction: Reading 1
Theater (2nd floor), 4:00 p.m. - 5:30 p.m.

Chair: Marvin E. Williams, University of the Virgin Islands, St. Croix

Marion Bethel	Vincent O. Cooper
Howard A. Fergus	Laurence Lieberman
E. A. Markham	Mark Sylvester
Patricia Turnbull	

ARTWALK:
These Christiansted galleries are open tonight: Maria Henle's Studio, Gilliam-King Gallery and Artist's Co-op.

Sunday, October 27, 1996
(All sessions & meals to be held at Hotel on the Cay. The ferry leaves from the waterfront, near the Fort.)

Breakfast Focus Groups
8:30 a.m. - 10:00 a.m.

Eat breakfast and join discussion leaders, session chairs, critics and writers in further discussions on Saturday's topics as well as additional topics, such as:

- Puerto Rican Writers in New York
- Teaching Creative Writing
- The Language Continuum that Caribbean Writers Navigate Through
- Encouraging a National Literature

Caribbean Poetry and Fiction: Reading 11
Theater, 10:00 am - 12:00 p.m.

Includes *The Caribbean Writer* award winners: the *Daily News Prize*, the *Canute A. Brodhurst Prize*, and the *Charlotte and Isidor Paiewonsky Prize*.

Chair: Valerie Combie, University of the Virgin Islands, St. Croix

Opal Palmer Adisa	David Gershator
Merle Hodge	Lelawatee Manoo-Rahming
Jeanne O'Day	Geoffrey Philp
Thomas Reiter	Elaine Savory
Loreina Santos Silver (with Linda M. Rodríguez Guglielmoni)	
Jean Small	

Third Plenary Session: George Lamming
Theater, 12:00 p.m. - 1:00 p.m.

Lunch: 1:00 p.m. - 2:00 p.m.

The Caribbean Writer's 10th Anniversary Literature Conference is funded in part by a major grant from the Virgin Islands Humanities Council, an affiliate of the National Endowment for the Humanities, and by the Virgin islands Council on the Arts and the National Endowment for the Arts.

Special thanks to:

Dr. Orville E. Kean	Dr. Darshan S. Padda
Dean Juanita Woods	Mr. Wallace Williams
Ms. Clarice Clarke	Dr. Jozef Keularts
Ms. Jessica Thorpe	St. Croix Reading Council
Island National Insurance	Friends of the Florence Williams Library

Virgin Words, See How They Grow: the Growth and Development of Virgin Islands Poetry

Ruby Simmonds

In 1932 when Virgin Islands writer, J. Antonio Jarvis' first poetry collection, *Fruits in Passing*, was published, the literary movement known as modernism was already in vogue. Despite vast changes occurring on the poetic landscape in Europe and the United States, poetry in the Caribbean, including the Virgin Islands, however, was progressing at a much slower pace, and even African American poetry with which it shared a number of similarities was progressing differently.

Several factors account for this in the development of Caribbean poetry. First of all, the geographical isolation of the Caribbean from the continent accounts for the delay in literary and other trends reaching its shores. Secondly, the experience of colonialism created a different mindset among a people who had to first struggle for selfhood and then to seek some voice for that new-found self. Thirdly, the educational system of the Caribbean in the early 1900s was completely European, often with outdated textbooks being the primary source of information for young scholars. Indeed, Peter Blackman, in a 1948 article entitled "Is There a West Indian Literature?" offers several reasons for the derivative nature of Caribbean poetry. Among them is the fact that the English did not develop a new life in the islands with standards comparable to those existing in their homeland. Additionally, until well into the nineteenth century, there were no bookshops and in some islands not even a printing press, and the English children were sent home (to England) to school. When education was extended to the black West Indian, English patterns of thoughts and English canons of beauty were taught and accepted even at points where they were hostile to the self-respect of most West Indians. It was natural, then, for the writers to imitate what was available to them. It also seems logical that in their imitating, the writers would be anxious to prove themselves worthy by not straying from the forms and even the themes they had been taught to emulate. Marvin E. Williams, editor of a forthcoming anthology of Virgin Islands poetry, shares the following sentiments about the derivative nature of early Virgin Islands poetry:

> These writers represented a largely unvoiced people still locked into a prescriptive and proscriptive colonial society; yet they sought to inscribe their voice within a scribal convention that heretofore had denied them [that] possibility. That imitation

occurred is not surprising; that the master tongue remained vir-
tually uninfluenced by [that of the] islands was almost inevitable. (2)

These educational and geographical factors coupled with the social and
political intercourse extant between the Virgin Islands and Harlem, and the Virgin Islands and the Eastern Caribbean helped to shape the writing of these early
Virgin Islands poets. The book *European and African Influences on the Culture of the
Virgin Islands* quotes Virgin Islands musician, Hugo Bornn:

The influences that shaped the native music did not come solely
from successive waves of conquerors. Another source was the lively
inter-island commerce which existed throughout the nineteenth
century. Songs were carried from one island to another by migrant
workers, by ships' crews and cargo workers, and occasionally by political refugees. Some of the songs may still be discovered in different versions in many islands and generally it would be impossible
to decide which is the original version. (68)

It would appear that the influence exerted on the music of the Virgin Islands
resulting from contacts with its Caribbean neighbors, applied similarly to other
aspects of life and culture including literature. Additionally, some of J. P. Gimenez's folklore poems like "A Virgin Islander's Letter to Uncle Sam" clearly show
that there was significant commerce among the islands.

Although the islands were owned by Denmark, the education to which
early writers were exposed was British. Charles Turnbull, noted historian and
University of the Virgin Islands professor, indicated in an interview that education under the Danes was very religious. Bible stories, particularly those which
encouraged human love and kindness, were common. Much of the reading came
from the Psalms and Proverbs. He adds that even stories which were taken from
the Bible provided moral lessons. The beauty of nature was also stressed in
school. Additionally, he states, there was a heavy dose of English literature.
Nonetheless, despite the predominantly British leanings, students were exposed
to some American literature, particularly Oliver Wendell Holmes and Walt
Whitman. Memorization was a significant part of the learning process, yet students were also encouraged to write their own poems. It would seem, then, that
having been thoroughly immersed in a certain type of literature, students, in their
own compositions, would imitate that to which they had been exposed. Certainly, the influence of their early education is evident in the writings of three
forerunners of Virgin Islands poetry, J. Antonio Jarvis, Cyril Creque, and J. P.
Gimenez.

Another factor which helped to shape the style of writing coming out of
the Virgin Islands in the 1920s and 1930s was the interaction with educators
from the Eastern Caribbean. While most teachers in the Danish schools were
local, a number of them, as noted by Turnbull, either came from Antigua or, like
Emanuel Benjamin Oliver under whom Jarvis worked, had been educated there.
There was also the practice of sending teachers in training to Antigua in the then

British West Indies (then considered the center of learning in the Caribbean) to complete their educations, so that Virgin Islands teachers to a large extent were exposed to much the same literature which shaped the literature of the rest of the Caribbean.

However, not only was the literary experience through education similar, but the peoples of the Caribbean shared the common heritage of dehumanizing enslavement, and many of the influences which shaped the literature of the Caribbean in general were also responsible for determining the face of Virgin Islands literature. The experiences of enslavement and colonization, for critics such as Louis James, were in large part responsible for the type of poetry produced by early Caribbean writers. Indeed, James maintains that West Indian literature has grown out of the explosive tensions of diversity (32) and in his estimation is perhaps the richest and most varied field of writing in English to emerge since World War II (10).

The Caribbean poetic tradition, of which the Virgin Islands is a part, begins with the oral literature of the enslaved Africans and includes not only writers of African descent, but the colonizers and their descendants as well. While there are some songs in African languages, by the end of the eighteenth century, the Caribbean-born slaves used the English vocabulary available to them. This tradition includes the "jamma" or work song, featuring the call-and-response structure which came from Africa. The satiric song, which ridiculed some aspect of the slave masters' lives, is also a part of this as are adapted folk songs. In the Virgin Islands this tradition was expressed in the carisos, a form of song used to send messages between different plantations and sometimes to ridicule other persons. It is also the one form of Virgin Islands literature which immortalizes a number of Virgin Islands heroes, "sheroes," and historical events. This oral tradition was expanded with the inclusion of hymns which arrived with the missionaries, and later with increasing literacy came the newspapers which were often read aloud. Likewise in the Virgin Islands, the local hymns such as "Brother Hopeful" and the sacred songs and solos referred to as Sankeys make up a significant part of the oral tradition.

It would appear that since the Virgin Islands oral tradition, through the cariso songs and the Sankey and other hymns, developed much the same way as that of the rest of the Caribbean, it would follow that the development of the scribal tradition, the pastoral—a form which extols the beauty of the landscape—is very evident in the works of early writers such as Jarvis, Creque, and Gimenez. Interestingly, Jarvis, in describing St. Croix in his book, *The Three Islands*, says "Driving east toward the Centerline is a drive for a painter in search of the plains of Arcadie or the scene of Millet's Angelus, for the country spreads out in spacious field and low land for miles in all directions" (11). This classical allusion is indicative of Jarvis' knowledge of the Romantics, and their possible influence on him.

200

In addition to treating the landscape, much of the Caribbean poetry written during the late nineteenth and early twentieth centuries dealt with natural cataclysms such as hurricanes, earthquakes, and volcanic eruptions, another feature evident in early Virgin Islands poetry. Other features of early Caribbean poetry evident in the writings of the Virgin Islanders include Gimenez's use of vernacular and attention to the Afro-Caribbean belief in obeah. Like the writers of Guyana, who developed a vigorous tradition of patriotic verse toward Great Britain designed to strengthen new bonds and new allegiances, the Virgin Islands poetical forefathers were generous in their tributes to the United States, its military might, and its leaders. There was also, particularly on the part of Creque, attention to developing a sense of patriotic pride in the Virgin Islands itself. According to Paula Burnett, all the territories shared this sense of patriotism to a certain extent, just as they shared the Victorian tradition of loyalty to Britain (1). This is the same tradition carried on by the writers of the Virgin Islands.

Additionally, early Virgin Islands writers were part of a tradition characterized by Lloyd Brown as "[T]he double-consciousness of an emerging poetic tradition which is still rooted strongly in entrenched loyalties to the literary forms and imperial sovereignty of England, but which is simultaneously beginning to respond to the growing social and ethnic pressures of the late nineteenth century and early twentieth century" (24-25). Interestingly, however, this dual consciousness takes a different form in the Virgin Islands. While writers in the rest of the Caribbean were beginning to address their own social plight, Virgin Islands writers were expressing a greater affinity with the struggles of Black America. It seems, therefore, that the Virgin Islands, while walking with the shoes of its geographic siblings on one foot and those of its political cousins on the other, managed to walk with its own gait, thus forging its own footprints in the sand. In this vein, therefore, it is appropriate to examine the relationship which existed between the Virgin Islands and Black America generally and Harlem in particular.

The Virgin Islands' relationship to Harlem goes back to the early 1900s when Virgin Islanders became active in a number of movements in the mecca of Black American life. The Virgin Islands connection to literary movements in Black America are many. Significant among these connections is the fact that both Jarvis and Creque had poems published in *Opportunity*, a major black publication sponsored by the Urban League. Jarvis also wrote a poem in tribute to Marcus Garvey, the Black Moses of the Harlem Renaissance period. Thus, the interconnections between the Virgin Islands and Harlem during the early 1930s show an influence of culture and literature. In fact, among Jarvis' poems are three which address Harlem specifically, "Harlem Comedy," "Harlem Tragedy," and one reminiscent of Claude McKay's "Tropics in New York," "On Spring in Harlem." Additionally, he wrote a poem in tribute to Paul Laurence Dunbar. The impact of the New Negro Movement on the Virgin Islands is not unusual, for in his book, *Harlem's Danish-American West Indians, 1899-1964*, Geraldo Guirty, a Virgin Islands journalist who lived in Harlem for many years, indicates that there was a branch of Marcus Garvey's United Negro Improvement Association in St. Thomas. He also notes that among the subjects of political activist Rothschild Francis's black achievement lectures were Paul Laurence Dunbar, George Washington Carver, Phillis Wheatley, Booker T. Washington, Frederick Douglas, Harriet Tubman, and Sojourner Truth, suggesting that the populace of the new territory of the United States was being kept abreast of Black American history.

Nevertheless, although some of the major cultural and literary links lie in the Caribbean and Black America, there were also other influences on Virgin Islands writing. For example, Jarvis acknowledged the influence of Longfellow and Byron on his style. Edward Richards recalls in an interview that once when Jarvis was evaluating his (Richard's) work, Jarvis admitted that Richards' work would stand out because it was written in free verse and didn't follow a pattern. He acknowledged that Richards' work was unlike his own which was patterned after Longfellow and Byron.

While much of the connections seem to have been made with Jarvis, it is important to note that because of his position as an educator, journalist, and publisher, Jarvis wielded much influence in the community. Other writers frequently gathered at his home for discussions. In fact, according to those who knew him, Jarvis's home Tivoli, was a center for the exchange of intellectual ideas. Rufus Vanderpool, cultural historian, recalls that anybody who wrote took their work to Jarvis for evaluation. In his words, "He was the divining rod."

It would appear, then, that the words flowing from the pens of Virgin Islands writers were to a large degree dependent on the words which washed to the islands' shores from both their political affiliates and their geographic neighbors. However, those diverse influences, when mingled with the context of Virgin Islands culture, served to produce a poetry that is the Virgin Islands' alone.

Certainly, Creque, Gimenez, and Jarvis were not the only Virgin Islands poets writing in the first half of the twentieth century, but they are certainly the earliest and in many ways set the tone for others to follow. Other early writers included Wilfred Hatchett, Gerwyn Todman, Isidor Paiwon (pen name for Isidor Paiewonsky), Valdemar Hill, Sr., Erica Lee, Aubrey Anduze, and Edward Richards, all of whom published at least one volume of poems. These later writers were all influenced by the first writers. Over the years, Virgin Islands poetry has changed, manifesting greater diversity than the works of the early poets. For example, Cornelius Emanuel, while following the vernacular tradition started by Gimenez, provides a different picture of the everyday life of the Virgin Islands in poems such as "The Legend of 'Tampo'" and "The 'Downtown' Senate (Bar Normandie in Frenchtown)." Some of the later poets, in particular Althea Romeo and Bertica Hodge, received their poetic initiation as students at the then College of the Virgin Islands in the 1970s, where their work impressed poets, such as Judson Jerome and Allen Ginsberg. Of the period that produced these writers, poet and former professor David Gershator says, "The tension today between Americanization and West Indianization provides fertile ground for the poets of

202

the 70s. These poets are aware of the complexities of West Indian life and the economic, cultural, and political cross-currents in and around the islands" (412). Significantly, the duality of which Gershator speaks is the same double consciousness which shapes the work of the early twentieth-century Virgin Islands poets.

Two conditions which impact on the growth and development of a literature are access to publication and criticism. Jarvis sought to provide both—publishing through the Art Shop and the *Daily News* and criticism through the scholarly gatherings held at his home. Over the years various magazines have served as outlets for poetry in the Virgin Islands, but there has been no one consistent vehicle devoted to highlighting this area of creativity. Among the magazines which have featured poems are *The Virgin Islands Forum*, *Virgin Islands View*, and *The Voice*. However, none of them is any longer in publication. Nonetheless, University of the Virgin Islands students today have an outlet in the student literary magazines, *Sea Moss* and *Leeward Breezes*, while other members of the academic community contribute to *The Caribbean Writer*, so there are some avenues available to poets desirous of getting their work in print.

Fortunately, there is more attention being given to the literary works of the Virgin Islands and certainly the upcoming anthology of Virgin Islands poetry will go a long way in helping to showcase the writers of the Virgin Islands, as it covers the early writers, Creque, Gimenez, and Jarvis, as well as present day poets, such as Wanda Mills and Carol Henneman. On the island of St. Croix, retired prison warden, Richard A. Schrader, has published a collection of poems and has been involved over the last five or six years in producing several small anthologies of works by St. Croix residents. Today's panel, highlighting the work of Virgin Islands poets, is yet another step in the process of recognizing Virgin Islands literature as part of the Caribbean canon. The writers featured here today have each in their individual ways helped the roots of Virgin Islands poetry to descend a little deeper and the branches of our literary tree to spread a little wider. Their words indeed are a vital part of a literature that is dynamic, as these Virgin words continue to grow.

Works Cited

Blackman, Peter. "Is There a West Indian Literature?" *Life and Letters and the London Mercury*. 59 (1948): 96-102.

Bornn, Hugo. *Resources for a Program in Music Study*. Ann Arbor: University of Michigan, 1965. 108-115. In Project Introspection. *European and African Influences on the Culture of the Virgin Islands*. U. S. Virgin Islands: Department of Education, 1973.

Brown, Lloyd W. *West Indian Poetry*. Boston: Twayne, 1978.

Burnett, Paula, ed. *The Penguin Book of Caribbean Verse in English*. Middlesex, England: Penguin Books, 1986.

Gershator, David. "Poetry of the Virgin Islands: Past and Present." *Revista Interamericana Review* 2 (1972): 408-414.

Guirty, Geraldo. *Harlem's Danish-American West Indians, 1899-1964.* New York: Vantage, 1989.

James, Louis, ed. *The Islands in Between: Essays on West Indian Literature.* London: Oxford University Press, 1968.

Jarvis, J. Antonio. *The Three Islands.* St. Thomas, V. I.: The Art Shop, 1935.

Richards, Edward. Personal interview. 29 December 1994.

Turnbull, Charles W. Personal interview. 5 January 1995.

Vanderpool, Rufus. Personal interview. 28 December 1994.

Williams, Marvin E., ed. *Yellow Cedars Blooming: An Anthology of Virgin Islands Poetry*. Unpublished manuscript.

Writings on the General Theme of "Cosmopolitan Pig"

John M. Figueroa

First I'd like to thank Erika Waters and the other people in charge of this conference for asking me to send them a video. They invited me to come and speak but, honestly, I'm not fit enough to do that, and I have to thank Mr. Rix of the Open University for coming to my house to help me. When I was recently in Jamaica I found much to my surprise that they were still on to something that they've been doing for a long time. They're trying to find the greatest Jamaican play and they're trying to give out a prescription for it. They're saying, as Errol Hill once said, "There can be no real Caribbean play without a procession." I won't go into the problems that that would create but I want to read a few poems which show, I suppose, as most of you know, that I don't agree with that point of view at all. If you get a good writer who has lived in Jamaica or is a Jamaican and has experiences that would appeal, he can write a very good play and I do know that many people are writing plays in Jamaica.

However, the first poem I'm going to read to you is an old favorite, a short poem called "At Home the Green Remains." Now it seems to be in every anthology that has anything of mine. That's why I'm reading it, not because I think it's a wonderful poem. It is a sonnet and there are those who feel a Jamaican writer should not write a sonnet. They say it's English. Of course it's not English at all. This sonnet was created in Italy and then English and French poets imitated it.

At Home the Green Remains

In England now I see the windows shake
And see beyond its astigmatic panes
Against black limbs Autumn's yellow stain
Splashed across tree-tops and wet beneath the rake.

New England's hills are flattened as crimson-lake
And purple columns, all that now remain
Of trees, stand forward as hillocks do in rain,
And up the hillside ruined temples make.

At home the green remains: the palm throws back
Its head and breathes above the still blue sea,
The separate hills are lost in common blue
Only the splendid poinsettias, true
And crimson like the northern ivy, tark,
But late, the yearly notice to a tree.

The next one I'm going to read makes a point about this idea of people writing only about their own culture or their own country. It's called "Cosmopolitan Pig" and is dedicated to George Lamming. (George has never said anything about this to me.) Some of you will remember that once upon a time the slogan was "Workers of the World Unite," but then powers of the countries like the Soviet Union started to speak of socialism and they called anyone who was interested in anything other than their own country, "cosmopolitan," and if this was being broadcast from Moscow, the degrading word "pig" had to be added, so such writers were "cosmopolitan pigs."

Cosmopolitan Pig
(For George Lamming)

A sculptured poem
Or long-lined church
Clean the line with rhymes
That chime but hardly show,
The poem in another language
From another time,
The church at Brou
Geometry in stone
Or at Les Baux
Out-crop of bauxite soil
Before that earth became
Red mother of metal.

Irrelevant to those
Who hate to see
Beyond the dust beneath their feet
Who dare not look within
Lest they find dreams
That stretch across the earth
Like air
Sympathies covering the globe
More urgent than missiles
Festering with hate.

The stone I break from Carib hills
To make a pot or build a church
Binds me to the Pyramids
And megaliths in Egypt or Peru
The church I love at Brou
Is part of that

Geometry of the sea
That rolls upon itself
In blues and greens
At Tower Isle
Or solidifies in whites
About the Crane.

What is Barbados, or Peru
Provence or Rome
But places which Any Man
Can make their home?
Home is too human
Work, making, building
Too much part of us
To be particular

No sharp stroke shaping stone
No bend of metal or curve
Of well-kept hill
No plotted field of cane
Or wheat or rice;
No garden by the railroad
Or formal as the French
No Ife bronze
Or illuminated script
Is alien to me

The next one is called "For the Girl Dancing on the Spanish Steps in Rome." It was written in Rome. The Spanish Steps connect one of the great, old houses with a view of Aneto. In the old house that afternoon they were playing what you might call I suppose avant-garde music and I walked down from that out onto the grass heading for the steps to go down into Rome and then I saw a group of students, who were clapping time. One of them came out of the bunch and started to dance. She danced in a very interesting way, in semi-circles turning to the left and as soon as she had neared the main circle she turned back to the right.

For the Girl Dancing on the Spanish Steps in Rome

Release, release the spirits of the dead
Unwind, unwind the winding sheets.
Untie, untie arthritic thighs
That mar the geometry in my head.

You bend the knees and spit the spell
Many dream the spiral conch to hold
And ageing men withhold their sighs
Sensing young breasts that rise and swell

Like morning tides the moon defeats
The moon directs us "forget the dead,"
And lunatic we breed against the cold
forget the happiness as we grow old.

Release, release the spirits of the dead
Unwind, unwind the winding sheets.
Your arms and legs, your mount that moves the world,
Struggle like a flutter-by from
The world to waving wings of light.

Unlock the graves and quicken the dead
To dance upon the Spanish stairs
I have not eyes, the dead no airs,
To be superior to the fugue you tread.

Release, release the spirits of the dead
Unwind, unwind the winding sheets.
Untie, untie arthritic thighs
That mar the geometry in my head.

Call up, call up my son to dance
To climb the Spanish stairs from death
Your spinning spell of touch and breath
Hole the sticky web from chance
From snapping or blindly catching
Insects it hardly wants,
Call up, call up
My son to dance.

Against the death your dance
Defeats at moments on the Spanish steps
There is no lasting motion,
Majorities do not rule the ocean,
But if we must go down the stairs
At last to the Piazza
Your dancing soothes us there
Or loses us in moments
of woven exaltation.

O dance and dance all night
And spin the web, the spell,
What does it matter
That morning light
Will find us dead-
With dignity because
You danced, you danced all night.

The whirling conch draws up the spirits
Like Da Vinci's flying wheel.
Your swirling elbows are loose then tight
An upward flame solid in the night

Low, then high swirling upward
With your tossing head you steal the fire
And the fluting of the whirling shell
You loosen the hardened shape
With your motion

Release, release the spirits of the dead
And spin the web, the spell
Untie, untie arthritic thighs
That mar the geometry in my head.

Call up, call up my son to dance
To climb the Spanish stairs from death
It is your winding spell of conch and breath
That holds the fragile web from chance.

We must go down the Stairs at
Last to the Piazza
Your dancing soothes us there
What matters it if morning light
Should find us stiff in death?

You wove the breathing spire
You fought with time and death
You swirled and smiled in the night
At us who did admire
But could not find the faith
To dance and weave and light the fire.

This is a rather short poem and those of you who know Spanish literature will see traces of Lorca in it. One of the criticisms of a poem or a novel that always amuses me is that people find that other poets or novelists often influence the writer too much. I don't know what's the use of having a love of literature and reading widely if the people you read do not affect you.

Goodbye. . .Despedida

The boy leans on a coconut tree-
He's shaped like it without its leaves-
Tears the thick skin oily as the sea
And sucks the juicy flesh with carnal ease.

He does not know that leaves will fall
That long before a seed arranges
New roots he'll not hear us call,

Insensate as any sand to futile sound
He will not smell the sea, nor oranges
Lighting up his final ground.

The next one engages an attitude which affects even our best writers. You know there was once a series of articles which wanted to show that Derek Walcott was not the poet that people thought he was because he wrote "I AM" in capitals. Apparently a Caribbean writer of the highest quality may not write "I AM" in capitals. Many of these articles were, of course, in support of one of our greatest writers, Eddy Kamau Brathwaite and as Brathwaite doesn't write in capitals, those who favored him had to show that Walcott was not so good because he wrote in capitals. Now one day, Walcott's brother, Roddy—who is a good dramatist and playwright and well-known in his own country but not so much abroad—was walking in the country and a man stopped him and asked, "Aye, you is Roddy? Teacher Alex son?" Roddy and Derek are twins and the mother's name is Alex. She is a well-known teacher and headmistress in St. Lucia.

Problems of a Writer Who Does Not Quite. . .

Roddy Broder, Teacher Alix son,
Bwoy, you no hear wa de lady say?
Watch de pentameter ting, man.
Dat is white people play!

Wha de hell you read Homer-
A so him name? - fa!
Yu his from the horal tradition
And must deal wid calypso and reggae na!

Mek I advise yu boy
If you trouble white people toy
Especially as yu win big prize an ting
Yu arse going swing

Like Metronome, yu'd say,
But a black boy should play
Widout dem mechanical aids
Full of rydhm like all true spades.

(Eh a since when yu tun black?
Yu note-book does say yu never did notice
Whedder the sore was black or white day dat wear de poultice,
But de lady slap "black experience" in yu back!)

See what dat pentameter and ESSAY do
Yu bwoy! Long time I school yu
To break
        up yu
Lines
        Lines
                Lines
Like dat black writer Poe, black like his raven

Bruck it
      up
         man an' wid de drums
                    de drums
De tinti
        nab   u
                       la
tion of de drums, de drums

Black bwoy black bwoy
                black
Bwoy

211

No more of the loud sounding sea
or the disjecta membra
Homer, Horace are not, are not for you and me
Colonials with too high a diction
instead of simply drug addition

Roll that spliff and break it up!
The simply diction, the lower registers
Are quite enough for colonials

Even if they snatch prizes from
The new
                    Imperialists.

Now the next poem is a different kind of poem. It was written for Louis Arnaud Reid, one of the best English-Scotch philosophers. I had the pleasure of working with him at London University. When I saw the reflection of the cathedral in the Seine, I was traveling from Nigeria to Jamaica, and I was not well at all and rather worn-out. So I stopped in Paris and I spent about five days there resting. On this evening when I was going to leave France, I was sitting on the bank of the Seine, and I saw and reflected upon the reflection of Notre Dame in the Seine.

On Seeing the Reflection of Notre Dame in the Seine

A man builds better than he knows
The cathedral, stone before floodlight's invention,
Through floodlight's shimmering reflection
On matted water long after renews perfection
A man builds better than he knows.

What he seeks is not hereafter
But everlasting now well done
The answer in stone or images
Built for the now that is forever
With every invention finds further perfection.

He finds the poem, the cathedral
The image, the tune, the stone
So sweetly stretched the tension—
That is perfection—in stone
He cuts stone's dreams, and the world's and his

A man builds better than he knows.

A poet at the crossroads
In a strange land,
Caught by his long forgotten song
As it falls from a curtained window,
Suddenly hears it as I see
This night's reflection
Steady in the moving stream
Knowing that he builds well
Who builds better than he knows.

This next one was written quite a time ago. Now I don't usually like saying things about poems that I've written. I usually like just to read them, but once a gentlemen who didn't like my poems but kindly came to readings I was giving, shouted at the end of one of the poems, "John, this stuff sounds better than I thought it would, but I like to mix a little bit of prose with my poetry." What he meant was that he didn't like poetry going on and on. I got out of saying anything because I got so tired of people saying that they remembered the exact moment they were belching when they decided to write a poem.

Girl in the Moonlight

I turned the steep corner and there she sat
In the moonlight on the ledge,
Her head against the skies and over the ledge
Of that rocky bench her legs dangling.
She looked to the valley, sometime flooded,
Now filled with moonlight, to the skies, where wrangling,
Crows fly by day and tonight the quiet clouds.

She sat there alone and seemed to bare
Her face to the moonlight and the breeze.
What girl is this, I thought,
Ledge-seated, alone, on the hill-top above the trees?

Is she as pure as the cloud-foam of the skies
Which the good ship moon has ruffled up?
As the stream that in the valley lies,
Carefree? Is it longing that brings her out
Alone, alone against the skies:
Or, having too much what others seek,
Does she look for surcease here
Alone in the moonlight on the peak?

John M. Figueroa

The heart that loves this heart that throbs
In time with songs of crickets and of frogs
Is probably pumping blood into the sea
Where the sunken freighter has left its logs
And a longed for head that bobs
Or like the birds that in feed-time fly
Through this valley in search of a resting place
Has her heart soared only above the dry
And yellow grass and rests tonight in dreams
Or rain tomorrow and a green watering place?

Yet, picture-framed by clouds against moon and stars,
Hair flowing from the upright head,
This girl, frozen thus for memory by one quick glance
To me is dead, is dead, is dead:

No use to probe the secrets of the scars.

The heart might open for as long as a meteor glides
Then it clamps closed, rigid as a dead crab's claw,
And the trailing glory is gone
And the stars that began to swim
Are stony-fixed.

As earth through every tree,
From base to leaf-top, through every forked branch
And veined leaf stretches for the sun,
So heart for heart.

And when the heart-sun arises
There is sap-trill:
And when the heart-sun sinks in the night-sea
There is sap-clot:
And in the heart-year
All days are short,
All nights,
Long.

She sits there ever, beyond my reach,
Alone on the hill-top by night,
By day in the crowded valley alone,
Save in the sharp coming of some short dawn;
Or when in an eye's flash,

The cloud veil rent,
The naked sun speaks to the trees.

     This next poem is quite different. It's for a West Indian poet who is not much known, Danny Williams. When I heard that he had died in a car accident during Carnival, I was much disturbed, and I wrote these few words for him—and for us.

For Danny Williams

Cassava and plantains
Nourished you.

Now your body nourishes them.
Your bones will build
For unsuspecting youths
Bodies as coo-coo build yours.

Your poems gentle in your way
Seeped through our foo-foo stuffed bodies
Enlightening them. They will lift
Our youth quietly to see our skies.

Goodbye, Danny, goodbye;
Still "the clouds are a flock of sheep
Grazing over the fertile vault".

Still our human bodies
Turn plantains and cassava
Into love and poetry.

Walk good, Danny, walk good
We walk with you Danny
We walk with death.

"The uncertain seine, a bundle of nerves,
               molests the sad sand"

We walk with you, Danny,

We walk with life

"Christmas Breeze," which many of you may know, brings me back home. It also points out the differences in language use. What we call "cold," the English call "cool," etc.

Christmas Breeze

Auntie would say "Ah! Christmas breeze,"
as the Norther leapt from the continent
across Caribbean seas,
across our hills
to herald Christmas,
ham boiling in the yard
plum pudding in the cloth
(Let three stones bear the pot;
and feed the hat-fanned fire).

This breeze in August cools a Summer's day
here in England.
In December in Jamaica
we would have called it *cold,*
Cold Christmas Breeze,
fringing the hill tops with its tumble
of cloud, bringing in
imported apples and dances
and rum (for older folk).
For us, some needed clothes, and a pair
of shoes squeezing every toe.
And Midnight Mass:
Adeste Fideles!

Some Faithful came—
and why not?—a little drunk,
some overdressed, but
ever faithful.
Like Christmas breeze
returning every year, bearing
not August's end, nor October's
wind and rain but, Christmas
and 'starlights'
and a certain sadness, except for Midnight Mass
and the Faithful
('The Night when Christ was born')

I miss celebrations, but I miss most
the people of faith
who greeted warmly every year
the Christmas breeze.

This last one is "For Palinurus, the Lost Helmsman" for a Roman, if we can call him that. He was a helmsman on the boat of Pious Aeneas, and as Palinurus fell asleep he wakened to realize that the boat wasn't going in quite the right direction. So he, of course, felt that this was the work of the gods and in fact at the end of the story they had sent down someone to put Palinurus to sleep.

For Palinurus, the Lost Helmsman

Too much you trusted the calm of the sea and the skies
Too much, Palinurus, you trusted.
We were hugging dreams of how sweetly
The waves were crooning against our bows—
Your splash into water joined the voices
That secured our dreams.
Too much you trusted, helmsman; your passengers
Slept too well.

Now naked, unknown, unknowing the sea,
your body will drift to the beach;
To some beach, somewhere, calm, yellow and unknown.

Well, that's about as much as I can capture. You must have noticed a rather croaking voice which I never did have, but a few nights ago I fell in my bedroom and had to be left on the floor warm and wrapped up, of course, for about five hours until a good friend came and helped lift me up on the bed. Since then I have not been quite myself. I slept all day yesterday in preparation for this. Anyway, if it's not too early may I wish you a "Happy Christmas" as well as a successful conference. I was going to say "Walk Good" but I understand that is not used anymore. I cannot remember the one word with which I should greet you. Adios.

Este ojo que me mira/This Eye that Looks at Me: Power Structures

Linda M. Rodríguez Guglielmoni

How to classify *Este ojo que me mira*: Is it a *bildungsroman*, remembrances (*memorias*) as the subtitle of the book suggests, or perhaps a testimonial/historical autobiography/novel exploring the life of a Puerto Rican woman and the colonial history of her island? *Este ojo que me mira* narrates both story and history through a series of scenes. Each of these represents a recollection and unfolds a chronological exposé of the first seventeen years of Loreina Santos Silva, a twentieth-century Puerto Rican poet, essayist, and narrator. The recollections begin with the tortuous birth of the writer and end with her self-imposed migration to New York City, an action which in its own way represents another difficult birth for the young Santos Silva.

As the title indicates, in *Este ojo que me mira*, an eye follows Santos Silva throughout her first seventeen years. This eye captures moments of the writer's life and, while it allows a re-creation of her life, it also fragments it. The construction of the text as a series of scenes reflects this fragmentation. The text created is postmodern: the self has been scattered and searches for a coherent identity through an analysis of past incidents. The uncensored eye that observes Santos Silva takes "snapshots" of the author's life, and as the unforgiving eye of the camera, it captures and reveals the beautiful and the grotesque in like manner. In her book's dedication Santos Silva explains that she wrote about herself inspired by an exhibition she visited at the National Art Gallery in Washington, D.C.: *"Inspirada por las caras de Sam, trazo las mías con el impulso de la palabra"* (Inspired by the faces of Sam, I forge mine by the power of words). This exhibition showed the self-portraits of the American artist, Sam Francis. Truly, Santos Silva, through the power of words and the innovative narrative technique represented by a disembodied cinematographic eye, transforms her life's story into art.

The fragmented portrait constructed in *Este ojo que me mira* is reminiscent of a Cubist painting. But, in addition, as classical portraits often do, such as Diego Velázquez's *Las Meninas* (1656) or Jan Van Eyck's *The Marriage of Giovanna Arnolfini* (1434), the text surrounds its main subject with other humans, animals, plants, architectural structures, and other objects that allow the beholder to better comprehend the cultural background and social status of the person or persons occupying center stage. For example, in the chapter entitled *"Juegos geométricos"* we can see the Puerto Rican women who worked in the cigar making industry some forty or fifty years ago. *"Juegos geométricos"* ("Geometrical Games") describes how these women sat together during long work days, hanging up row after row of tobacco leaves, telling stories, singing, and rolling cigarettes for

218

themselves from the top quality tobacco, *corona*. Clearly this chapter reveals the writer's high social status since these women worked for Santos Silva's grandfather, owner of large stretches of land and a lucrative cigar-producing industry. In this chapter we also see a typical childhood incident. The young Santos Silva, wanting to imitate the grownups, begins to roll cigarettes for herself, and enjoying the geometrical patterns that the smoke creates, ends up smoking fifteen cigarettes, overdosing, and nearly dying.

Also, portrayed in *Este ojo que me mira* are the women who cared for the young Santos Silva, Mamita Moncha and Grandmother Serafina. Mamita Moncha is the great grandmother who came to Puerto Rico from Holland when she was eleven years old. Mamita Moncha, as many of the other female characters we encounter in the book, is a care-giver and teacher to the young Santos Silva. Mamita Moncha familiarized the young girl with the beauty of the land and its vegetation by taking her on walks as described in the following passage:

> Little Mother Moncha, you, my beloved great grandma, and me,
> we would walk through the countryside delighted by its wonders:
> the flaming red of the wild flowers in the early morning, the banks
> of the river blooming with rose apples and bellflowers, the song
> of the flowing streams, the mystical trees in communion with the
> clouds, the onomatopoeia of the crickets and frogs, the songs of
> the birds in an unexpected early morning orchestration.[1] (14)

While Mamita Moncha teaches the young Santos Silva to love nature, Grandmother Serafina prepares the girl to appreciate the importance of a formal education. This grandmother persuades her husband, abuelo Ramón, to move the family down from the tobacco plantation to a house in the city in order that the young girl may more readily attend school. Grandmother Serafina encourages the girl to study, undoubtedly motivated out of love but, moreover, because she had come to understand that only through the process of education would Puerto Ricans gain the necessary tools to solve the dilemma of the island's political status.

On the other hand, one must not come to the quick conclusion that *Este ojo que me mira* is a portrait of innocence, of an idyllic childhood spent in the countryside with loving family members. As has been stated before, the portrait constructed in the text shows a fragmented self. This process of fragmentation begins in the struggle of labor since through birth humans lose their place in a paradise-like womb, their state of innocence, and subsequently are thrown into life. In the book life is visualized as a hell and as a fire which consumes the energy of every single living cell. The birth sequence, "*Golpeando el vacío*," ("Punching the Emptiness") describes Santos Silva's introduction to life:

> This eye knows that in these times nobody thinks of the inferno
> that will fall on me, of the inferno I will live with. My mother and
> aunt look me over to see if I am all there, as all mothers do. This
> eye sees me with closed fists punching the emptiness, screeching

219

because they will throw me to those borrowed wombs: cribs in hospitals, cribs in towns, cribs out in the Island, cribs out in the universe, and they will throw me at those invisible daggers that puncture with wounds of pain and laughter. To be honest, flowers, mourning, and funerals should be held when one is born, during that despairing exit, with an array of weeping women who should fill buckets with their tears lamenting the unceasing struggle ahead, the fire that will burn out the last drop of energy.[2]

From the passage one may surmise that there is no joy in birth or that the possibility of achieving happiness in life does not exist. Succeeding events demonstrate the validity of the writer's image of birth as an entrance to hell.

First, Santos Silva is falsely viewed by the town's people as being the outcome of her aunt's alleged affair, since the aunt and Santos Silva's mother move to the capital city of San Juan in order to escape from the abusive behavior of Santos Silva's step-father. Then a drunk man sexually molests Santos Silva early in her childhood. The grandfather never shows any affection towards Santos Silva; and her relatives, fearing that he might harm her, hide her when he visits. But, while this same grandfather condemns his daughter, eventually driving her to madness, and thrice attempts to murder her own daughter, young Santos Silva, he keeps several concubines and has a collection of illegitimate children.

Finally, disease and death constantly encroach on the young Santos Silva. Her cousin goes blind, apparently after playing with a stray dog and developing an eye infection that can only be cured with eye drops prescribed by a local health healer, or *curandera;* and a child dies when a horse runs over it in front of her grandmother's house. In both cases Santos Silva was the potential victim. The young Santos Silva also suffers directly from the island's colonial status when her teacher beats her for not being able to recite her ABC's in English.

Este ojo que me mira not only narrates the life of a Puerto Rican woman, but moreover, it narrates part of her island's colonial history. The story of Santos Silva and her family parallels Puerto Rico's twentieth-century history. This history is seen as individuals living within an extended family structure, but a structure which lacks a caring, loving—one could say—a legitimate father figure. Santos Silva's family must contend with the legacy that history has bequeathed to them. This legacy includes not only 400 years of Spanish colonialism but also the beginnings of a new type of colonialism in the form of a forceful American presence in Puerto Rico which began in 1898 with the Spanish-American War. Culture, patterns of development, and power structures began to change in Puerto Rico with the American presence on the island.

In *Este ojo que me mira*, the grandfather openly and vehemently favors an American presence in the island. He is also the character that evidently signifies patriarchal dominance and abuse. Santos Silva's mother is mentally and physically abused and eventually destroyed by patriarchal forces which are to a great extent embodied by the figure of the grandfather. The grandfather thinks only of his own gratification and does not hesitate to use his compatriots, his wife and other family members, other women, and the land to increase his capital and consolidate his position of power. As so many people in positions of power, the grandfather lives off the work of the "others" in the Third World, often criminally underpaid women, such as the women described in the cigar scene, *"Juegos geométricos."*

Certainly, the women's oppression portrayed in *Este ojo que me mira* has an economic dimension that is part of the relationship between the grandfather and the other women in his life. Their dependency on his economic wealth makes them his victims. The grandfather benefits both from the old power structure created by the élite, wealthy, land-owning families, the *hacendados*, and from the new power structure created by North American capitalist investment. The grandfather's own daughter, Santos Silva's mother, is the most conspicuous victim of his legacy of patriarchal abuse. She dies tortured by the thought of killing her own daughter so that she would not suffer her grandfather's abuse. Moreover, the grandfather, demonstrating that he is an illegitimate father figure, allows the destruction of his daughter's trunk that held within it the symbols of Puerto Rico's nascent nationhood, the then illegal national flag and photos of Albizu Campos, who presided over the Puerto Rican Nationalist Party in the 30s and became a political prisoner.[3] Although the trunk is destroyed, its memory is not lost to the young Santos Silva, and she inherits the ideals of independence once symbolically held in the contents of the trunk. This inheritance allows her to keep alive within her an alternative narrative of Puerto Rico's history.

After her mother's death, a profound longing for her mother's love, a love thwarted by the same patriarchal forces that caused her mother's death, marks the existence of the young Santos Silva. In the narrative we can observe some attempts at destroying these patriarchal forces; for example, the *hacienda* sitting in the middle of the tobacco fields is set on fire by one of Santos Silva's uncles. The destruction of that which symbolizes injustice, abuse, and economic exploitation becomes only that, a symbolical act, which does not liberate Santos Silva or her family from her grandfather's tyrannical oppression. Eventually, Santos Silva, escaping from another figure of patriarchal tyranny, her godfather, travels to New York City because *"quiero demostrarle a mi padrino que los seres humanos no son posesiones, son caminos"* (113) ("I want to demonstrate to my godfather that human beings are not possessions, instead that they are pathways.") She tells herself that she is nobody's possession: *"Mi padrino tiene que entender que no soy posesión de nadie"* (112) ("My godfather must understand that I am nobody's possession.") Ironically, the United States and the City of New York become for the young woman a means to freedom, an escape from the stifling patriarchal forces back home. Just before leaving Puerto Rico, Santos Silva begins to dream of the famous female figure that welcomed and gave hope to millions before. She dreams of the Statue of Liberty on Ellis Island in this manner:

I give myself up to the fantasy of a new world, to the fantasy of
the giant woman, with her arm held up high. (*Me entrego a la
fantasía de un mundo nuevo, a la fantasía de la gigante mujer, con el
brazo en alto.*) (112)

When she finally travels to New York, Santos Silva becomes part of the growing
Puerto Rican diaspora, one more foreigner among the many foreigners that
inhabit the city, and this gives her an intense, albeit, brief sense of happiness:

In the Great City I am in ecstasy looking at the collage of
foreigners, I am one more among them. (*En la Gran Urbe me
extasío con el collage de los extranjeros, soy una más entre ellos.*) (114)

Anonymity in New York City does give Santos Silva the long-sought freedom
from patriarchal dominance, but she pays a price for this. Shortly after arriving
in New York, the city becomes for Santos Silva a land of exile, marginality, and
loneliness, filled with people suffering mental illness and people with ques-
tionable characters.

The city, however, is also filled with business opportunities and, becoming an active participant in the American capitalist enterprise, Santos Silva
goes to work. First, she works for a Jewish businessman who teaches her about the
Holocaust and the Jewish people, the other diaspora; and then for a pragmatic toy
seller who tells her that the best way to keep children happy is to give them toys
every two weeks. Thus Santos Silva begins to gain new experiences that perhaps
she would not have had if she had stayed in Puerto Rico. She also decides to
continue her formal education, and the narration ends precisely when Santos
Silva symbolically becomes a winged creature and flies back to the university to
complete her bachelor's degree. Thus, an advanced education becomes a road to
autonomy and perhaps will allow the young woman future access to power
structures in the Western world. Although with significant differences in tone
and intention, *Este ojo que me mira's* ending echoes the final scenes of other recent
novels written by Caribbean women, such as Esmeralda Santiago's *When I was
Puerto Rican*, which ends when the protagonist is admitted to Harvard University,
and Jamaica Kincaid's *Annie John*, which ends with Annie leaving for London to
study nursing.

In *Este ojo que me mira*, Santos Silva, in a similar reconstructive process as
the painter Sam Francis who inspired her, by the power of words transforms her
life into art. Moreover, her book, which is proof of her ability to innovatively
utilize linguistic symbols and narrative techniques, has allowed her to resist the
patriarchal power structure and colonial oppression that came so close to destroying her.

Notes

[1] The translations here are mine. The original reads as follows: "*Mamita Moncha, tú, mi bisabuela querida, y yo, caminábamos por los campos deleitadas con sus maravillas: el rojo fulgor de las amapolas silvestres cuando despierta la mañana, las orillas del río florecidas de pomarrosas y campanas, las corrientes cantarinas de las aguas, los místicos árboles en comunión con las nubes, las onomatopeyas de los grillos y los sapos, las canciones de los pájaros en una orquesta matinal insospechada.*" (14)

[2] The original: "*Este ojo sabe que en estos tiempos a nadie le importa un infierno lo que yo pese, a nadie un infierno lo que yo mida. Mi madre y mi tía me rebuscan a ver si estoy enterita, como lo hacen todas las madres. Este ojo me ve con los puños cerrados golpeando el vacío, armando tamaña gritería porque me van a tirar a esos vientres ajenos: cunas de hospital, cunas de pueblo, cunas de Isla, cunas de universo, me van a tirar a esos puñales invisibles que asestan los golpes del dolor y la alegría. A la verdad que los florones, baquinés y funerales se deben hacer cuando uno nace, a esa desesperada salida, con un fracatán de lloronas que lloren a cántaros el emplazamiento de esta lucha irredimida, de este fuego en que se extingue la última gota de energía.*" (1)

[3] See Ronald Fernandez, *Prisoners of Colonialism: The Struggle for Justice in Puerto Rico*, "Political Prisoner #0001." Monroe, ME: Common Courage Press, 1994: 17-58.

Work Cited

Santos Silva, Loreina, *Este ojo que me mira: ciclo 1: memorias.* San Juan, P. R.: Editorial de la Universidad de Puerto Rico, 1996.

Puerto Rican Literary Experience in New York: An Overview

Hilda Mundo-López

DIVERSITY is the word that best describes Puerto Rican literature in New York: linguistic, thematic and stylistic diversity.

Puerto Ricans have been in New York since the late nineteenth century, when Puerto Rican intellectuals founded, along with Cuban patriots, the Puerto Rican and Cuban Revolutionary Party. It was the most important New York-based organization supporting the independence of both Cuba and Puerto Rico from Spain. An increasing number of Puerto Ricans came to the United States after the Spanish-American War in 1898, the independence of Cuba and the Platt Amendment in 1902, and the Jones Act which imposed American citizenship on the people of Puerto Rico in 1917. These newcomers organized communities that have evolved into today's Spanish Harlem ("El Barrio"), Lower East Side ("Loisaida"), "Patchoge" and others. During 1930 - 1950, a great number of skilled and unskilled Puerto Rican workers, especially tobacco makers, organized a political leadership which, in turn, became the New York City Hispanic labor movement's backbone. Community members interested in world-wide literature and politics gathered around factories and working class organizations (see *Memoirs of Bernardo Vega*).

From this first influx of migrants (1890 - 1940), Puerto Ricans in New York have inherited *A Puerto Rican in New York and Other Sketches* (1961) by Jesus Colón; *Memorias de Bernardo Vega* (1977), *Down These Mean Streets* (1967), *Savior, Savior, Hold my Hand* (1972), *Seven Long Times* (1974) and *Stories from El Barrio* (1978), all by Piri Thomas. Other literary pieces pertaining to this trend are the works by Nicholasa Mohr: *Nilda* (1973), *El Bronx Remembered: A Novella and Other Stories* (1975), *In Nueva York* (1977), *Felita* (1979), *Rituals of Survival: A Woman's Portfolio* (1985), and *Going Home* (1986). These books are the foundation of a Puerto Rican fiction in the United States written in English.

Jesus Colón and Bernardo Vega left a valuable record of what life was like for the first New York Puerto Rican residents. They created a first-hand history of the development of the Puerto Rican community in New York. Nicholasa Mohr and Piri Thomas portrayed the experiences of youngsters coming of age in their struggle to accept or reject the values of U.S. mainstream society. They clashed against, rejected or accepted these values while living within the "homey walls" of a more traditional culture. At home, not only did they encounter cultural differences, but also linguistic restraints, and a memory stream of an island already gone—the Paradise of the Caribbean, Piri Thomas' island of honey and milk.

The second wave of migrants, often referred to as "the big migration," arrived in New York between 1945 and 1970, when one third of the entire population of Puerto Rico left the island to settle on the mainland. This migratory influx was the aftereffect of the Second World War and Operation Bootstrap, an economic plan geared at industrializing the island of Puerto Rico. Piri Thomas' island of honey and milk—the Caribbean Paradise—was undergoing a rapid economic and urban transformation: from monocrop agriculture, the economic trend veered to industrial investment along with extended urbanism. Those not necessarily benefiting from these economic policies were encouraged to migrate. Displaced from land and property, most Puerto Rican peasants, artisans and seasonal workers settled in those Puerto Rican communities already developed in the U.S. mainland.

Facing linguistic, ethnic, racial and economic barriers, a new generation of poets emerged, poets who lived within the limits of two worlds and two cultures; hence, the theme of identity pervades their writings. Many are the voices expressing a poetics emerging from within these margins. For monolinguals, their style has most likely been perceived as lack of linguistic ability and command, often presupposing lack of critical skills' and illogical reasoning. Not until recent years have these writers received their deserved recognition as cultural workers.

For those who grew up, were born and raised in New York, possibilities of expression are many. They can write in Spanish or English. They can also re-create the bilingual code-switching of daily speech. Their diverse linguistic techniques trademark their *"differance."* After 1950, the literature of this second generation of Puerto Ricans is marked with certain "aberrations," such as wondering in what language to write—standard Spanish, standard English—or what degree of bilingualism is just right to convey meaning. To them, writing in Spanish risks literary marginality in the U.S. and Latin America. Most of these writers were deprived of educational opportunities in the language of their parents. They do not recognize themselves as exclusively emerging from a dominant Spanish literary experience which they can turn to in search for literary models. They feel distant from the social and linguistic experiences of Puerto Rican islanders. Spanish is for them the language of the heart; it allows for cultural identification, but it is not necessarily regarded as the only language through which to express their identity. English, although the language of "cultural betrayal," is also the language through which they were "miseducated." Therefore, Spanish/English bilingualism becomes part of the linguistic idiosyncrasy of this second generation of Puerto Ricans who grew up in the most disadvantaged sectors of mainland urban enclaves.

Most young Puerto Rican writers find themselves sharing common deprivations. They all share incomes below poverty levels. They use bilingual expressions molding community speech, yet are unfit to conform within monolingual English or Spanish language standards. They share a poetic tradition emerging from oral discourse more than from written literature. These features characterize "Nuyorican" writers, a generation of writers which sprang up in the seventies and gathered around the "Nuyorican Poets Café" and the "New Rican Village." This generation of poets and playwrights was first anthologized in Miguel Algarín and Miguel Piñeiro's *Nuyorican Poetry: An Anthology of Puerto Rican Words and Feelings* (1975). Later on, their poetry was published in Efraín Barradas' *Herejes y Mitificadores* (1981), and most recently in *Puerto Rican Writers at Home in the USA* (1991), an anthology edited by Faythe Turner.

Alternating both languages, as some Chicano writers also do well, the Nuyorican poets expanded literary expression far beyond monolingual paradigms. Linguistic code-switching broadens and enables literary meaning far beyond the constraints of linguistic standards. María Esteves, Louis Reyes Rivera, Tato Laviera and Pedro Pietri are, among them, the most prolific.

The poet speaks a language of his/her own dialectical interchange, dependable and harmonious, somehow resolving the political instability of the alienated self by legitimizing his/her contradictions. Sandra María Esteves expresses this in Spanish:

> *Pienso en mi tierra*
> *los barrios de Nueva York*
> *mi madre calle*
> *a donde se crió un tipo nuevo de este mundo*
> *el puertorriqueño que no habla el español*
>
> *(I wonder about my homeland*
> *New York barrios*
> *my motherly street*
> *giving birth to a new world character*
> *the Puerto Rican who doesn't speak Spanish)* (19)

Miguel Algarín assumes and resumes the linguistic tension in "Inside Control: My Tongue":

> *if the man owns the world*
> *oh white power hidden*
> *behind every word I speak*
> *if the man takes me into his*
> *caverns of meaning in sound*
> *if all my talk is borrowed*
> *from his tongue, then I want*
> *hot boiling water to wash*
> *out my mouth, I want lye*
> *to soothe my soiled lips*
> *for the English that I*
> *speak betrays my need to be*
> *a self-made power* (58)

For the Nuyorican poets, New York barrios are the new land where identity is recovered. They alternate English and Spanish whenever necessary since being bilingual is "like eating rice and beans" (*"como comer arroz y habichuelas"*), a matter of survival. A most rejected practice, written code-switching is, nonetheless, their most cherished and mastered stylistic literary strategy.

In Tato Lavieras' poetry, cultural alienation takes on a positive dimension; it allows for survival. In a sense, it connotes a most cherished difference. Most of his work emerges from and reconciles with the street corners of "Loisaida" (Lower East Side), the "new motherland" where the "sweet melodies" of conga rhythms evoke an encounter with culture, thus, with self-identity:

> *congas strong cuchifrito juice*
> *giving air condition to faces*
> *unmolested by the winds and the*
> *hot jungles of loisaida streets* (39)

As in oral discourse, the appropriation of Spanish words within an English text reinforces cultural institutions such as dance, food, ways of addressing and/or naming people, that if translated, lose emotional content. Nuyorican poets belong to the rhythm of their *barrios*, to the loud shouts of their own imagination. It is for the *barrios* they sing.

After 1980, a sudden revival of short stories, novels and autobiographies permeates Puerto Rican English writings in the United States. Besides Piri Thomas and Nicholasa Mohr, the literary scenario is shared by other writers. Ed Vega's *The Comeback* (1985) narrates the life of a Puerto Rican-Eskimo hockey player in the United States. His *Mendoza's Dreams* (1987) is "a book of short surrealist fantasies about Puerto Rican Horatio Alger's heroes." (Turner 319) *Sleep of the Innocents* (1991), by Carole Fernández, is set against a civil war background in Soledad, a fictional Central American country somehow archetypal of Central American countries under civilian and military unrest during the 1980's. Most recently, Esmeralda Santiago's *When I Was Puerto Rican* (1994) reflects upon the issue of Puerto Rican identity before and after Esmeralda's migration and settlement in Eastern U.S. For the most part, these two women writers have recently been acknowledged as their work has emerged at the peak of the current Latino Literary Renaissance.

In the United States, the literary tradition of Puerto Ricans has three diverse modalities: 1) the writing of those who utilize English as their primary linguistic tool; 2) a strong tradition of writers in Spanish; and 3) the hybrid style of the Nuyoricans, with command of English, Spanish or a well-balanced code-switching. The recent anthology of Puerto Rican poetry in New York, *Papiros de Babel* (1994), edited by Dr. Pedro López-Adorno, is a major contribution to the legacy of Puerto Rican Spanish poets in New York. It traces the poetry of Puerto Ricans who were either born and raised or settled in Puerto Rico, New York, Boston, or New Jersey. The anthologized poets have all contributed to the Caribbean and the American literary tradition since the early twenties, and probably, earlier. From Clara Lair (1895-1974) to Martín Espada (1957-), the most prolific Puerto Rican poets are represented in this text.

Spanish Puerto Rican writers have faced a stronger marginality within the literary U.S. market. Besides *Memoirs of Bernardo Vega*, by Bernardo Vega, and *Spics*, by Pedro Juan Soto, important intellectuals, poets and fiction writers such as Jose Luis González, Guillermo Cotto Thorner, Manuel Ramos Otero, Alfredo Villanueva Collado and Jose López Heredia (born and raised in New York) are still untranslated (and thus, still unknown to U.S. English-dominant audiences), notwithstanding their dual literary contribution to the United States and the Commonwealth of Puerto Rico.

The Nuyorican writers bridge these two secular traditions. Only recently have Puerto Rican writers in either language come together and shared their cultural and literary experiences. After almost a hundred years under U.S. domination, they now work collaboratively, understanding and bridging the cultural and linguistic diversity of Puerto Rican writers from both island and mainland. Puerto Rican literature and Puerto Rican intellectuals are undergoing a dramatic (traumatic?) encounter in their literary *encuentros*. The literary work of Puerto Rican writers from metropolitan U.S. has only recently been considered by Puerto Rican writers and critics from the island of Puerto Rico. It was easier for intellectual islanders to acknowledge Pedro Juan Soto's *Spics* as a masterpiece of Puerto Rican literature in New York, than it has been recognizing Tato Laviera, Sandra María Esteves or Nicholasa Mohr's work.

Aside from cultural heritage, linguistic considerations have constrained a more dynamic sense of a national literary configuration. In order to construct the one hundred years of the colonial literary self, the history of Puerto Rican literature must reflect the full one hundred years of U.S. colonialism; the displacement of its writers, and the various linguistic strategies they have abided by. From island or mainland, Puerto Rican writers express a national idiosyncracy still colonial, not yet post-colonial. In this light, I have explored the stylistic and literary contributions of Tato Laviera, Sandra María Esteves, Pedro Pietri and Louis Reyes Rivera, Nuyoricans of excellent linguistic and literary skills.

Works Cited

Algarín, Miguel. "Inside Control: My Tongue." *Nuyorican Poetry: An Anthology of Their Words and Feelings*. Miguel Algarín and Miguel Piñero, eds. New York: William Morrow, 1975. 58.

Esteves, Sandra María. "Esclavitud." *Yerba Buena*. New York: Greenfield Press, 1980: 19. (Translation by Hilda Mundo-López)

Laviera, Tato. "The New Rumbón." *La Carreta Made a U-Turn*. Houston: Arte Público Press, 1981: 39.

Turner, Faythe, ed. *Puerto Rican Writers at Home in the USA*. Seattle, Washington: Open Hand Publishing, Inc. 1991. 319.

The Thematics of Diaspora and the Intercultural Identity Question

Sandra Pouchet Paquet

"It may be that the first impulse of West Indian writing is not towards nation, because that is another device that conceals our identities."

Derek Walcott

The thematics of diaspora in the Caribbean is complicated by the fact that Caribbean writers and scholars have been at great pains to represent the region, historically and culturally, as diasporic space—more commonly in terms of the competing claims of African, Asian, and European ethnicities.[1] Diasporic space represents the Caribbean in specific histories of conquest and settlement, population movements, exile and migration. It exists in tension with the concept of community inscribed within sites of ancestral dwelling .[2] It follows that diasporic cultures are heavily invested in mediating the cultural values of travel and dwelling and, in the Caribbean, there is the added dimension of mediating competing ethnic inscriptions of lineage in any given territory. This self-conscious, often contentious cultural diversity is important to any discussion of national and/or cultural identities in the Caribbean, and complicates issues of cultural localization in what we are now identifying as Caribbean diasporic literature, that is, literature generated in ethnic Caribbean communities outside the region, the transnational literature of a new generation of hyphenated Caribbeans, as in the Guyanese-British Fred D'Aguiar, Haitian-American Edwidge Danticat, and Cuban-American Cristina García.

This brings us to the conjunction/disjunction of culture and nation and the role of literature in developing a consciousness of community within the nation state. There is no question that the ideal of a national literature has a role to play in the development of a national culture, and that the nation state provides a legitimate legal framework for developing and defending the resources of a community, however its boundaries are defined. But a Caribbean literary culture, broadly or narrowly defined, enjoins transnational affiliation rather than national solidarity. It shifts focus away from the ideal of a national literature as rooted and self-determining to focus instead on hybrid cosmopolitan experiences that tend to blur, if not erase, the physical boundaries of the nation state.

If the idea of a regionally defined Caribbean literary culture links island to island, nation state to associated state and colony, Anglophone to Dutch, Francophone, and Hispanic, African ethnicities to Amerindian, Asian, and European, then the idea of a Caribbean diasporic literature further revises the modalities of inside and outside, national and transnational relations. The thematics of diaspora highlights the Caribbean text as product of a heterogenous legacy of values and experiences, and underscores the interdependencies generated over time by colonial, postcolonial and neocolonial cultural and institutional practices.[3] Caribbean diaspora redraws the lines of culture and community beyond the political boundaries of the nation state and even the region. A methodology for interpreting diasporic literature, one might argue, inevitably privileges intercultural identity as a transnational phenomenon that reaffirms established colonial links between Caribbean literary production and the metropolitan centers of Europe and continental America. It identifies the Caribbean as a traveling culture, as a site of dwelling *and* travel (Clifford 105). James Clifford explains in "Traveling Cultures" that, in his privileging traveling cultures for ethnographic purposes, his "goal is not to *replace* the cultural figure of the 'native' with the intercultural figure of 'traveler'. Rather the task is to focus on concrete mediations of the two, in specific cases of historical tension and relationship" (101). A similar case might be made for negotiating the thematics of the Caribbean's complex history of travel, exile, migration, immigration, and specific population movements within the region.

The idea of a growing Caribbean diaspora is not welcomed by everyone. In "The Emerging West Atlantic System," Orlando Patterson sees the development of what he calls the "postnational" environment of Miami, for example, as a threat to the political and economic integrity of the nation states of the Caribbean (260). On the other hand, Kwame Appiah, writing from the African diaspora, appears to welcome a "second wave" of postcolonial novels that not only reject the legitimating narratives of imperial history, but what he calls the neocolonialist nationalist project: "Far from being a celebration of the nation, then, the novels of the second stage—the postcolonial stage—are novels of deligitimation: rejecting the Western *imperium*, it is true; but also rejecting the nationalist project of the postcolonial national bourgeoisie" (152). The perceived disjuncture between nationalist legitimation and cultural production is not new to Caribbean literary discourse, but foregrounding Caribbean diasporic literature privileges variations of errantry over dwelling and effectively reconfigures the conjunction of literature and nation.[4]

In "Traveling Cultures" James Clifford asks the question: "Who determines where (and when) a community draws its lines, names its insiders and outsiders?" (97). By way of a response, I propose to explore some variations of nomadism and errantry in relation to settlement and territorial possession thematized in V.S. Naipaul's *A Way in the World* (1994) and to explore related issues in a sampling of the works of a new generation of writers, for example, Fred D'Aguiar's *Dear Future* (1996), Edwidge Danticat's *Breath, Eyes, Memory* (1994), and Cristina García's *Dreaming in Cuban* (1992), where the junction between diaspora and homeland is articulated, not dissimilarly, as a site of ongoing negotiation.

In *A Way in the World*, V. S. Naipaul thematizes a distinctly "post-nationalist" response in the text's mapping of its own cultural and intellectual inheritance.[5] In *A Way in the World*, the intertwining, overlapping tropes of return and quest are managed by a narrator who, as traveling native, is something of a shape-shifter, assuming a series of interrelated roles as the returning native, world traveler, native informant, writer inscriber, reader, researcher, quester, and native dweller. His psyche is split into then and now, child and adult, narrator and character in a parodic replay of the often reiterated Caribbean quest for psychic reintegration. Driven by the narrative's interior logic, native space is a multi-dimensional frame of reference for the hybrid native traveler. It is identified as the island of Trinidad expanded to include its hinterland/heartland refashioned as Guyana, Venezuela, Brazil, and Columbia. The idea of national boundaries becomes meaningless as a way of mapping native space since this is actually determined by the narrator's conception of return and the nature of his quest for aboriginal space: "Over a number of journeys I began to think of Venezuela as a kind of restored homeland" (*Way* 220). Given the narrator's level of sophistication in respect to the historical density of place, native space extends to the most widely separated transhistorical boundaries, even as they are sublimated in the transhistorical codes of Nature as aboriginal landscape.

Naipaul's foregrounding of travel as cultural practice resituates culture as a site of dwelling in the representation of native space.[6] Cultural dwelling is perceived as subject to ceaseless transformation. He notes the new Mohammedans squatting where hundreds of years before "had been Cumucurapo, an aboriginal Indian place" (40); illegal immigrants from smaller islands and the 1897 inscription of Queen Victoria's Diamond Jubilee & the Centenary of the British Conquest of Trinidad at Point Galera, named by Columbus, an aboriginal place "cleansed of its past" (76); Woodford Square where East Indian derelicts have been replaced by Africans, and is the site of tumultous political changes (31); and Cedros, where once "aboriginal Indians were masters of these waters. They no longer existed; and that knowledge of currents and tides had passed to their successors. . .descendants of agricultural people from the Gangetic Plain" (223). Considered in specific historical relation to population movements in the region, cultural dwelling assumes the transitional quality of travel encounters; national boundaries appear peripheral to cultural identity.

Reinforcing this representation of native space in *A Way in the World* is the inscription of cosmopolitan native travelers who parallel, anticipate, and critique through repetition the narrator as ex-centric native. The most obvious of these are Lebrun, a Marxist writer and revolutionary on the run, whom he identifies as a precursor; Blair, a fellow traveler for whom the ethnocentric, race-based quest for identity dead-ends in East Africa; and Sorzano, the East Indian from Trinidad, who has acquired "a new land, a new name, a new identity, a new kind of family life, new languages even" (228), and who makes a pilgrimage to Trinidad for special prayers from the Hindu scriptures for a son in trouble. By focussing on hybrid cosmopolitan experiences that intersect with his own history of travel, displacement, and quest, the narrator creates a self-referential space for the portrayal and understanding of related concepts of culture and travel.

In *A Way in the World*, travel is construed as a discourse, a genre, and a basis for comparing the different cultures that traverse and constitute the Caribbean. Native place is a site of arrivals and departures, of local/regional/global encounters involving dominations, resistances, commerce, intercultural penetrations, and ideological appropriations. The native traveler leaves home and returns in ongoing interaction with a variety of different cultures. He is both islander and exile, dweller and traveler; in him the cultural figure of the native and the intercultural figure of the traveler overlap and intertwine.[7] His insularity is conceived as exploration and transforming encounter.[8] Predictably, these turn on the quest for aboriginal landscape, identity, origins, ancestry, psychic reconnection, and rebirth. The novel sequence begins with the overlapping tropes of return to one's native land and quest for an aboriginal landscape ("an aboriginal Indian place," "the aboriginal island," "the untouched aboriginal island," "a crowded aboriginal Indian island," "a fabulous aboriginal landscape") in a tropological refashioning of a Caribbean myth or desire for psychic integration.[9] Together, these tropes articulate a cross-cultural poetics that resists a nationalist, ethnic, racialist quest for unique origins. Aboriginal space privileges precursors over ancestors, displacing ancestral desire for organic cultural differentiation with a cultural chronotope that privileges a poetics of landscape in a quest for "the beginning of things"(218), and a discourse of travel as a way of inscribing cultural flux as an identity marker.[10]

In *A Way in the World*, Naipaul inscribes the Caribbean as a culture of travel and dwelling; both constitute what comes to be seen as Caribbean experience.[11] This provides a useful framework for reading D'Aguiar, Danticat, and García as well, though each maps a distinctive continuity with Caribbean origins in Guyana, Haiti, and Cuba.[12] Fueled by a self-determining affiliation with the Caribbean as site of ancestral dwelling, their claim to a cultural lineage inscribed in the territories of the region reaches across the ruptures and densities of memory and place. In their novels the Caribbean is a site of displaced dwelling, whether "home" is currently in the United States or the United Kingdom. In the case of D'Aguiar's *Dear Future*, Danticat's *Breath, Eyes, Memory*, and García's *Dreaming in Cuban*, a sense of Caribbean beginnings and cultural dwelling is invented and preserved in the representation of childhood as site of original dwelling, an enduring marker of birthright and cultural inheritance. Fred D'Aguiar explains the process of retrieving a Guyanese childhood in an interview with Frank Birbalsingh:

> Each memory is exactly as I remember it when I was there, and each now has an emotional weight for me, because I played in those trees and ran on that red sand road, which is now paved, while the trees have been cut down. I was aware of creating an

emotional map of a place and of superimposing it on a geography
that no longer existed. (138)

"Relation is spoken multilingually," writes Glissant in *Poetics of Relation*
(19), and for each of these writers the representation of Caribbean home is multi-
voiced and multilingual. As Glissant observes, the root is monolingual—Spanish
for García, Haitian Creole for Danticat, Guyanese Creole for D'Aguiar—but the
act of reconnection employs the language of the periphery, the cultural margin
that is another world, in this case, the United States and the United Kingdom.

García's *Dreaming in Cuban* returns Pilar, a young Cuban American, to her
native Cuba, from which she is forcibly removed as an infant, and to the arms of
her Cuban grandmother: "As I listen, I feel my grandmother's life passing to me
through her hands. It's a steady electricity, humming and true. . .Women who
outlive their daughters are orphans, Abuela tells me. Only their granddaughters
can save them, guard their knowledge like the first fire" (222). Continuity of
being for Pilar is steadily reestablished around interactions of language, memory,
and place:

> I've started dreaming in Spanish, which has never happened before.
> I wake up feeling different, like something inside of me is changing,
> something chemical and irreversible. There's something about the
> vegetation, too, that I respond to instinctively—the stunning
> bougainvillea, the flamboyants and jacarandas. The orchids growing
> from the trunks of the mysterious ceiba trees. (235)

In D'Aguiar and Danticat, this intimacy is established at the outset of
their respective novels, generating an originary Caribbean consciousness as root,
foundation, and ancestral inheritance. The Caribbean is a concrete place of childhood dwelling to D'Aguiar's Red Head and Danticat's Sophie. It encompasses
growth, self-awareness, and the development of personal and cultural compe-
tencies in respect to language, food, flora, fauna, politics and government, and
family—grandparents, aunts, uncles, cousins, roads through wilderness, villages,
and towns. At-one-ness is established in the representation of childhood as a
special kind localized dwelling, a narrative focal point, a part through which one
could represent the cultural whole. As Kwame Appiah observes: "The accumu-
lation of detail is not a device of alienation but of incorporation" (71). A person
out of place can thus be represented in place; inheritance as prelude rather than
destination.

In D'Aguiar, Danticat, and García, the travel trope is linked to the trope
of the divided family. Children leave to join their parents; they are transplanted
to another landscape; they are separated from siblings, parents, grandparents.
Their modes of departure and their destinations enact different diasporic worlds
at the juncture of diaspora and homeland, engendering a diasporic consciousness
shared by traveler and dweller. D'Aguiar registers the psychic dependency of a
child left behind in a letter addressed to his uncertain, unstable Future:

Life took my mother and three brothers from me and I put up with
what I had left, my elder brother, and lived that life. You should
know, dear future, that I laboured on in the belief I would see them
again. . .Work this one little thing for me. Let me know that you
have given my people some sign of my continued existence. (205).

The transition to the United States for Danticat's Sophie and García's
Pilar enacts an ongoing in-betweenness, a continuous negotiation of conflicting
identities and interdependencies in ethnic Caribbean communities and in the
spiraling dialectic of travel and return. For Danticat's Sophie, the future is a
consciously wrought refashioning of Haitian cultural values as Haitian-American;
a Haitian-American future that is at first resisted but later enacted as a point of
personal and cultural liberation. She achieves this with the blessing of her Haitian grandmother. Having challenged her grandmother about why Haitian
mothers "test" their daughters, she is told that "she must liberate herself from the
legacy and burden of pain" (157). Continuity of being achieved, García's Pilar
speculates on the vagaries of diasporic consciousness, the interplay of here and
there, identification and distanciation: "sooner or later I'd have to return to New
York. I know now it's where I belong—not *instead* of here, but *more* than here"
(236).

It seems fair to say that diasporic consciousness as thematized by writers
as different as Naipaul, D'Aguiar, Danticat, and García, speaks to an ongoing
negotiation of cultural identity, modeling forms of Caribbeanness that work
against nationalist legitimation. "Identities," writes Kwame Appiah, "are complex and multiple and grow out of a history of changing responses to economic,
political, and cultural forces;. . .they flourish despite our misrecognition of their
origins;. . .their roots in myths and lies; almost always in opposition to other
identities" (178). It is clear that diasporic consciousness challenges and under-
mines expectations of socio-cultural homogeneity in the Caribbean where these
expectations endure. Assessing its impact in the formulation of Caribbean
cultural identities is difficult if only because diasporic consciousness of one form
or another is endemic in a region that has been defined historically, geogra-
phically, and culturally as gateway, bridge, and archipelago. In the wake of
postcolonial nationalist consolidation in the region, Wilson Harris's "gateway
complex" is perhaps a useful descriptor in that it leaves open the possibility of a
permanent co-existent plurality:

Such a gateway complex means, in fact, that one stresses a
discontinuous line—the missing links as it were—between cultures
rather than a hard continuous dividing wall. Such a discontinuous
or dotted line means, in effect, that one has no dogmatic evolutio-
nary walled creed of superiority and inferiority. One is, in fact, intent
on an original overlap or viable frontier between ages and cultures. (26)

Notes

[1]Much has been written about the thematics of a Caribbean diaspora and intercultural identity. In respect to a distinctly Caribbean literary discourse, I have in mind the works of Antonio Benitez-Rojo, Kamau Brathwaite, Carole Boyce-Davies, Maryse Condé, Paul Gilroy, Edouard Glissant, Stuart Hall, Wilson Harris, C.L.R. James, George Lamming, V.S. Naipaul, among others.

[2]In *Caribbean Discourse*, Edouard Glissant observes: ". . .what makes this difference between a people that survives elsewhere, *that maintains its original nature*, and a population that is transformed elsewhere *into another people* (without, however, succumbing to the reductive pressures of the Other) and that thus enters the constantly shifting and variable process of creolization (of relationship, of relativity), is that the latter has not brought with it, not collectively continued, the method of existence and survival, both material and spiritual, which it practiced before being uprooted" (15).

[3]Despite cultural indigenization and the efforts of cultural enterprises like *The Caribbean Writer* and several distinguished regional and national presses, the Caribbean writer is still dependent on European and North American publishers and readers.

[4]See Edouard Glissant, *The Poetics of Relation*, especially 11-22.

[5]These observations on V. S. Naipaul's *A Way in the World* are developed further in relation to George Lamming's *Natives of My Person* and Antonio Benitez-Rojo's *The Sea of Lentils* in another article of mine, "*Documents of West Indian History*: Telling a West Indian Story" (*Callaloo* 20. 4).

[6]"Once traveling is foregrounded as cultural practice then dwelling, too, needs to be reconceived—no longer simply the ground from which traveling departs, and to which it returns" (Clifford 115).

[7]Naipaul's "native" traveler is a complex historical subject, neither a cultural type nor a unique individual, and in this respect is similar to George Lamming's "native" cosmopolitan traveler in *The Pleasures of Exile*, C.L.R. James's in *Beyond a Boundary*, Claude McKay's in *A Long Way from Home*, and Naipaul's in *The Middle Passage*.

[8]Both Benitez-Rojo and Glissant are defensive about the idea of insularity as a positive rather than a negative value, for example: "Ordinarily, insularity is treated as a form of isolation, a neurotic reaction to place. However, in the Caribbean each island embodies openness. . .A Caribbean imagination liberates us from being smothered" (Glissant 139); "The Antilleans' insularity does not impel them toward isolation, but on the contrary, toward travel, toward exploration, toward the search for fluvial and marine routes" (Benitez-Rojo 25).

[9]"The ordinary thing, the almost arithmetical constant in the Caribbean is never a matter of *subtracting*, but always of *adding*, for the Caribbean discourse carries, as I've said before, a myth or desire for social, cultural and psychic integration to compensate for the fragmentation and provisionality of the collective

Being" (Benitez-Rojo 189).

[10]"The *poetics* of landscape, which is the source of creative energy, is not to be directly confused with *the physical nature* of the country. Landscape retains the memory of time past. Its space is open or closed to its meaning" (Glissant 150).

[11]Naipaul's quest for aboriginal space and cultural heartland is a personalized adventure; it is usefully compared Glissant's concept of *reversion*: "not a return to the longing for origins, to some immutable state of Being, but a return to the point of entanglement, from which we were forcefully turned away" (26).

[12]"Identity is no longer completely in the root but also in relation" (18) observes Glissant in *The Poetics of Relation*.

Works Cited

Appiah, Kwame Anthony. *In My Father's House: Africa in the Philosophy of Culture*. New York: Oxford University Press. 1992.

Benitez-Rojo, Antonio. *The Repeating Island: The Caribbean and the Postmodern Perspective (La isla que se repite)*. Trans. James E. Maraniss. Durham: Duke University Press. 1992.

Birbalsingh, Frank. "An Interview with Fred D'Aguiar." *Ariel* 24.1 (January 1993): 133-148.

Clifford, James. "Traveling Cultures." *Cultural Studies*. Eds. Lawrence Grossberg, Cary Nelson, Paula Treichler. New York: Routledge. 1992: 96-116.

D'Aguiar, Fred. *Dear Future*. London: Chatto & Windus. 1996.

Danticat, Edwidge. *Breath, Eyes, Memory*. New York: Soho Press. 1994.

García, Cristina. *Dreaming in Cuban*. New York: Alfred A. Knopf. 1992.

Glissant, Edouard. *Caribbean Discourse: Selected Essays (Le Discours Antillais)*. Trans. J. Michael Dash. Charlottesville: University Press of Virginia. 1989.

___. *Poetics of Relation*. 1990. Translated by Betsy Wing. Ann Arbor: University of Michigan. 1997.

Harris, Wilson. "History, Fable and Myth in the Caribbean and Guianas." *Caribbean Quarterly* 16.2 (June 1970): 1-32.

James, C.L.R. *Beyond a Boundary*. 1963. Durham: Duke University Press. 1993.

Lamming, George. *The Pleasures of Exile*. 1960. Ann Arbor: University of Michigan. 1992.

McKay, Claude. *A Long Way From Home: An Autobiography*. 1937. New York: Harcourt. 1970.

Naipaul, V.S. *The Middle Passage: Impressions of Five Societies—British, French, and Dutch—in the West Indies and South America*. 1962. Harmondsworth: Penguin. 1975.

___. *A Way in the World*. 1994. New York: Vintage. 1995.

Patterson, Orlando. "The Emerging West Atlantic System: Migration, Culture and Underdevelopment in the United States and Circum-Caribbean region." *Population in an Interacting World*. Ed. W. Alonso. Cambridge: Harvard University Press. 1987: 227-260.

Paquet, Sandra Pouchet. "*Documents of West Indian History*: Telling a West Indian Story." *Callaloo* 20. 4 (Fall 1997).

Caribbean Children's Literature for the Elementary Classroom

Darwin Henderson

The noted historian and literary critic, Edward Kamau Brathwaite, has described the Caribbean as

A 2,000 mile arc of jewel-islands; brown and green; jumping like porpoises from Florida, outward and south to the South American coast; some 5,000 fragments, varying in size from Cuba—through Jamaica. . .and Trinidad. . .to sand spits the size of Friday's footprint. . .The island/fragments are themselves the tops of a sunken cordillera; an ancient mountain range, once a part of mainland America, which swung out catastrophically from that double continent's western spine; Rockies and Andes; out to the Atlantic through the gape of Yucatan to end, perhaps, in what was once Atlantis. (quoted in Bello, 245).

This definition serves us as we explore Caribbean children's literature. This definition of the islands becomes the foundation of the history and the development of a literature which is Caribbean. While time does not permit me to trace the development of the history of that literature, according to Yahaya Bello,

the predominant historical force informing the literature of the West Indies is that of struggle and resistance. The people of the region have struggled for centuries, first against a system of slavery and its remnants, and against the continuing social, cultural, political, and economic domination of their former colonial rulers. (247)

Long years of struggle have given birth to cultural independence, a cultural reaffirmation of the people embodied in the Caribbean literary aesthetic. Thus the literature reflects the victories of resistance: the right to use indigenous language patterns in various literary genres and the right to one's own culture and way of life.

Anansi, the most well known of all Caribbean characters in children's literature, encompasses and reflects the struggle against oppression. Through his guile and cunning, Anansi defeats the powerful and strong and thus employs his own will and strength to resist those who would visit injustices upon him. No collection of Caribbean folklore would be complete without him.

While Anansi's roots are with the Asante of West Africa, according to Yahaya Bello, "Anansi is known throughout much of the Caribbean as a surprisingly benevolent trickster par excellence" (248). Like the Anansi stories, other Caribbean folk tales, legends, and animal stories are composed of an African root.

However, these stories have additional elements from all over the world. For example, tales from India, the former colonial influences of England, France, Spain, Holland, and the indigenous Amerindians, add variety to a common African story source.

The folk tales, myths and legends were preserved by village elders and storytellers; similar to the African griot, the stories were handed down generationally. The stories served as community entertainment in conjunction with passing along of valuable moral and ethical lessons. The writer Jan Carew states:

There is a dearth of material for our children which would give
the images of themselves. When I say 'our children,' it is the
Black children everywhere who need this. And I'm interested in
giving the children's stories a kind of ideological underpinning.
This is a tradition we inherited from Africa which should be maintained in the folk tales. For instance, Afro-American folk tales are
lessons in survival by Black people. Brer Rabbit has a great fear of
enemies. He survives best in a community. If he goes by himself he
is the victim of predators. . .So I'm interested in transforming visions through stories. . .For instance. . .I attempt to bring back a
kind of African aesthetic about age and beauty to counter the
Western idea that all beauty must be young, have a toothpaste
smile, high bosom, long legs, blond hair. When you get older they
fade out. Whereas in Africa the tradition was for the aged to acquire more status and respect. (quoted in Warner-Lewis, 39)

Caribbean children's literature is represented by a wide range of genres: legends, folk tales, animal stories, illustrated books, poetry, historical and realistic fiction. This literature is characterized by the struggle of the Caribbean people to continually define themselves and develop their culture. In contemporary realistic fiction, for example, the adolescent character's struggle is mirrored in the regional struggle for cultural, economic and political independence. These works not only provide valuable literary experiences for children, but expand their cultural literacy and make it easier for them to live in an increasingly multicultural society. Currently a growing sense of pride and unity throughout the Caribbean has increased the need for children's books by and about Caribbean people.

The following illustrated children's picture books are divided into categories which seem to exemplify the various themes found in these books about Caribbean culture: life on the island, family, tales of magic and mystery, Anansi stories, and poetry.

My Little Island

The books in this category are testimony to the beauty and life in the Caribbean. Frané Lessac's *Caribbean Canvas* is a stunning collection of her paintings of island life in Antigua, Barbados, Grenada, St. Kitts, and Nevis. West Indian proverbs and poems from a dozen poets compliment this pictorial journey. Likewise, Lessac's *My Little Island* provides the reader with an introduction to life lived on an island with fresh realistic scenes which reveal the special qualities of the tropical setting. In Lessac's *Caribbean Alphabet*, four commonly used words throughout the island region are used for each letter of the alphabet. As in her other books, Lessac's folk art style portrays island people in a variety of activities.

In Jenny Stow's *The House That Jack Built*, a sense of the tropics flows through the vibrant illustrations, which give new life to the familiar cumulative rhyme. Irving Burgie, the composer of "Day-O" and "Jamaica Farewell" has combined these and other Caribbean folk songs in *Caribbean Carnival: Songs of the West Indies*. Included with each song are easy piano and guitar arrangements which invite the reader to sing along. Repetition and word play characterize the text in Phillis Gershator's *Rata-Pata-Scata-Fata: A Caribbean Story*. Junjun, the daydreamer, uses a magical chant to complete his chores in this highly imaginative and playful story. What a joyful celebration of life on my little island.

Mothers, Fathers, Aunts, Uncles, Cousins, and Grans

In Katherine Orr's *My Granpa and the Sea*, deeply held feelings about family are represented by a young protagonist. Similar emotions are evoked as other Caribbean child characters interact with their mothers, fathers, grandparents, and extended family members in this category. In Charlotte Pomerantz's *The Chalk Doll*, Roses's mother relates childhood memories of resourcefulness and a happy childhood while growing up in Jamaica. Rita Mitchell's *Hue Boy*, although small for his age, learns upon his father's return home after a long absence, that his pride makes him feel tall. Warmth, comfort, and the joy of togetherness are evident in the Caribbean counting book, *One Smiling Grandma* by Ann Marie Linden. The text rhymes and allows for the counting of various objects, people, animals or plants. This is a vibrantly colored book which evokes the lush tropical setting of Barbados. A unique and playful relationship between grandma and grandson is depicted in rhythmic language in Ashley Bryan's *Turtle Knows Your Name*. Carolyn Binch's all-American *Gregory Cool*, with his baseball cap and sneakers, has many new experiences while away in the tropical Caribbean visiting his Grandpa, Granny, and cousin Lennox in Tobago. In *So Much* by Trish Cooke, Mom and baby are home alone in the afternoon when Auntie, Uncle, Nanie, Gran-Gran, and the cousins come to visit. They all want to love, kiss, and squeeze the baby because everybody loves the baby *So Much*. The setting for

James Berry's *Celebration Song* is Jesus' first birthday. The world comes to celebrate in this lyrical, exuberant song-poem. Caribbean language and culture are celebrated in this setting, too, with warm expressionistic artwork which extends the text beautifully.

Spiced with Magic

Indeed, there is magic in the telling! In Lynn Joseph's *A Wave in Her Pocket: Stories from Trinidad* and its sequel, *The Mermaid's Twin Sister: More Stories From Trinidad*, Tantie tells stories in the context of everyday life experiences. When Tantie begins her tales, the language comes alive with the richness of expression. These tales read aloud extremely well. They seem to jump from the page into your mouth and ears and beg to be retold. The versatile storyteller James Berry offers six stories in a Jamaican setting in *The Future-Telling Lady and Other Stories.* The importance of healers, picnicking ghosts, and magic which makes a young girl's brother invisible and takes sibling rivalry to another dimension are included in this portrait of life for young readers. In Diane Wolkstein's *The Banza*, readers are introduced to the banjo which originated in Africa. The instrument found its way to Haiti in the eighteenth century as a hollowed-out calabash with hemp strings called a banza. This is an authentic retelling of the warm, funny Haitian folk tale with a sophisticated edge. Like Lynn Joseph's stories, this one begs repeated tellings. Critically acclaimed author, Robert D. San Souci, draws upon African, European, and South American traditions and imagery in the tale of romance, intrigue, and courage on the lush island of Martinique in *The Faithful Friend*. Indeed, there is magic in the telling and magic in the listening as well.

Anancy, Anansi: The Spiderman

James Berry's *Spiderman Anancy* is a retelling of the West African spider tales in colorful Jamaican patterns. This collection finds the spiderman involved in such timeless situations as domestic disputes, political upheaval, and the attempted murder of his main adversary, Bro Tiger. Philip Sherlock has modified the dialect in *Anansi, The Spider Man* while not losing the character and flavor of the islands in this collection of 15 West Indian tales. Threatened by Fish and Falcon, Anansi is saved by his sons in Gerald McDermott's *Anansi The Spider*. Nyame, the God of All Things, assists the rogue Anansi in a resourceful manner which allows Anansi to put the moon in the sky.

Come On Into My Tropical Poetic Garden

A beautiful brown-faced baby girl is born on a lush green island. Her hair is the color of the blossoms of the flamboyan tree. She takes an imaginary flight-journey throughout the land and returns home to the familiar flamboyan tree. Arnold Adoff's rhythmic, yet gentle, verse in *Flamboyan* is accompanied by brilliant tropical-hued illustrations. Lynn Joseph's *Coconut Kind Of Day: Island Poems* captures a day in the life of a Trinidad girl from her morning walk to school until bedtime, when she fears "the jumbi man go eat you up / and spit you 'cross the island.'" Grace Nichols captures the richness of the lush landscape of the Caribbean in *Come On Into My Tropical Garden*. The twenty-eight poems in this collection evoke the natural wonders of the Caribbean and most importantly, the lives of growing children. Monica Gunning's *Not a Copper Penny in Me House* is a quiet collection of poems which reflect a cycle of events on a Caribbean island. Celebrations, holidays, hurricanes, shopping in the market, picnicking, and walking to church are all depicted in free verse, complemented by Frané Lessac's extraordinary folk art illustrations. John Agard and Grace Nichols have gathered *A Caribbean Dozen: Poems from Caribbean Poets* in a collection which features thirteen acclaimed poets. Each poet introduces his/her selections with an essay or brief description about his/her work, and the poet's photograph is included.

In their introduction to the collection, Agard and Nichols state,

The voices of these poets are informed by the rhythms and flavors
and textures of a Caribbean childhood. Though many of them now
live in metropolitan places in the U.S.A., Canada, and Britain, their
formative meeting with the magic of the world happened under tropical skies where fireflies were shooting stars, and English nursery
rhymes and fairy tales mingled with the tricky doings of Anancy
spiderman and ghost stories about duppies and jumbies with turned-
back feet. (11)

In 1992, Ashley Bryan published his first collection of original poems, *Sing to the Sun*. They are tender, joyous, playful, and close to the African root. Ashley Bryan celebrates all life in these poems: children, grannies, mommas and daddies, birds, and even flowers. The reader is treated to free verse, rhythm, rhyme and the blues in this collection along with Bryan's vibrantly colored illustrations. Mother Goose with distinctively Caribbean nuances? Yes. John Agard and Gene Nichols offer traditional and original nursery rhymes in *No Hickory, No Dickory, No Dock: Caribbean Nursery Rhymes*. This modern rendition will make a great addition to existing Mother Goose collections:

Come on into my tropical garden
Come on in and have a laugh in
Taste my sugar cake and my pine drink
Come on in please come on in. . .

While the list of books discussed is in no way comprehensive, these books exemplify a growing body of literature which represents the various cultures in the Caribbean. This literature is currently enjoying its much deserved position among other books which are viewed as multicultural. Ironically, while the books are published and marketed in the United States and Great Britain, they are seldom seen in the Caribbean. However, children's books about the Caribbean represent a current trend which appears to continue to grow and "illuminate the cultures of the Caribbean" (Dixey and Mahurt 28).

Works Cited

Agar, J & Nichols, G. (1994). *A Caribbean Dozen: Poems from Caribbean Poets*. Illustrated by Cathie Felstead. Cambridge, Massachusetts: Candlewick Press.

Bello, Yahaya (1992). "Caribbean American Children's Literature." Violet J. Harris (Ed.) *Teaching Multicultural Literature In Grades K-8*. (pp. 245-265) Norwood, Massachusetts: Christopher-Gordon Publishers, Inc.

Dixey, B. & Mahurt, S. (1995). "Caribbean Culture." *The Five Owls*, 10, 2, 25-32.

Joseph, L. (1990). *Coconut Kind of Day: Island Poems*. Illustrated by Sandra Speidel. New York: Lothrop, Lee & Shepard.

Nichols, G. (1990). *Come On Into My Tropical Garden*. Illustrated by Caroline Binch. New York: Lippincott.

Warner-Lewis, M. (1987). "Jan Carew Interview." *Journal of West Indian Literature*, 2, 37-40.

A Story to Tell

Phillis Gershator

When a librarian or teacher offers children books to read or reads to them, we know that the story must grab, hold, enlighten, entertain. We hook the kid with a bit of plot or a situation or an evocative title. We also know that variety is important, diversity in all its aspects—genre, style, subject, pace. Diversity includes a range of stories about all sorts of people. We need these books for every reading level, and when it comes to picture books, we also need positive, humanistic, creative visual images, not insulting or stereotypical ones.

Working at the St. Thomas Public Library in 1969, I was frustrated and embarrassed by the lack of picture books featuring local people. Later, when I worked as a children's librarian for the Brooklyn Public Library in the mid 70's, the situation had improved. Books were being published by and about African-Americans, but there were still very few books with the Caribbean as a setting or about West Indian characters.

That situation has changed dramatically in the last few years. My own publishing experience reflects the growing interest in the region: out of a total of eleven published and forthcoming books, six of them have Caribbean themes. Five represent various styles in the tradition of read aloud picture books. One is a realistic easy-to-read chapter book for second graders.

I thought this would be a good opportunity to describe some of them; and if you have any questions, about the books or the process of writing and publishing, please ask.

To start with folk tales, and something of a departure from the traditional Anansi stories, *Tukama Tootles the Flute: A Tale from the Antilles* (Orchard, 1994) features a two-headed giant. I freely adapted it from a tale told by a St. Thomian to Elsie Clews Parson, who included it in her *Folk-lore of the Antilles. French and English, Part II* (American Folk-Lore Society, 1936). For the song, which kids can repeat when the story is told, I used the language of children's chants. Synthia St. James did the bold, striking illustrations in her distinctive style, emphasizing the rhythm and repetition of the story. This was the first picture book this popular artist illustrated. Lucky for me! It was very well received, and *The Bulletin for the Center for Children's Books* selected it as a Blue Ribbon Book in 1994.

As I've read and studied folktales from around the world, trying to analyze just what it is that makes a good story, I came across one of the most accomplished storytelling people ever, the Mende of West Africa, who have four criteria. Every good Mende story has to include one or more of the following: 1) humor, 2) "fitting lies" (imagination), 3) an opportunity to sing and shout, and 4) a demonstration of evil defeated. I keep them in mind when I reread a story I've written, usually much later, days or weeks or, better yet, months after the first flush of creation, because then I can be more objective. I also keep in mind my own experience telling stories to children, mostly in the library and classroom, and what works best: Repetition and participation, the noisier the better. Conflict between good and bad. Overcoming a problem or disadvantage, like size. Jokes, however gross and slapstick. Magic.

Speaking of magic, *Palampam Day* (Cavendish, 1997), another story with a folkish feeling, a whimsical tall tale, is a collaborative effort with my husband, who speaks several languages and is attracted to West Indian speech for its richness and variety of influences.

On one imaginary day, everything starts talking, including the fruits and vegetables. This worries the young hero of the story, naturally, who finds it impossible to eat anything that talks. He goes to a wise old man who tells him that this day occurs only when the moon is blue, and that if he goes home and says: "The moon is blue. / Paladee, paladoo. / Fungee, fish and kallaloo," and then says "Goodnight":

> the moon will set. The sun will rise. Things will go back to the way
> they were. Parrots will repeat what people say. Dogs will bark the
> night away. Cats will meow whenever they please. Frogs will croak
> on hands and knees. Coconuts, sweet potatoes, bananas, fish, and
> mangoes will be quiet again. Can you remember the words?

Of course, Turo remembers the words and it turns out just as the wise man predicted. "The moon set! The sun rose!. . .The island was quiet again, very quiet—so quiet Turo could hear the palm trees whispering in the wind down by Coconut Beach."

Enrique O. Sanchez, who is from the Dominican Republic, illustrated the story. His palette is colorful; his characters are appealing. Magical skies, suns, moons, and plants let us know that this is no ordinary day.

Rata-Pata-Scata-Fata: A Caribbean Story (Little, Brown, 1994) is a realistic story with just a dash of magic, or so the main character thinks, as he makes a series of wishes which amazingly all come true. He even convinces his mother to make a wish, and her wish comes true, too.

Holly Meade did the illustrations using a collage and torn paper technique with a special kind of paper that leaves a white edge when it's torn. The white edges give the illustrations a light, airy feeling. Her depiction of local flora and fauna, not to mention traditional architecture, tells something about the color and beauty of the Caribbean. A Japanese publisher is translating *Rata-Pata-Scata-Fata* for that market. Children in Japan will learn a little about the Caribbean and have a positive cross-cultural experience, in the same way our kids learn a little about Japan from storybooks. They'll discover that children everywhere have things in common, and that part of the fun is discovering the ways they're different—games, favorite foods, clothing, environment, etc.

The same holds true for *Sweet, Sweet Fig Banana* (Whitman, 1996), the picture book closest to my own experience. Most children (and adults) can identify with growing a plant and sharing the harvest. Here a little boy grows a banana plant. His mother wants to sell the ripe bananas at Market Square, but he saves some to give to three friends: the hat man, the fraico man, and the librarian, who then encourages him to make his own picture book about the banana plant. A fourth grader reviewed this book for an upstate New York school library system. It's my favorite review. She wrote: "I never thought about how bananas grow until I read this book. Reading this book made me want to have a garden and go to the market like Soto did. I like how the librarian had Soto write the story of the fig banana, and now I am reading the book."

The story has an agenda, a plug for reading, of course, *and* for drawing. Drawing is not only a creative, expressive activity in its own right, it facilitates and enhances the ability to read and write. Even with older kids, studies have found that art activities had positive results in the area of reading interest and competence. The story was also directly inspired by one of my student's younger brother, who hung around with his mother at Market Square. I wondered what he might do there all day. I already knew what he might do at home: watch a banana grow, just like me.

A Haitian artist, Fritz Millevoix, set the story in Haiti, illustrating it in a naive, detailed, colorful style. One reviewer wrote, "The pictures shimmer." They do, in the bright Caribbean sun.

Sugar Cakes Cyril (Mondo, 1997) is a short chapter book. Four of the chapters focus on typical island experiences: making sugar cakes, watching an eclipse of the moon, finding and decorating a Christmas cactus, and watching a whale at Coki Beach. The story is wrapped up, beginning and end, in the universal experience of sibling rivalry and regression. Cedric Lucas, an artist and art teacher who often visits these islands, did several black and white illustrations and color cover.

Mondo, the publisher of this book, sells to bookstores, but also directly to schools, taking a grade-oriented approach, marketing the books in sets for specific reading levels. Part of being flexible in writing for children is fitting into these categories.

I've written other stories set in the Caribbean for third and fourth grade readers, combining fantasy and reality, and someday I also hope to place them with a publisher. It's more work than non-writers think—lots of rewriting and revision, rejection, and then more revision, more rejection, and then, even if a story is accepted for publication, *more* revision.

I titled this presentation "A Story to Tell" from a local proverb: "A story to tell, no time for telling." Like many a cryptic proverb, this one can have several meanings and implications for behavior.

One is that we can never know the whole story. Knowing this, we will be more questioning and less judgmental. There is always more to learn, more reason to keep reading. This is good news for the storyteller. If the whole story is not known, we can imagine it. A few plots, countless permutations.

"A story to tell, no time for telling" can also mean there's a lot to tell, but time is running out. I take this as an exhortation to get busy: to get busy collecting stories to preserve the best and / or most meaningful parts of our cultural backgrounds (plural); to get busy writing stories, both to express ourselves creatively and convey our beliefs; to get busy reading stories to children so they can also become readers—and writers.

Exhortations aside, what really keeps me at this is the fun, challenge, satisfaction, even the high of writing a story, and the hope that my work will give children pleasure, the same pleasure *I* got from books as a kid.

Strategies for Teaching Caribbean Literature: Focus on Caribbean Poetry

Gayle V. Dancy-Benjamin

Virgin Islands students are very unique individuals. They live on islands that are American enclaves caressed by the Caribbean Sea. The V. I. student has a duality of spirit, one associated with the nuances of a small American city with its values and mores of American life and the other associated with the rich flavor of language, music, food, mores and values of Caribbean life.

It is imperative that we, as educators, become sensitized to the quality of this duality of spirit that our students possess and as we teach them we must embrace all the domains in which they exist. Poetry is the key that allows us to inspire, imbue and uplift the intrinsic spirit of the Virgin Islands student. More importantly, Caribbean poetry offers the students a wellspring of pride in the knowledge and exploration of their Caribbean spirit and their rich, cultural heritage as members of the family of the African diaspora.

"Poetry," as expressed in the *Prentice Hall Gold Edition of Literature*, "is a highly charged form of literature in which every word is packed with meaning" (545). Every power-packed word on the written page makes poetry a vehicle of expressive power and response for students to explore and develop a voice of their own. Caribbean poetry opens new vistas of learning and new ways of expressing their duality of spirit and experiences.

Caribbean poetry generates expressive energy that uses both standard English and what Edward Kamau Brathwaite calls "nation language" to electrify the Caribbean spirit. Brathwaite states in "History of the Voice" that

First of all, it is from. . .an oral tradition. The poetry, the culture
itself, exists not in a dictionary but in the tradition of the spoken
word. It is based as much on sound as it is on song. . .The noise that
it makes is part of the meaning, and if you ignore the noise (or what
you would think of as noise) then you lose part of its meaning. (17)

Students love "the noise" of Caribbean poetry; they love to read and perform it and even though confronted with difficulty in syntax development, they love to write it.

Caribbean poetry also offers the ultimate in the study of the power of the written word. Caribbean poetry can foster students to become empowered with a medium of expression with which they can feel comfortable. For the teacher it becomes an enjoyable, educational technique that imbues students with a sense of positive self-esteem and literary acumen.

To achieve the goal of teaching Caribbean poetry in the classroom, the following strategies can be used that will help both the teacher and the student to achieve the optimum in the learning experience of studying and writing Caribbean poetry.

Model Lesson Plan for Teaching Caribbean Poetry

Subject: English 9   Unit: Poetry: Caribbean Poetry
Lesson: "Comparative Poetics"   Time: 50 minutes

I. Comments:
   A. A discussion of the poetic structure of "rap" and "reggae" music will assist students in understanding poetic form found in music.

   B. An analysis of the songs *Dangerous Minds* by Coolio and *Africa Unite* by Bob Marley will assist students in identifying the themes found in both songs and assessing their similarity or dissimilarity.

II. Objectives: Students will be able to:
   A. Identify the poetic structure of both "rap" and "reggae" music.
   B. Analyze both songs and identify rhyme scheme, symbolism, mood and figurative language (simile, metaphor) found in each.
   C. Identify themes found in both songs.
   D. Respond in writing to the similarity or dissimilarity of the themes found in both songs during the final ten (10) minutes of class.

III. Concept / Content:
   A. Concept: poetic structure of "rap" and "reggae"
   B. Content:
        1. rhymed verse **spoken** to a distinctive beat = rap
        2. rhymed verse **sung** in a distinctive style and beat = reggae
   C. Concept: identification of poetic devices and terms studied in previous lessons
   D. Content: Poetic devices and terms
        I. rhyme scheme
        2. symbolism
        3. mood
        4. figurative language
              a. simile
              b. metaphor
        5. lyric poetry
   E. Concept: similarity / dissimilarity of themes found in both styles of music
   F. Content:
        1. analysis of thematic structures / identification of themes found in each
        2. response in writing similarity / dissimilarity of themes found in each

249

IV. Procedure:

A. Teacher will lead students in a discussion of rap and reggae music.

B. "Dangerous Minds" and "Africa Unite" will be played for the students to first analyze music for poetic structures found in concept/content.

C. Students will identify poetic structures when randomly called upon by teacher.

D. Both songs will be played a second time so that students will be able to assess the themes inherent in each song.

E. Each student will then demonstrate his/her assessment of the similarity or dissimilarity of the themes found in both songs by writing a full page essay. The essay is to be written on loose-leaf paper and handed in at the end of the period.

V. Assignment at home:

A. Write a rap or a reggae song illustrating an issue in your community or school you feel strongly about

or

B. Prepare the first draft of a three paragraph essay discussing why you believe that Bob Marley's "Africa Unite" written in the late 1970s is as relevant to today's youth as Coolio's "Dangerous Minds" recorded in 1995.

VI. Materials

A. Notes on poetic terms and devices from previous lessons

B. Loose-leaf paper/pens

C. CD's or cassette tapes of rap, "Dangerous Minds", and reggae tune, "Africa Unite"

D. CD player/cassette player

Virgin Islands Poetry Analysis

Instructions: In cooperative learning groups analyze the following poem by Virgin Islands poet, Bertica Hodge-Hendrickson. Each group must answer **all** questions. The first group to complete the assignment will receive ten (10) bonus points. The group that has all questions answered correctly will receive twenty-five (25) bonus points.

"Yellow Cedar"
by Bertica Hodge-Hendrickson

Pop
Pop
Little bells
Yellow bells
Ring out your beauty.

I admire you
Like a lover
Afraid to speak
For fear you will
Go away and
Never bear
Beauty anymore.

Seeds in bean pods
Burst open
Like the dawn of spring.

They fall
to the ground
Pop
Pop
Plop.

And scatter
Where they
Nourish on tropical ground.

When rain clouds gather
Little trees grow
Round your feet,
A colony of your kind
Lives on
To add yellow,
To shine like the sun
If we let them.

1. This poem is written in _____ verse because it is unrhymed poetry.
2. Examples of onomatopoeia are found on lines ___, ___, ___, ___, and ___.
3. Similes are found on lines ___, ___, and ___.
4. What images are presented by this poem?
5. After reading this poem, what do you think is the author's reason for writing this poem?
6. What is the mood of this poem?
7. Is this poem a narrative poem, a dramatic poem, or a lyric poem?
8. What is a lyric poem?
9. Identify the theme of this poem.
10. Using the art supplies given each group, draw and color the images illustrated in the poem in the space provided.

Additional Strategies for Teaching Caribbean Poetry at the Secondary Level

I.   Listening to calypsos
       A. Identify poetic structures
       B. Identify satire
       C. Identify the *double entendre*

II.   Writing calypsos/raps

III.   Publication of poetry anthologies
       A. Publish classroom collections of students' poems
       B. Disseminate to Media Centers and other classes

IV.   Printing of poetry newsletter
       A. Inspire other students—write poetry
       B. Spark poetry contests

V.   Preparation of pictorial poetry journals

VI.   Interpretation (artistic) of literature
       A. Poetry Quilt—poems placed on colorful backing
       B. Poetry Mural—poems & drawings / pictures displayed

VII.   Presentation of oral reports
       A. Caribbean writers (poets)
       B. Caribbean islands
       C. Caribbean foods

VIII.   Discussion series
    A. Major concerns of Caribbean writers
        1. Use of language
        2. Publication
        3. Frame of reference
    B. Common motifs found in Caribbean literature
        1. Migration
        2. Spirituality
        3. Family relationships
        4. Cycle of disillusionment
        5. Politics (defiant/satirical)
        6. Social differences
        7. Racial differences
        8. Nationalism
        9. Identity/culture
        10.Tourist haven
    C. Use of Humor
        1. Paul Keens-Douglas
        2. Louise Bennett
        3. Arona Petersen

Works Cited

Brathwaite, Edward Kamau. *History of the Voice: The Development of Nation Language in Anglophone Caribbean Poetry*. London: New Beacon Books. 1984.

Coolio. *Gangsta's Paradise*: "Dangerous Minds": Soundtrack. Universal City, California: MCA Records. 1995.

Hodge-Hendrickson, Bertica. "Yellow Cedar." St. Thomas: V.I.P.: College of the Virgin Islands Literary Magazine. 1970.

Marley, Bob. *Natural Mystic*: "Africa Unite." Jamaica: Tuff Gong, Island Records. 1995.

Prentice Hall. *Prentice Hall Literature, Gold Edition*. New Jersey: Prentice Hall, Inc. 1989.

The Caribbean Play in the University of the Virgin Islands Classroom and Suggestions for Further Reading

Patricia Harkins-Pierre

The University of the Virgin Islands has a rich history of exploring Caribbean culture through literature, including plays by Caribbean writers who, as University of the Virgin Islands President Orville Kean has stated, "speak for, speak about and speak to the peoples of the region."

For example, all Humanities majors at U.V.I. are required to take a two-semester Senior Seminar (HU 497-498) in which they explore multidisciplinary topics, then present papers based on their research. In 1995-96 the seminar topic was "Ancestors"; in 1996-97 the topic will be "Sports." Student presentations may focus on Caribbean oral or scribal literary traditions, both verbal and non-verbal communication in any language used in the region, journalism, art, dance, theatre. The students study the past in order to understand the present and speculate about the future. Storytellers and scholars in various disciplines, from on and off-campus, have lectured in the seminar, which is open to visitors from other divisions and from the community. When Derek Walcott returned to U.V.I. after winning the Nobel Prize in literature, he was a guest lecturer. His classic play *Dream on Monkey Mountain* was being performed at the Reichhold Center for the Arts, and Walcott urged U.V.I. students to write and stage their own plays. Reichhold's director, playwright David Edgecombe, has also spoken to seminar students and guests, emphasizing the important role Caribbean drama can have in the cultural and economic future of the region.

Personally, it seems to me that educating my students as much as possible about every facet of their rich literature is an important part of my responsibility as an English teacher at a Caribbean university in the latter part of the twentieth century. This includes educating them about the history and availability of Caribbean plays in print. David Edgecombe has often asserted that "Drama is not regarded as part of Caribbean literature, or at least, not an important part" (*Heaven & Other Plays* 13). And it is true that even when Derek Walcott was awarded the Nobel Prize there was no recognition of his long and distinguished association with theater. None of his books of plays was cited. The University of Miami's Caribbean Writers' Seminar, established in August 1991, has never featured a playwright or offered a course in drama. Even in the Caribbean itself there were only two West Indian plays placed on the CXC syllabus in 1995 (Dennis Scott's *An Echo in the Bone* and Trevor Rhone's *Old Story Time*). Most recently, the University of the West Indies (Cave Hill Campus) has announced a Summer

Workshop in Caribbean Creative Writing, but drama is not an option for the students.

My own commitment to teaching and promoting Caribbean theater has increased as I have learned more about it. As a new teacher at U.V.I. in the fall of 1989, I joined the Little Theater "family," appearing in a few minor roles, working on the set, and backstage. My students, whether they are in literature or composition courses, are encouraged to take part in auditions, go to play readings, attend dress rehearsals, and/or join the stage crew. We attended Little Theater productions (produced by Dennis Parker and Rosary Harper) of such West Indian classics as *Ti-Jean, Moon On A Rainbow Shawl* or Mustapha Matura's *Playboy of the West Indies,* and the students write reviews of the plays we have seen. We were also privileged to attend the premier production of David Edgecombe's play *Heaven.* Now that U.V.I. has a thriving student newspaper, *Uvision,* we are able to submit our reviews to the editor for possible publication—as well as submitting scripts of one act plays.

The courses in which I have taught West Indian drama at U.V.I. are Elements of Literature, Caribbean Literature, and such selected topics courses as Introduction to Shakespeare, Creative Writing, and Mythology. Since these are English courses, I have emphasized the use of language in the scripts and have chosen to teach plays that read well. I like to supplement the use of printed texts with performances on audiotape or videotape (such as the film version of Jean Rhys' *Wide Sargasso Sea*). My students also learn to find resources on CD Roms and through the Internet. Class discussions and student writing are important components of the classes. We also act out scenes, and students "try on" the roles of playwright, director, actor, technical crew. Combining traditional literary and theatrical approaches to drama has worked well for us.

A representative but far from complete list of playwrights and plays I have featured follows: Alwin Bully (Dominica): *Good Morning, Miss Millie, Nite Box* and *McB*; David Edgecombe (Montserrat): *For Better, For Worse*; *Heaven*; *Makin It* (originally titled *Son Of A Bitch*) and *Marilyn*; Errol Hill (Trinidad): *The Ping Pong*; Kendel Hippolyte (St. Lucia): *The Drum-Maker*; Errol John (Jamaica): *Moon On A Rainbow Shawl*; Earl Lovelace (Trinidad): *Jestina's Calypso*; Derek Walcott (St. Lucia): *Drums and Colors*; *Dream On Monkey Mountain,* and *Ti-Jean.*

In my experience, it is more difficult to find published plays by Caribbean women. However, I have enjoyed teaching the work of these playwrights: Tulip Fleming (Antigua): *Coming To Terms*; Gladys Stuart (Belize): *Dog and Iguana*; Telcine Turner (the Bahamas): *Woman Take Two,* and Cicely Waite-Smith (Jamaica): *Africa SlingShot.* In the future I hope to include the work of such influential women as Una Marson and Patricia Cumper.

I am especially interested in teaching Caribbean plays that, in John Thieme's words, "explore the nature of West Indian identity and at the same time fuse a broad range of cultural influences to produce a distinctly West Indian drama" (*A Handbook for Teaching Caribbean Literature* 86).

Suggestions for Further Reading:

Agostini, Melindsa. "Who Dat!!!: A Play in One Act," U.V.I. Humanities Bulletin. No. 6 1990. 2-5.

Bonwell, Charles C. and James Eison A.. "Active Learning: Creating Excitement in the Classroom." (ASHE-ERIC Higher Ed. Report No. 1, 1991). Washington, D.C.: 1991.

Bully, Alwin A. *McB.* 1989. Unpublished.

Corsbie, Ken. *Theater in the Caribbean.* Intro. Trevor Rhone. London: Hodder and Stoughton. 1984.

Dadydeen, David. "Unit Ten: Derek Walcott." *A Handbook for Teaching Caribbean Literature.* London: Heinemann Ed., 1988. 86-95.

Daniel, Alecia. "Sharon Guess What!: A West Indian Play." *Uvision* (U.V.I. student newspaper). Tuesday, March 26, 1996: 6.

Edgecombe, David. *Coming Home to Roost: a play in two acts.* Plymouth: Montserrat. 1988.

___. *Heaven and Other Plays.* Frederiksted, V.I.: Eastern Caribbean Institute. 1993.

Francis, Dale. "Full Moon." *Sea Moss*: Student Literary Magazine. 5 (1993): 14-20.

Hartigan, Patti. "The Passions of Derek Walcott." *American Theatre.* May/June 1993. 14-19.

Hill, Errol. *The Jamaican Stage 1655-1900: Profile of a Colonial Theatre.* Amherst, Massachusetts: University of Massachusetts Press, 1992.

Lee Wah, James. *Carray! A Selection of Plays for Caribbean Schools.* London: Macmillan Ed. Ltd. 1977.

Lovelace, Earl. *Jestina's Calypso and Other Plays.* London: Heinemann. 1984.

Noel, Keith, ed. *Caribbean Plays for Playing.* London: Heinnemann, 1985.

Ogilvie, W. G. "Derek Walcott et al." *West Indian Plays for Schools.* Intro. Jeanne Wilson. Jamaica: Jamaica Publishing House. 1979.

Stone, S. J. Stone. *Studies in West Indian Literature: Theatre.* London: Macmillan Caribbean, 1994. (See the excellent Selected Bibliography)

Teytaud, Anton C. *Sarah & Addie: 19 Short West Indian Plays.* St. Croix, Christiansted. 1978.

Turner Telcine. *Woman Take Two: A Play in Three Acts.* London: Macmillan Caribbean. 1994.

Walcott, Derek. "Drums of Revolt." *Caribbean Quarterly*, 7 (1961): no p.

___. *Dream on Monkey Mountain and Other Plays.* New York: Noon Day Press. 1970. 81-166.

BOOK REVIEWS

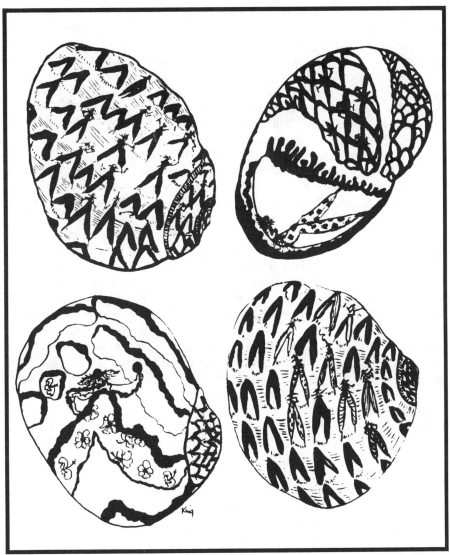

Judith King

Derek Walcott, *The Bounty*. New York: Farrar, Straus & Giroux. 1997. 37 pages. hc. $18.00

Walcott's writing has very often engaged with Europe to revision that continent's global cultural influences, working out of an affectionate intimacy which nevertheless in such texts as *Pantomime* (first performed 1977) and *Omeros* (1990) locates Europe's culpability in the history of colonisation, transatlantic slavery and their aftermath. It is, however, a conversation with less political edge and less overt literary affiliations than Seamus Heaney's poetic construction of a divided Ireland. Heaney, Walcott's friend and fellow Nobel Laureate in poetry, comments on the inside cover of Walcott's latest poetry collection, *The Bounty*, that the ". . .Walcott line is still sponsored by Shakespeare and the Bible. . ." It is perhaps partly a generational concern, of those who came to maturity as colonialism was formally ending across the imperial British world, and the huge shadow of the middle-class British literary tradition fell across those gifted with language. The decision had to be either to turn into that shadow and engage with it or to try to move at least to the edges of its influence from which to locate and defeat the co-option, by embracing other ancestral verbal traditions. Walcott has certainly, over his career, paid attention to the collective voice of resistance of the ordinary man (mostly the man) in his own culture, but he has also quite centrally embraced the shadow within his most creative space.

The Bounty is no exception. The title poem is a very moving, powerful elegy to Walcott's mother, Alix, which engages with the figure of John Clare, the English poet of nature and the countryside (1793-1864) who went mad in 1837. This is the densest of Walcott's poems, its warp and weft stunningly confident and outrageously various: "Between the vision of the Tourist Board and the true / Paradise lies the desert where Isaiah's elations / force a rose from the sand. . .the bliss of John Clare / torn, wandering Tom, stoat-stroker in his county. . ." The rhythm is confident and practised: surprises come thick and fast and subvert the comfort of the seamless lines. Clare, with "(f)rost whitening his stubble," blesses not only his own English winter world but the "shadows of the beach road near where my mother lies." The lines get even more high-spirited. One example may stand to indicate Walcott's major strategy of taking customary poetic strategies of juxtaposition and repetition to their limits, within his audacious refiguring of elements of terza rima into his own idiosyncratic interlocking rhymed tercets:

. . .so, John Clare, forgive me
for this morning's sake, forgive me, coffee, and pardon me,
milk with two packets of artificial sugar,
as I watch these lines grow and the art of poetry harden me
into sorrow as measured as this, to draw the veiled figure
of Mamma entering the standard elegiac. (5)

That the surprises are deliberate and come from close to home may be judged from Walcott's comment in his Nobel lecture that "visual surprise is natural in the Caribbean": in this poem, surprise is a major component. The pyrotechnics of the verse seem to be shy of conjuring Alix Walcott except for brief moments:

the poet's grief is even more elusive. But the poetry plays that grand elegiac note which was established by Milton in *Lycidas* or Tennyson in *In Memoriam*, where the point is not the death of an individual, however important, but an essay on mortality and the ephemeral quality of human relations, feelings and life itself: ". . .the dread of death is in the faces / we love, the dread of our dying, or theirs."

The rest of the volume is slightly less impressive only because it must come after such a wonderfully shameless demonstration of the master craftsman's fluency in his own aesthetic language. The second section begins with a self-elegy, ". . .Here lies / D.W. This place is good enough to die in." It really was." (19). Here the verse paragraph turns us in the direction of a poetic essay, complexly and at times tightly rhymed. There are some dangers to this confidence: the first poem in the section "Parang" rustles over commonplaces without being sufficiently unusual in its reading of them (". . .the night wind in your eyes like a woman's hair," and "the stars that are no longer questions"). Walcott has long had a weakness for romantic conventions when his verse is not quite entirely awake, though his exercises are far better than many poets' full throttle performances. But as the volume moves on, the impressive global cultural references and conceptual control finally diminish into a quiet ending in which, in a rare moment, the rhetorical defences of this most elusive of poets come down and he finds another space:

> . . .not the expected wonder
> of self-igniting truth and oracular rains,
> but these shallows as gentle as the voice of your daughter,
> while the gods fade like thunder on the rattling mountains. (77)

I have no space here to explore this rich volume fully. Sufficient to say that for those who know Walcott's work, there are many satisfying revisits to major themes: ". . .the two languages I know. . ./ . . .my love of both wide as the Atlantic is large", and ". . .after the motion / of history, every object we named was not the correct noun". For those who do not, the sheer performative power of this poetry could not be a better place to begin to understand Walcott's importance.

Elaine Savory
New York, NY

Caryl Phillips, *The Nature of Blood*. New York: Alfred A. Knopf. 1997. 212 pages. hc. $23.00.

Caryl Phillips is a product of the 1970s with its analysis of power in terms of race, gender, sexuality, and class, to which he has brought a strong sense of history, especially of the relationship between dominance, exploitation, slavery, and prejudice. *The Nature of Blood* returns to the similar experience of the Jews and Blacks in the two Venice chapters of *The European Tribe*. *The Nature of Blood* begins in Cyprus towards the end of World War II when the Jewish refugees were being turned away from Palestine by the British. It ends in Israel decades later with a "hero" who, after having left his wife and child in the United States so he can fight for a homeland, is aging, lonely and nostalgic.

This is a book about memories, desire, history, ethnicity, isolation, love, and imagining "home." The literary imitations, interruptions of the fictional frame, and interweaving of stories are Brechtian in breaking uncritical involvement with the characters and aiding objective analysis and judgment. A central story about a Jewish family destroyed by the Nazis is mirrored by a retelling of *Othello*, the history of the Jews of fifteenth-century Portobuffole (who fleeing persecution in Germany were allowed to settle near Venice and were once more victimized, a background of *The Merchant of Venice*), a portrait of refugees becoming Hagannah soldiers, and a conclusion with Ethiopians discriminated against in Israel. There are notes on the history of Venice, and a psychiatrist recounts research into survivors of concentration camps.

Phillips shows history's contradictions. During early capitalism usury was a sin but borrowing was necessary for ventures; the more successful strangers are in rising in society and becoming assimilated, the more likely there will be resentment and violence. While Jews were needed in Venice to lend money, the people resented them and the Church wanted to destroy them. Such contradictions continued. The acculturated German Jews remained a people without a home whom the Nazis wanted to destroy. The Jews in Israel, however, brought with them European racism in their treatment of the Ethiopians who are disliked and whose customs are viewed as primitive instead of similar to the original Jews.

The Nature of Blood avoids the simplicities associated with black protest writing and postcolonial critique of the West. While it shows how groups treat those felt to be alien, and how social hierarchies use and keep power, it recognizes the force of loneliness, isolation, and the need for love, and belonging. Such emotions energize life but can be dangerous and self-destructive. Othello's isolation and loneliness in Venice drive him towards the dangers represented by Desdemona and hope of assimilation. The success of the German Jews made many blind to the threat of the Nazis. Throughout the novel men rise in society by gaining the love of women towards whom they later behave badly and, like Othello, destroy.

It is Phillips' ability to tell such related stories that makes him one of the better writers of our time. The short, often-fragmented sentences, the consciously monotone voices, the lack of humor and imagery, contribute to an interiority, which like the minimalism of Samuel Beckett suggests much. Behind this complex novel there is Phillips, the black British West Indian, at home neither in England nor his parents' St. Kitts.

Bruce King
Muncie, Indiana

Opal Palmer Adisa, *It Begins With Tears*. Oxford, England: Heinemann Caribbean Writers Series. 1997. 239 pages. pb. $13.95.

Opal Palmer Adisa's *It Begins With Tears* is a magical tale about the inhabitants of Kristoff Village, Jamaica. In this, her first novel, Adisa has created a seamless world that connects the eternal and the ephemeral, where words bridge the gap between these seemingly disparate dimensions.

The novel opens with an introduction to various characters, Devil and She Devil, Angel and Arnella, then plunges into the turmoil caused by the return of Monica, a retired Kingston prostitute, who wants a new life: "She made a promise to herself never again deliberately to take another woman's man, just because she could." But for a woman like Monica, things are never that easy and her emotions soon get the better of her. She seduces Desmond Burton and steals the attention of Ainsworth McKenzie. The wives, Grace Burton and Marva McKenzie, take notice and as their husbands grow more distant, they blame Monica and retaliate. Their vicious and violent attack on Monica destroys the equilibrium of Kristoff Village, and the elders, guided by Mr. and Miss Cotton, rescue the village from a destructive spiral into madness and death.

Miss Cotton and Mr. Cotton, drawing on the collective wisdom of the community—this is the novel's greatest strength, its exploration of the web of relationships in the village—create a communion between the men and women, women and women, the living and the dead. The women led by Miss Cotton join in a ritual of forgiveness that releases the women from their shame about their past, their bodies and fears about the future. The men, too, have their own rituals, but these are not as fascinating, nor are they described with the same deftness as the scenes between the women. In a climactic episode, Monica, despite the upheaval that her actions have caused, is welcomed back into the circle of women.

It would be misleading, however, to suggest that the novel is merely a saga of unchecked passions, for Adisa also gives her story a spiritual dimension. In Kristoff Village, the bonds between the living and the dead are never broken, and the past and the present co-exist in a continuum of love and care—heaven and earth are one: Devil and She-Devil, with the help of God and Sabbath Angel, plan the wedding of their son, Brimstone, and his fiancee, Tallawah; and Monica speaks freely with her dead mother, offering her reasons for running away from home and accepting her mother's apology for her harsh treatment.

It Begins With Tears creates a mythical realm and invents its own moral universe. Throughout the novel, Adisa never wavers from the origins—Herstory as counterpoint to Aristotelian esthetics. Anyone reading *It Begins with Tears* won't want to leave Kristoff Village.

Geoffrey Philp
Miami, Florida

Wilson Harris, *Jonestown*. London: Faber & Faber. 1996. 234 pages. $15.95.

The name *Jonestown* triggers memories of cultism, charismatic leadership, and catastrophe propelled by suicidal megalomania. But Wilson Harris's perspective on megalomania takes an unusual twist in his recent novel, *Jonestown*. Readers looking for a well-crafted, fantastic tale that blends science fiction with ancient myths of reincarnation are in for a surreal experience with Wilson Harris's tale.

Harris's dream fiction invites the reader to explore a metaphysical world defined by reincarnation and the human collective unconscious, modified by popular science fiction notions of a "quantum leap" that link past and future. This story also merges individual human identities, neutralizing the effect of geographical, cultural and historical distance. This Guyanese author's metaphysical "dreambook," therefore, portrays all forms of individual and communal violence as ultimately suicidal, hence, absurd.

The novel is set in New Amsterdam, Guyana (formerly British Guiana), scene of the infamous 1978 Jonestown massacre, a modern human tragedy that serves as the concrete source of inspiration for the author's fertile imagination. Francisco, possibly Harris's alter ego, reflects that New Amsterdam, Guyana, stands as a decrepit memorial to "Spanish, French, Dutch, British colonization across the centuries." The narrator, who is also author of a "Dreambook," reflects on the irony that Guyana itself, though almost as large as Great Britain, has a declining population of less than a million—the result of conquest and colonialism. This "decline, which is due in large part to emigration. . .energizes the imagination into an apprehension of earlier peoples, aboriginal ghosts whose presence is visible still in their nomadic living descendants. . . ."

Francisco's next observation draws our attention to Harris's notion of multiculturalism, an expansive concept that starts with Guyana and ends with the entire human race: "Thus the mixed peoples of African or Indian or European or Chinese descent who live in Guyana today are related to the aboriginal ghosts of the past. . .if not by strict biological kinship then by ties to the specter of erosion of community and place which haunts the Central and South Americas."

Some of Harris's ideas challenge a reader's tolerance for Jungian imagery; for example, the theme of "over-arching ghosts." Francisco notes that:

this overarching Ghost throws some light on the play of
extinction within my Dreambook. I was driven in my flight
from Jonestown to reflect on myself as an "extinct" creature.
I dreamt I had been robbed of my native roots and heritage.
I suffered from a void of memory. I belonged to the peoples
of the void. . .[but this] "extinction" imbued me with breath-
lines and responsibilities I would not otherwise have encom-
passed. I became an original apparition in my wanderings
with over-arching ghost. . .in visualizing my own "nothing-ness"
as intangible "somethingness."

Concerning the theme of detribalization of human society, Harris's I-narrator asserts: ". . .a capacity prior to violence makes one see how tribal are pacts of institutions founded on coercion and conquest. . .to glimpse this abhorrent tribalism is to begin to question all one's premises and to look backwards into the mists of time for alternative creations, alternative universes, alternative parallels. . ." This story reminds me of one of Borges's characters in *Fantastic Stories*. Francisco Bone reflects Harris's notion of interchangeable identities, by sharing identities with Jonas Jones and Deacon. Francisco, referring to the time when Jones tries to shoot him, says:

> I prayed. . .that it would seize him in the twinkling of an eye
> before he fired. . .I remembered in the nick of time and my
> fingers clutched Deacon's stomach, pulled forth the bullet,
> inserted it into his hand and gun. Thus I appeared to complete
> the deadly circuit between Jones, Deacon and myself. . .

Throughout his narrative, Harris underscores the irrationality of conquest, imperialism, and colonialism, and all forms of megalomania. Harris's narrator, Francisco Bone, narrowly escapes the fate of those who succumb to the megalomania of Jonas Jones.

Finally, some familiarity with the ideas of transcendental idealism and the mythologies of Central and South America would facilitate a close reading of this book. However, Harris's talents as a storyteller, the potency of his poetic image, and his mastery of descriptive detail make the work compelling reading in its own right.

Vincent O. Cooper
St. Thomas, USVI

Mayra Santos-Febres, *Urban Oracles*. Translated from the Spanish by Nathan Budoff and Lydia Platon Lázaro. Cambridge, Massachusetts: Lumen Editions, Brookline Books. 1997. 129 pages. pb. $15.95.

Mayra Santos-Febres has become an internationally acclaimed Puerto Rican writer since the publication in 1991 of her first two poetry books, *Anamú y manigua* and *El orden escapado*. And now with the publication of *Urban Oracles*, readers will have access to an English translation of *Pez de Vidrio*, the 1994 winner of the *Letras de Oro* prize, awarded by the University of Miami and the Spanish Ministry for Exterior Affairs.

Santos-Febres's *Urban Oracles* explores the interaction of desire and frustration that permeates modern Puerto Rican society. In "Resins for Aurelia" a man, longing for the unattainable, yearns to feel the arms of his beloved's corpse lovingly wrapped around him. In the story "Abnel, Sweet Nightmare," an aging woman briefly alleviates her loneliness by becoming a voyeur. "God, oh God, why have you forsaken me?" she cries, caught in a metropolitan bus inching forward through the San Juan afternoon traffic, fearing she will not reach her apartment window for her 6:15 ritual to observe the man of her sexual fantasies coming out of the shower and meticulously dressing himself. She arrives late only to discover that he, too, another lonely inhabitant of this Caribbean urban jungle, is waiting for her and that he, as much as she, needs this daily dosage of communication with another human being even if it has to be carried out through concrete, steel, and glass.

Certainly Santos-Febres's collection, through a language that meshes body, soul, and spirit, intelligently deals with some key issues of Puerto Rican contemporary society, such as race, social status, sexual orientation, and political status. The collection has been categorized by its publishers under the heading *Erotica*, and oddly enough also under *Latin American Studies*. The stories certainly deal with sexual desire, but should Santos-Febres and the island she writes about be compartmentalized as part of Latin America? Nothing about life in Puerto Rico can be easily defined, especially Puerto Rican identity. Issues such as Puerto Rican identity and the island's political status are intimately related to sexual desire in skillfully constructed stories like "Dilcia M." In "Dilcia M," a story "for all the Puerto Rican political prisoners jailed in federal prisons by the U. S. government since 1980," an imprisoned, frustrated young Puerto Rican woman becomes a metaphor for the colonized body of the island of Puerto Rico. Nevertheless, though the story pays homage to Puerto Rican political prisoners and their struggle for an independent Puerto Rico, it also questions the fervor of a Dilcia M who, for an ideal, will give up family, friends, and love. The story leaves us asking ourselves if such a sacrifice is valid or verging on the perverse. In all, *Urban Oracles* may be read as a call for the liberation of both Puerto Rican sexual identity and national territory.

Urban Oracles should have a wide appeal to readers interested in women's studies, Caribbean, Puerto Rican, and American studies. The collection represents a unique opportunity to read in English the prose work of one of Puerto Rico's young and talented writers.

Linda M. Rodríguez Guglielmoni
Mayaguez, Puerto Rico

Cecil Gray, *Lilian's Songs*. Toronto, Canada: Lilibel Publications. 1996. 116 pages. pb. $6.00.
Anthony Kellman, *The Long Gap*. Leeds, England: Peepal Tree Press. 61 pages. pb. £6.95.

Cecil Gray and Anthony Kellman have a great deal in common. Both of these Caribbean men are serious poets whose work has already received very favorable responses. They are didactic poets in the best sense of that maligned phrase. That is, their poems are vehicles that carry forward the eloquent weight of their values and beliefs. They are formalists who are also comfortable writing free verse and are often attracted to oral, folk, and popular traditions. Some of their poems are highly lyrical but others are written in dialect and can even be quite prose-like. Noted American writer Nancy Willard's critique of Anthony Kellman's work could be equally applied to Cecil Gray's: "[Their] poetry combines the rhythms of Caribbean music with a splendid gift for metaphor and form. You will find yourself wanting to read these poems out loud."

Lilian's Songs is Cecil Gray's second book of poems. His first volume, *The Woolgatherer*, was published by Peepal Tree Press in 1994. Howard Fergus, reviewing *The Woolgatherer* in *The Caribbean Writer*, Vol. 9, wrote of Gray's "powerfully apt imagery" and "flexible attitude of rhyme." These attributes are clearly evident in the three sonnets that make up the title piece of *Lilian's Songs*. The sonnets are woven into a tribute to the poet's mother. The first begins, "My mother, Lilian, was silken black / wearing pride like the tribal regalia / queens in her great-grandfather's Africa / were bedecked with. Pain's counterattack." Lilian's dark face, "stirred up weather / that pitched her adrift, a lost refugee," yet "she kept coaxing from life / the notes she needed to soften the strife" while "she plait[ed] her woolly hair." Lilian's "woolly hair" is the unifying symbol of black hope and pride that braids the three sections of the sequence together. Part 3, or sonnet 3, ends with a rhyming couplet that spells out his black mother's victory over circumstances and change: "Lilian's songs will always remind me / woolly plaits weave strong strands of dignity."

The Long Gap, Anthony Kellman's book, is overtly like Cecil Gray's *Lilian's Songs* in several ways. For example, *The Long Gap* is also Kellman's second volume of verse; his earlier collection was titled simply *Watercourse*. Like Gray, Kellman's poetry was first published in book form by Peepal Tree Press, which has a well-established history of recognizing and promoting the work of accomplished Caribbean writers. And like Gray, Kellman proved himself to be a master of "apt imagery" and "flexible. . .rhyme." The title poem of Kellman's *The Long Gap* will remind readers of the title piece of Gray's *Lilian's Songs* although Kellman's poem does not follow the formal structure of Gray's sonnet sequence. Instead, it consists of one long strand of verse paragraphs that employ subtle, often internal rhymes rather that overt end rhymes, and passages that are sometimes more prose-like than lyrical. Yet it, too, is a rich tapestry of family history woven into images and sounds, and like Gray, Kellman's references to music are key to understanding his message. As the narrator moves through the landscape of his childhood he reports, "I wrestle with an angel from that past" resolved "Not to leave with the song only part sung / not to leave without saying goodbye" to "Mother, bearer of all things, / lover of all things." Kellman's poem, like Gray's, ends on a note of hard-won victory as he turns away from the memory of his mother, who "calmly expire[d] at seventy-six" and turns to greet his young daughter—"I say: 'Everything will be all right just now' / and I look on the sunlight just now."

"Reggae, ruk-a-tuk, samba, calypso" music "throbbing 'pon de stereo'" and the "braid-dripping head" of a Barbadian fisherman's wife, "shining in the Caribbean moon" ("Fishing Song") are images that haunt the self-exiled Anthony Kellman. He finds himself continually traveling, both figuratively and literally, "between the gnarled skyscraper and the water's edge" ("A Dancer to the Gods"). But always, "Home is where islands are." ("A Churn In the South") Cecil Gray also feels torn between two cultures, though the source of his pain is not because he had to leave his beloved Caribbean in order to prosper as a scholar and writer. Rather, like Derek Walcott, he has discovered, "A wide road stretches behind like a thong history / wants to strap on me" ("Sides of My Road"). If he walked back down one ancestral path he would meet African "legends. . .in ivory and iron" in "forests the Niger would redden;" with tribal warfare; if he walked down the other path he would gaze on European "grey cobbled cities with cathedrals / like jewels, and hamlets. . .soaked red" with "disputes." Cecil Gray laments, "Hate crosses and recrosses my road. . .draw[s] straight lines to keep. . .the races apart, / their snipers aim shots at freaks like me." In order to escape the crossfire, the poet must "push forward," "full of strange wine" "dipped / from the world's brimming cisterns of joys and sorrows" ("Songs Becky Taught Us").

It is hard to do justice to one complex book of poetry in a short review, much less adequately explore two such resonant books as *Lilian's Songs* and *The Long Gap*. There are at least as many interesting differences as likenesses between Cecil Gray and Anthony Kellman's latest collections. Gray's volume is nearly twice as long as Kellman's, which may be explained by the fact that Kellman is teaching English and creative writing full-time at Augusta State University in Georgia while Cecil Gray has retired from his post as Director of the In-Service Diploma in Education Programme at the University of the West Indies. He only began writing verse seriously after his retirement in 1983. Before that, he was too busy "producing 25 textbooks for use in West Indian schools" to concentrate on poetry.

This reviewer is grateful he decided to do just that and that Kellman finds the time as well. I can honestly say these two books are the work of two gifted poets. As Gray writes, "I am always rereading / the words of the master, / tongue-strumming the metres / . . .re-startled by metaphors / that peel open places we know and show us what / they are made of."

Patricia Harkins-Pierre
St. Thomas, USVI

Jennie N. Wheatley, *Pass It On! A Treasury of Virgin Islands Tales.* St. Martin: House of Nehesi Publishers. 1996. 91 pages. pb.

Pass It On! is a miscellany of "stories"—vignettes of experience told with a sense of fun and the urgency of excitement, aimed at the junior high school level. Fact and legend seamlessly intertwine in a delightful children's collection set in Tortola, British Virgin Islands. Eleven Boysie incidents are in two parts, the first centering on his growing up, the second on his escapades into the cultural history of the village. The pivot of the collection is the somewhat idyllic household of the country village: Grandpa in rocking chair biting his pipe, grandson on mat soaking up family history, and Grandma flitting like a bird between them. The somewhat precocious Boysie connects this center to the circumference of village life. It is a world of tragedy and comedy, of inter-island trade and treasure hunting, a world in which the pulse of the oral tradition beats strong. Still it is not a parochial world, for Boysie's escapades are in tune with the excursions of many a Caribbean youngster growing up in the second quarter of the century. Our hero prefers the beach to Sunday school, gets in trouble with his school principal, and must submit to the fingers of the village massager, then bear the consequences of early initiation into "mannish" pursuits.

Caribbean literature, though increasingly less so, is still at the periphery of many a Caribbean classroom. However, *Pass It On!* is intended as supplementary reading material for the author's own junior high school students.

Wheatley plants her episodes foursquare in the landscape and seascape of the Virgins. The pieces describe the links between Tortola and St. Thomas, the Virgin Islands and Santo Domingo, links of legal trade and brazen inter-island smuggling. They show movement not only of goods but also of people and are a faithful record of folk history preserved for future generations. The author freezes these snapshots of history in time and preserves them for posterity. The face of the islands today reflects features of this past.

The level is appropriate for silent reading in the classroom or children reading at home in the quiet hour. Stories are about four to five pages in length on the average. Teachers will find in these pages material for many a lesson in social studies. "Boysie in School" is a wonderfully crafted play in two scenes, quite suitable for performance. In "Eclipse Wedding," the most elaborate piece in the collection, the writer gives her readers the flavor of the traditional wedding. The story is woven into the historical event of an actual eclipse that occurred in the islands in 1897 so that Leah's wedding and the eclipse become one.

One of Wheatley's stated objectives is to "explore and expose the richly dynamic varieties in language patterns in Caribbean literatures." The author interweaves more formal language with the informal dialect, and readers hear a more relaxed voice, a more natural voice. On occasions, there is the inclination towards historical reportage.

Along with the "historical" documentation giving authenticity to many stories, the author provides Boysie's family tree and even a map of the British Virgin Islands. All of us can enjoy Boysie's growing up, for the boys are boys everywhere, and the islands in many ways are more similar than different.

Trevor Parris
St. Thomas, USVI

Rabindranath Maharaj, *The Interloper*. Fredericton, New Brunswick: Goose Lane Editions. 1995. 181 pages. pb. $14.95.

Most of the stories in this collection shift between the author's native Trinidad, here called Caura, and Canada, where he now lives and teaches. The book takes its title from a story about a new Canadian immigrant who is cautioned by an already established cousin, "Try and don't interlope in these people territory too much." Like *The Gra* and *Bitches on All Sides* it belongs to the type of migration literature established early on by Lamming and Selvon in which

West Indians of more wit than education interact among themselves in a new and unaccommodating environment. In this well-defined genre, situational humor is reinforced by clever use of dialect and by low-key satire of the host society.

Maharaj handles this genre effectively in the stories just mentioned, but what is most striking about his work is his use of the West Indian experience to explore migration in historical, psychological, and even philosophic terms. The narrator of "The Other," son of West Indian descendants of East Indian laborers, migrated to Canada with his parents while still a young child. So what is he? "Hyphenated Canadian, Native Indian, South Asian, or Indo-Caribbean?" Migration, far from being a simple shift of locale, is perceived as a series of concentric orbits formed by the gravitational pull of spheres in constant motion. Pakistani and East Indian immigrants in Canada, descendants of the two great migrations from the Indian subcontinent, preserve their historic enmity, and neither group is willing to relate to distant cousins from the West Indies. Maharaj's migrants carry within them the histories of past migrations, which operate like genetic inheritances.

The need or desire to return to one's roots, real or imagined, is strong in these stories. Angus, the narrator of "Never Forget," is a descendant of Red-legs, highlanders from Scotland who had been captured by Cromwell and settled in Barbados. Angus's great-grandfather had bought land in Caura, where he prospered; but as he grew into senility he began singing old Scottish songs and expressing a wish to "return" to Scotland. And Angus's father still dreams of "returning" to Barbados. "It *is* possible to exist in one place and live elsewhere. . .[E]very departure forces you nearer to your point of origin." Migration is fraught with ambiguity; Janus-like, the migrant must look before and behind. Indeed, the only protagonist who consciously severs his ties to Caura, the subject of "Kevin's Log," ends tragically, "a stranger caught between two worlds, with nowhere to go."

Maharaj underscores the migrant's separateness by references to the interloper, the other, the stranger. And the use of these terms, once established, enables him to extend and universalize the concept of migration. In "The Assault of Strangers" Rose, postmistress of a small university town in Canada, feels more and more isolated as population shifts alienate the town's original inhabitants: "I blame the strangers for changing us all." But populations shift not only from place to place but also through time. As Rose, a spinster approaching 50, becomes the target of adolescents taunting her with their crude sexuality, she is forced to recognize herself as "this crazy old stranger." And the parents in "Photographs" become aware that their daughter is "growing apart from them, gradually becoming some stranger." Standing still, one may be left a stranger by the world's migrations.

A short review cannot do justice to the depth and complexity of the stories in *The Interloper*. Although not the most memorable book on West Indian migration, it breaks new ground in its self-conscious expansion of a theme basic to modern experience worldwide. The portrayal of West Indians of different ethnic backgrounds is convincing, and in most of the stories plots and themes are well integrated.

The limitations of the work are characteristic of fiction by young writers. The most obvious limitation is the author's reliance on personal experience for his material. Personal experience can, of course, be the stuff of excellent writing as it is in "Snowfall," a poignant, lyrical response to news of a sister's cancer. The problem is that while most of the stories are set in Canada, the characters are almost all West Indian; the author makes no real use of the possibilities of dramatic interaction between West Indians and Canadians. This may reflect the isolation of the West Indian community in Canada, but artistically it means lost opportunity.

A second flaw is the occasional sacrifice of story to thesis. This is most obvious in "Nothing Personal," in which four characters, each representing a different position, debate the appropriate West Indian response to Canadian violence.

Finally, the author's love of language sometimes gets the better of his literary judgment. The intellectual and linguistic humor of "Being an Account of the Upward Mobility of B. S. Roget" seems more pretentious than funny, and the attempts at putting on style in "Changes" sound forced. But these are small quibbles about a generally well-written and interesting book.

Eugene V. Mohr
San Juan, Puerto Rico

Joan A. Medlicott, *Belonging: A Caribbean Love Story*. Alexander, North Carolina: WorldComm. 1996. 222 pages. pb. $13.95.

If one were to examine the literature of the United States Virgin Islands written over the last fifty years, one would find poetry collections, historical accounts, political biographies, folktales and jumbi stories, some short stories, and a growing number of novels. Among the newer offerings of the latter genre is *Belonging: A Caribbean Love Story* by St. Thomian Joan A. Medlicott. In this tale of young love, Medlicott has crafted a story replete with obeah, hurricanes, violent seas, generations-old secrets that finally come to light, death-bed confessions of interracial copulation, intrigue, discovery—and the need for belonging.

Set in St. Thomas, United States Virgin Islands in the 1950s, *Belonging* is a story of discovery. It is the story of Peter Hamlin, the young architect who comes from the mainland in search of his roots, of which he only recently learned from his mother on her deathbed. However, he discovers more than he had bargained for, because in his quest, he unearths some truths about his mother which creates a dilemma for him. This story is also the story of Iris Borinkov, a native of St. Thomas, who although she has known her family and grown up with much knowledge of her heritage, discovers some of the dark secrets of her family as well. These two characters' love is the catalyst for the discovery, and it is also the element which makes them able to handle the knowledge which they acquire and make the choice they deem to be correct.

Nonetheless, this story goes beyond young love, for it explores the intricacies of the Borinkov family, whose contributions to the political and economic life of the islands are legendary. It also examines the greed, hypocrisy, and racial prejudice which are part and parcel of the elite segment of the society. As the name suggests, the story is about belonging or one man's desire to belong. However, it addresses the false sense of security afforded those who think they belong to a particular family, a particular segment of society, and whose sense of belonging can be shattered by the truth.

In her handling of the concepts of secrets and discovery, Medlicott is part of a feminist tradition which speaks to women breaking the silences which have kept them imprisoned for generations. The women of this novel have been the keepers of the secrets and are the unearthers of the truth. Medlicott's use of water—the raging sea which almost takes Iris' life, the sea which takes Peter and Iris to St. John where another part of his heritage is revealed, and the hurricane, which wreaks destruction on the island—is reminiscent of authors such as Paule Marshall who utilizes the sea as an element of cleansing and purgation. In Medlicott's work, the devastation of the hurricane becomes the ash heap from which new, healthier relationships emerge once the truth is told. It provides the avenue for the record to be set straight and for forgiveness to be asked and granted.

However, as Penny Aylor-Freeman writes in the "Foreword" to the novel, "[I]t is also about the time, the way of life, the way of thinking that existed in the islands when author, Joan A. Medlicott, was growing up in St. Thomas." For that reason then it treats quite candidly the racial attitudes of both blacks and whites and clearly articulates the lengths to which some whites would go to conceal the stain of a heritage which includes being dabbed with the "tar brush." Significantly, it also addresses intra-racial prejudice. A statement by Rachel Borinkov, Iris' grandmother, as she shares with Peter her knowledge of life in the islands, captures one aspect of that prejudice. She says:

This island, this paradise you see here is venomous with racial bias. Yes, colored men and women on our island are well educated, own land and stores, run the government, yet even here where it appears so integrated, it is not we few whites, but they themselves that foster the racial attitudes that would bring confusion and pain to your children.

Nevertheless, the attitudes of whites toward blacks inherent in this former Danish colony are also evident in the relationship between Rachel Borinkov and her servants and also in the way she feels about Ivy Tolman, an obeah woman.

Medlicott captures and portrays a number of vital aspects of Virgin Islands life as she masterfully keeps her reader rapt in a fascinating story of attitudes, secrets, discovery, and the like. These morsels she ably wraps in the incredible beauty of St. Thomas, providing a package which draws the reader into a world to which, for that moment, he/she also "belongs."

Ruby Simmonds
St. Thomas, USVI

David and Phillis Gershator, *Palampam Day*. Illustrated by Enrique O. Sanchez. New York: Marshall Cavendish. 1997. 32 pages (ages 5-8). hc. $15.95.

Can you imagine a day when everything you encounter begins to talk to you? *Palampam Day* is the story of "the day all things find their voice and say whatever they feel like saying, in any language under the Caribbean sun." Turo, the young boy in the story, has a terrible day unable to eat or drink without having the food talk to him, and he just cannot bring himself to eat something that is *talking*. Then, he finds out that even his dog and cat are talking. Finally, a fisherman sends him to Papa Tata Wanga, the man in the village who "is very knowledgeable," to find out what is going on. It is Papa Tata Wanga who tells him that all the "roogoodoo" will end the next day when the full moon is no longer blue. To assist Turo, Papa Tata Wanga gives him the magic words and actions to help the night come quickly. "Go right home. Turn left. Turn right. Turn all around and say 'good night' . . .and sing: The moon is blue. / Paladee, Paladoo. / Fungee, fish, and kallaloo." Things return to normal in the morning and Turo "later ate his fill of coconut, sweet potato, banana, fish, and mango," and with this food, his stomach stops talking.

The illustrations by Santo Domingo native Enrique Sanchez are vibrant and colorful. They put life into the talking food and animals through the wide eyes and open mouths of coconuts, mangos, fish, and bananas. These characters speak the different languages that are found in the Caribbean, such as Papiamento, Creole, Spanish, French, Dutch, and English. An author's note on the last page gives meanings to the various words and expressions that add "flavor" to the story.

Palampam Day is an enjoyable story that children can relate to. They can identify with Turo's dilemma and laugh at the colorful characters as the noisy day progresses.

Valerie Bloom, *Fruits: A Caribbean Counting Poem*. Macmillan Caribbean, 1997. Illustrated by David Axtell. Unpaged (ages 4-6). hc. $16.95.

It is the measure of a good picture book that the words and illustrations together develop the book to be more than each taken separately. By placing this poem in a well-illustrated picture book, its message springs to life. The illustrations by David Axtell help to develop the plot and add a layer of meaning not possible with words alone.

This poem-picture book goes beyond simply counting objects and shares a day in the life of a greedy young girl. *Fruits* teaches children a life lesson about greed and does it without being didactic. It is obvious from the text and illustrations that the young girl has been told not to eat the fruit that is around the house. In the illustrations, she hides from adults and quiets her younger sister who is watching with great interest. In the end, she suffers the aftereffects of her disobedience and gets a stomachache after counting and eating so many fruits. She says, "Mek me lie down on me bed, quick. / Lawd, ah feeling really sick."

Along with the developed story line and the impressionistic illustrations, the language of the poetry leads the reader into the Caribbean setting: "One guinep up in the tree / Hanging down there tempting me. / It don mek' no sense to pick it, / One guinep can't feed a cricket." A short glossary helps young readers understand the localized names of fruits and specialized words. By the second page, however, we realize that the Caribbean language is most important to the development of Bloom's poetry in this outstanding picture book.

Sarah F. Mahurt
St. Croix, USVI

Jean 'Binta' Breeze, *On the Edge of an Island*. Newcastle-upon-Tyne, England: Bloodaxe Books Ltd. / Chester Springs, Pennsylvania: Dufour Editions, Inc. 1997. 96 pages. pb. $17.95.

Perhaps best known for her vital performances and popular recordings, Jean 'Binta' Breeze, in the tradition of storyteller Louise Bennett and dub-poet Linton Kwesi Johnson, is an artist of spectacular versatility and resonance.

She describes her latest work, *On the Edge of an Island*, as "stories of the present, not the past from somewhere behind God's back." Indeed, this collection of largely narrative poetry and prose possesses an immediate presence, an authentic sense of the people, time and place of which Sister Breeze writes.

Like the daughter-mother in *Return* who "had travelled all over the world performing, but still kept coming back, still couldn't cut the navel string that held her to the soil," the writer/performer cannot, nor wishes to be separated from the "rootsical" nuances of home—the land, the water, the songs, the proverbs, the words, the "riddym."

Yet, "dis yah likkle island" is fraught with poverty, injustice, disillusionment, madness, death:

    nervous spirit
    trapped
    between mountain and sea.

Ironically, what prevails is a sacred spirit of defiance, nurtured by the blood and sweat, the vision and promise of the ancestors, as is related for instance, in *Grandfather's Dream*. That same spirit sustains the generation of maroon children who have come to know that "rocky road / nuh frighten duppy. . .dark night / nuh badda rolling calf." So they press on—mothers and widows, farmers and fishermen, exiles and outcasts—journeying "in search of tings getting better," a little love, freedom, dignity and respect.

Shifting effortlessly from nation language to standard usage, Sister Breeze competently employs both scribal and oral strategies. One time she is Jonah "used by a gift of faith"; same time she is "like a warner woman in de market." Essentially, she is a performance poet and storyteller whose writing possesses that "audio/visual/kinetic integrity" which Carolyn Cooper attributes to her earlier classic *Riddym Ravings*.

In the poem "I Will Come" the artist in exile reclaims her voice and "tests it for range." And the range in *On the Edge of an Island* is astonishing. All strongly felt stories, they move from the quietly moving and spiritually profound to the wickedly humorous. From social commentary to sermon, kitchen talk to joke, all is "serious business." The breadth and complexity demonstrated, for example, by the handling of the cricket metaphor in the poem "Song for Lara" reveals artistry refusing to limit itself when a continent of "open space" is what is required to

> bus out a heaven gate today
> wid a certain majesty. . .
> from all dat cramping. . .
> breaking de boundary

In speculating on the future of dub-poetry, Linton Kwesi Johnson predicted that "the wheat will sort itself from the tares. The good ones will hopefully progress and go on writing different kinds of poetry and deepening their knowledge and their experience of poetry. . ." *On the Edge of an Island* confirms Jean 'Binta' Breeze as one of the "good ones." Nuf rispek due!

Patricia Turnbull
Tortola, British Virgin Islands

Cristina García, *The Aguero Sisters*. New York: Alfred A. Knopf. 1997. 300 pages. hc. $24.00.

It is only in the confusion or absence of any fixed aesthetic criteria that appreciation of literature becomes so difficult. In face of the issues regarding questions of mass and popular culture, on one hand, and considering the attention that women writers and minorities are receiving in the market place on the other, it is not surprising to find how relatively easy some "writers" become famous or fashionable. Or from a different angle, the book market accommodates all needs and preferences in existence, in a never-ending process of recycling. I wonder who Cristina García's readers are, where do they situate themselves, and to what referents do they respond. Because among other things, I consider *The Aguero Sisters* a potential soap opera script, or one of those box office hits from the worst of Hollywood although the sophisticated hard cover format of an edition that I could not stand to read a second time, might produce the delusion of quality.

The Aguero Sisters joins other publications by women from the minorities in the United States that sell well, and which correspond to a Cuban proverb that I will translate in its literal sense: "a lot of noise and very few nuts." What is surprising is how some Women's Studies Departments and Women's Associations promote these "writers," validating and conforming to a deterministic biological configuration or stimulating women to write because of their essentialist and priviledged knowledge, in this case what they consider to be women's experience from certain countries.

However, the novel itself, in García's case, reiterates line after line, all the well-known and even less well-known clichés about Cubans in Cuba, about Cubans in Miami, and about Latin Americans in general, including the Spanish, a result of her pretension of situating the narration in different localities, Cuba, New York, Madrid, and Spain, a recurring element of some postmodern fiction and film. I say pretension, since, after all, the characters' perspective forecloses relations of time or space in a quasi-archetypical distortion of basically everything they try to represent. Actually their conception or construction makes everything possible, just like special effects in commercial movies, regardless of consistency, verisimilitude, or the enigmatic plot García tried to convey, simulating the Aristotelian demands, that I do not make.

The Aguero Sisters' exotic and erotic stereotypes, parade of stock figures, exaggerations in the style of special effects—all constitute a mosaic of images already known either from already well-known Latin American novels, or from the news and comments shared by Cuban people and distorted by García to the point of caricature. I refer both to the plot and to the stereotypical characters presented.

The narration begins with the shooting. In 1948, their father shot their mother, covered it all, "and began to tell his lies." Lies and history, dates, events, a manuscript rescued by Constancia à la James Bond, inconsistencies—in this fictional untruth, everything is possible. But for whom? The rest of the novel is organized around the chapters referring to Reina, the goddess, a superwoman, who climbs telephone poles during the days and coconut trees at night to "mingle its milk with a little rum," insatiable for love-making, who has begun to suffer insomnia and whose lover can't "exhaust her sufficiently into slumber."

I wish I had the time and the space to show the laughable lines that this pseudo-novel contains, along with the characters' dependence on distorted views of faiths and rites.

From Cuba, the narration jumps to New York where Constancia, who is rich and married, sells cosmetics at a store where her sales "break all company records," although she "doesn't need to sell cosmetics," because her husband owns a tobacco store on Sixth Ave. Then the father's diary begins to interrupt the third-person description of the sisters' lives, in a more direct and personal style, but of course full of the lies he tells himself, beginning with his dedication to the protection of the Cuban flora and fauna when in "reality" he is just another predator justifying his crimes, including the shooting of Blanca. These parts from the father's perspective reappear throughout the narration although at the very end the trick is revealed, and Constancia, who has gone to Cuba to search for these memoirs, has found them and can't stop till she finishes reading them.

Finally, there is another first-person perspective, that of Dulce Fuerte (which means strong candy or desert), Reina's daughter, who begins her account with the following commonplace expression: "Sex is the only thing they can't ration in Havana. It's the next-best currency after dollars, and much more democratic, if you ask me."

Perhaps I should have begun here, by tracing a seamless line from that simplification to this "fucking safari" in the words of Dulce Fuerte, which leaves the reader surfeit and especially bored. Déjà vu from TV? In the kingdom of consumerism this novel should be rated, like movies, half a star and condemned to oblivion, but I do not wish to do that.

María Elena Alonso
San Juan, Puerto Rico

Roger Norman Buckley, *Congo Jack*. Mt. Kisco, New York: Pinto Press. 1997. 310 pages. hc. $22.95.

Congo Jack is the first fictional work of Roger Norman Buckley, a history professor at the University of Connecticut at Storrs. The book's dust jacket tells us that he has a doctorate from McGill University in British Empire history and is the author of several histories of Africans serving in European colonial armies in the eighteenth and nineteenth centuries.

Buckley's book is based on an actual event. In 1798, Congo Jack, an African slave, was recruited on the island of Dominica into the British Eighth West Indian Regiment, one of twelve regiments of African slaves created by the British government to compensate for the appalling loss of European troops from disease.

Three years after his recruitment, Congo Jack's regiment distinguished itself in a battle against the French on the island of St. Martin, and Congo Jack became duly proud of his participation and what he perceived to be his status above other laboring Africans by being one of Britain's warriors. His world came to an end, however, on April 9, 1802 when his regiment mutinied. Buckley's work is the story of Congo Jack's ensuing court martial and his coming to a resolution of his role as a black man in a European colonial army.

Buckley has considerable descriptive skills which he amply exhibits when picturing the lush landscape of Dominica and the "pellucid, blue-green water" that surrounds it. Although born in New York, perhaps because of his West Indian parents, he has a good ear for Caribbean speech. He is at his best, however, when using his talent as an historian to describe the battle scenes on St. Martin and the action during the mutiny. His discipline as an historian and his broad knowledge of African life at times produce a tendency to provide an over-abundance of detail, such as Congo Jack's tedious description of the facial tribal markings of the Hausas, the Pabirs, the Oyo nation, the Higis, the Borgawas, the Abewas, the Kajes, and the Fulanis.

My biggest disappointment with *Congo Jack* is that as a narrative it gives us the barebones of an historical happening without providing its readers with the elements we customarily expect from a novel. Buckley seems more intent on giving us historical description than developing a substantial plot. As a result *Congo Jack* lacks suspense. The white officers conduct the court martial as we would expect. Congo Jack and his alleged co-conspirators react as we would expect. The conclusion offers no surprises, and throughout the book there is a lack of dramatic tension between the characters resulting, in part, from our being told too often what has happened instead of being shown what is happening. Even Jack's love interest with the sensuous field slave, Jubba Lily, seems to have no role in advancing the plot; and their relationship lacks dramatic tension, largely because the two characters rarely speak directly to each other. Instead their interactions are usually presented in a stylized narrative form—printed on the page like parts in a play—that do not conform to the sounds of their natural voices. I found the switch from narration in standard English (and sometimes lofty, poetic prose) to elemental African slave dialect a jarring and distracting stylistic device.

The court martial is interrupted by "Jack's Story," a narrative of his life in Africa, his enslavement there, his sale to a ship captain, and his transportation to Dominica. The description of Jack's life in his village in Africa provides an interesting read, but I wish that Buckley had avoided any attempt at a detailed description of the Middle Passage. After countless historical accounts and works of fiction, drawings of slaves chained in the hold of ships, or motion pictures like *Amistad*—is it novelistically possible to enhance what we already know about the African holocaust? Because of Buckley's narrative style and plot deficiencies, I found *Congo Jack* hard to hold interest, but I think that it is a book that is better heard than read. *Congo Jack* is the kind of book that justifies the invention of audio books.

Roland B. Scott
Sandia Park, New Mexico

Kwame Dawes, *Shook Foil: A Collection of Reggae Poems*. Leeds, England: Peepal Tree Press. 1997. 75 pages. pb. £6.99

Few poets capture the mood of a generation. In *Shook Foil*, Kwame Dawes, "drawing on inspiration as diverse as Derek Walcott, T. S. Eliot and Lorna Goodison," attempts to define reggae and the major personality behind the success of the music, Bob Marley. That Dawes chose Marley as the primary subject to explore the dimensions of reggae is no coincidence, for it was Marley who taught my generation how to be Jamaican and Pan-African (as if the two terms were mutually exclusive), how to honor ourselves and others, and finally how to love.

Shook Foil opens with epigrams from G. M. Hopkins' "God's Grandeur" and Bob Marley's "Trench Town Rock," a signal that Dawes has set himself the task of reconciling the world of St. Augustine (best exemplified by Hopkins) who dubbed the genitals *pudenda* from the Latin *pudere* "to be ashamed" and Marley: "I'll push the wood / I'll blaze your fire / Said I'll satisfy your heart's desire," ("Stir It Up") for he recognizes the conflict in Jamaican culture which was similar to the dilemma of many church-going Christians in New Orleans at the turn of the century—how to be a good Christian and enjoy the honest-to-goodness funk of jazz bubbling up from Bourbon Street.

This conflict between spirituality and sexuality is fully dramatized in "Blessed are They Whose Ways are Blameless," "Some Tentative Definitions

VII," and especially in "How Can a Young Man Keep His Way Pure?" where the speaker laments: "I am too young now for middle ground / though I know I will die forever / if brought down when my mind is swamped / with the precepts of my libido. / I seek out purer paths." Excluded from Marley's vision of oneness in Rastafarianism, many of the personae in the poems fear the power of the music: "Everything get like water now / the way steady hands / curve round a sweat-smooth waistline, / guiding the rub, the dub, so ready" ("Some Tentative Definitions I"). Yet this was at the heart of Marley's subversive music, for he sought to unify mind and body—a bass line to move the body and lyrics to feed the mind—to make what he called "a godly thing" in his CD "Talking Blues". The speakers ache from the psychic war that plagues Caribbean culture—a result of the twin legacies from religions of the book that fear the body and its passions and religions of the mindful body that fear the atrophy of human passion.

Dawes finds a reconciliation (and rightly so) in "Rita." In this poem, Rita Marley emerges as an archetypal third world woman: higgler, rude girl, slave mother, and black sister. As a matriarch and seductress, "Naughty as hell, talking about feeling damned high," he praises her fortitude and strength:

You have
walked the walk well. The pattern is an old one.
I know it now. It's your time now, daughter.
Ride on, natty dread, ride on my sister, ride on.

By the end of the poem, he has created a portrait of a complete woman who is able to combine worldly and spiritual wisdom while still "rolling [her] backside like a teenager."

"Rita" also contains hints of violence that existed on the fringes of reggae and which moved to the center of the dance hall craze. Behind the sentiments of "One love, one heart, / Let's get together an feel all right" ("One Love / People Get Ready") there lurked a sinister side to reggae: "I can tell / those eyes have nodded to home spun executions" ("Meeting"). In "Some Tentative Definitions XIII" the "knife blade's edge" and the concomitant violence of the dance hall are subsumed into "the familiar sound of the guitar / *chekeh, chekeh, chekeh*."

In the midst of these meditations on death, disease, and dub, there are gems such as "Prayer for my Son": "My last prayer spoken / I wait for the bright miracle to flame / in the twilight of peace" which is simply the prayer of every father who has watched over the bed of a sick child.

Throughout the collection, Dawes captures the many dimensions of reggae from the psalmic to the prophetic that are yet to be explored by other writers and musicians. Reggae remains unparalleled in its ability to absorb other influences and remain true to itself and to capture beauty, pain, and pleasure in a one-drop *riddim*. Its syncopation suggests a break, a gap—somewhere to fall with the faith that you will be caught—and this is what gives reggae its redemptive value. To really enjoy the music, you must believe. The same could be said of *Shook Foil*.

Geoffrey Philp
Miami, Florida

Zoila Ellis, *On Lizards, Heroes and Passion: Seven Belizean Short Stories by Zoila Ellis*. Belize: Cubola Productions. 1997. 130 pages. pb.

Zoila Ellis dramatizes the Belizean search for spiritual and economic redemption with vivid realism. She accurately portrays the struggle for survival and self-knowledge shared by all Third World nations as her characters yearn for a more prosperous lifestyle, yet cling to their native culture.

The conflict of European-style Christianity with instinct is successfully conveyed in the first two stories. "The Teacher" is a disenchanted priest, assigned to a rural school after his breakdown on the altar. Surrounded by the honesty of country life, the teacher admits to the social forces which impelled him into the priesthood: "It was the fifties. A native priest had seemed an excellent idea. He had been an excellent idea—loyal, black, grateful." Ellis's distant narrative style suggests Teacher's discomfort with the structure of formal religion when he compares it to the heartfelt, authentic spirituality of rural Belize.

In "My Uncle Ben," the impending death of Candida's alcoholic uncle is as bewildering as the dualism of her religious background. Her mother brings her to pray at the native *dugu*, or drumming ceremony, while her father contacts a priest who threatened to "have us all excommunicated for devil worship." Ellis's narrative evokes childlike ingenuousness as Candida muses: "Uncle Ben could say prayers much better than Father Delaware because he did not make you want to go to sleep."

In stories of women burdened with economic struggle, Ellis relies more on the narration of detail than on an illuminating view of the women's interior selves. In "The Subway Takes Me Home," Carla's daily routine as an urban housekeeper is thoroughly described. Less clear are the inner conflicts of a woman who has left her family behind and the origins of her many racial and cultural biases: "nasty, corn tortilla and beans, Spanish," "rich Jews with more money than sense," "Kerubs are all alike," "Racist white so-and-so." Ellis is more prosaic than passionate with such language as "She let her anger cool and then changed into her uniform."

"White Christmas and Pink Jungle" evokes the joyous energy of a small town immersed in holiday preparations for "black cake an' ham an' turkey," but eighteen-year old Julia doesn't fully emerge as a character. Raising her baby alone after her boyfriend abandoned them, Julia agonizes in secret about her second pregnancy. Her wood-barracks home and sales clerk job represent grim economic realities lamented by Julia's co-worker: "We poor people go 'cross the border for cheap toys for we pikni." Still, Julia's anguish is not vividly conveyed by the narrative as she contemplates spending her hidden savings on an abortion: "Midday she came home for dinner, she looked at it and tried to decide what she should do."

In "A Hero's Welcome," Ellis succeeds in portraying the irony of an economically and morally depressed Belizean village, blind to its own strength and potential. A village "paralysed in an abyss of despair and disunity" pins its hopes on one of its favored sons when 'Mas Tom goes off, apparently to fight in a British war. Here, impersonal narrative style fits the story's lofty intent: to recount the gradual decline of Cotton Tree Village. Tom is transformed in his absense into an icon and news of his homecoming ignites a frenzy of preparation, described by Ellis in rollicking comic detail. The townspeople rush to organize, yet all this furor leads to disappointment when Miss Hetty encounters a bed-raggled 'Mas Tom: "This was the worst. . .no decent clothes, no wife, no teeth, and worst of all, no English accent." The town settles back into despair, still yearning for a hero: "He made us pull together, unite, cooperate, achieve," they mourn; "if only 'Mas Tom had come home." Implicit in their mourning of 'Mas Tom is their mistaken belief that their source of redemption is another, more de-veloped culture. With all the raucous energy of their homecoming preparations, the villagers unwittingly prove that cooperation and unity are within themselves.

In this collection of fiction, Ellis creates characters whose spiritual strength is rooted in the same country which inhibits their economic redemption, and her protagonists are of all ages and sexes, representing the wide range of Belizean society at home and abroad. Stylistically, though, Ellis needs to better adapt her narrative to suit each story's purpose. Tales of inner struggle might benefit from more use of the expressive Belizean creole speech which Ellis handles so well in her dialogues.

Gabrielle DiLorenzo
St. Croix, USVI

Kwadwo Agymah Kamau, *Flickering Shadows*. Minneapolis: Coffee House Press. 1996. 300 pages. hc. $21.95.

Disquieted by the possibility of disclosing too much about Kwadwo Agymah Kamau's first book, *Flickering Shadows*, one proceeds cautiously with comments. Without a doubt and nonetheless, *Flickering Shadows* is one of the brightest new spangles to appear in the literary heavens. In his premiere novel, Kamau writes with richness of voice, quiet authority and from a deep dedication to his characters. And what an exciting, delightful, amazing cast he gives us.

Transported to a fictional West Indian island where daily life on the Hill, in the gap, down the gulley and in the sugar cane brakes is hard but rhythmical, steeped in age-old unwritten laws, customs and attitudes, we are told, through the spirit-narrator Cudgoe, an amazing tale. The pace never slows. *Flickering Shadows* contains scores of brief but powerful occurrences. The hurricane. Cephus and the ball of fire: "And fear is a cold hand squeezing Cephus heart and he watching the ball of light, which he knows is a hag—the obeah woman that lives up the hill by herself and who does leave her skin and travel around the village at night sometimes like this."

Blasting for bauxite in the hills. Spirit Cynthia Gittens overhearing the sneak-dog conversation between corrupt Roachford and unscrupulous Craig. Intrigue and murders of political expediency. Roachford's "cane blade" speech. Kwame and Donald in their lookout tree. Cephus in the "flickering shadows" coming to terms with his vision. And we are taken to the house of the husky-voiced obeah woman, where the boychild Kwame learns he "has the gift." The exquisite episode of Lionel and his drum. The domino game outside the new church. The grisly account of Harold's death.

This is firsthand writing that enchants us with its melodious language, enthralls us with its depictions of simple joys (when a threadbare shirt is better than no shirt at all), a reverence for life because it is better than death—writing that pulls us in until we become participants. We learn about catching standpipe water and toting it up the Hill. And the descriptive portions are as smooth and enjoyable as chocolate pudding.

Flickering Shadows emerges as a work done with deep appreciation and deeper respect for cultural history, not a line ruined by sentimentality. It is at once long-poem, mystery, romance, play, musical, a tale of sexual infidelities, political greed and corruption, religious hypocrisy, souls and visions, signs and sighs. It vibrates with sights both pleasing and terrible. The plot is not really a "plot"; it is an intertwined series of events that track like an unmarked trail to a stunning, tragic, and unpredictable climax.

In an age when the arts have taken to the gutters or run for cover, it is refreshing to hear new voices that carry on the meaning of literary artistry and tell us all is not lost. This book displays one such voice; it is landmark literature written in the Bajan griot tradition. Tradition, yes; but Kamau, a native of Barbados, does not place the feet of his artistry in anyone else's footprints, not even Clark's, Lamming's or Marshall's. *Flickering Shadows* is not only a book to buy. It is a book to buy and give. Buy and keep. And pass on down. The drums are working.

June Owens
Zephyrhills, Florida

Bruce King (ed), *New National and Post-Colonial Literatures: An Introduction.* New York: Oxford University Press. 1996. 311 pages. hc.

New National and Post-Colonial Literatures is an auspicious collaboration between a talented editor and internationally known experts on the subject. Reading this book is like attending a first-rate literature conference—and you don't have to leave home.

The contributors include such authorities as Helen Tiffin and Gareth Griffiths, authors of *The Empire Writes Back* and co-editors of the *Post-Colonial Studies Reader*; J. Michael Dash, author of books on Francophone Caribbean literature; and Victor Ramraj, the editor of *ARIEL, A Review of International English Literature.* Clearly these critics were judiciously selected to represent various international perspectives on post-colonial literatures.

As King writes in his preface, the collection's focus is on the relationship between literature and language, creolity, colonialism, nationalism, cultural pluralism and marginalized groups within a nation. Each essay offers provocative insights and, what's more, the essays are readable, a necessary attribute if the book is indeed to be an introduction, as the subtitle proclaims.

While one wishes the Caribbean had more emphasis here since King himself has published widely on Caribbean literature, particularly on Naipaul and Walcott, and only Michael Dash represents the region as far as scholars go, this is a rich compendium of excellent work, highly recommended.

Robert D. Hamner, *Epic of the Dispossessed: Derek Walcott's Omeros*. Columbia, Missouri: University of Missouri Press. 1997. 187 pages. pb.

To my knowledge, this is the first and only full-length study of Derek Walcott's extraordinary epic poem, *Omeros*, which was published in 1992.

Robert Hamner, an English professor at Hardin-Simmons University who has written extensively on Caribbean literature, places *Omeros* squarely in the tradition of other great epic masterpieces, including *Beowulf*, *The Divine Comedy*, *Paradise Lost*, the *Iliad*, the *Odyssey*, and the *Aeneid*, and more modern incarnations such as *Leaves of Grass* and the *Cantos*. He argues that *Omeros* similarly represents its own age, and then goes on to devote chapters to the important elements in the poem, such as Philoctete's wound (a wound at the shin that does not heal), and the role of Helen, a symbol of St. Lucia, the island of Walcott's birth.

It is clear we are in the company of an expert, guiding us through this multi-faceted and complicated masterpiece. This is an impressive, valuable piece of scholarship, made more so by the extensive bibliography and detailed index.

Myriam J. A. Chancy, *Framing Silence: Revolutionary Novels by Haitian Women*. New Brunswick, NJ: Rutgers University Press. 1997. 200 pages. pb.

Here is another welcome literary critique, this one on fiction by women of Haiti, the first full-length study in English on the topic. But it is a collection with an agenda, as the author candidly explains: "I have purposely brought together novels whose authors contest the regimented view of Haitian history that has denied female existence. . ." and her analysis is a revisionist view of Haitian culture to redress the current trend of postcolonial criticism, which she feels "by and large, stifles any claims to the presence of feminism in the Third World."

Selective in her choice of authors, Chancy admits to rejecting certain important writers because their heroines, for example, "depict Haitian women primarily as martyrs." While Chancy's emphasis is admittedly focused on books that provide "empowering images" of Haitian women, her context remains the larger cultural and literary picture.

Her choices include Anne-Christine de'Adesky, Ghislaine Charlier, Marie Chauvet, Jan J. Dominique, Nadine Magloire and Edwidge Danticat (who published in *The Caribbean Writer* for many years). Chancy's introduction, which sets the stage by dramatically depicting a fictional woman's death and then provides an overview of the literary canon of Haitian women, is indicative of the compelling, skillful writing style.

The author is a descendant of Toussaint L'Ouverture; she was born in Haiti and brought up in Canada. Today she is a professor at Vanderbilt University in Tennessee.

Erika J. Waters
St. Croix, USVI

Patrick Chamoiseau, *Texaco*. Tr. Rose-Myriam Réjouis and Val Vinokurov. New York: Pantheon Books. 1997. 401 pages. hc. $27.00.

If one is fortunate enough to afford a Caribbean cruise to the Lesser Antilles, part of the tour will most likely include a one-day port of call in Fort-de-France, Martinique. As the ship slowly arrives to dock, the tourists will be mesmerized by the hills, dotted with small concrete houses to their left but oblivious to the history of the Texaco Quarter, which is the focal point of Patrick Chamoiseau's 1992 Prix Goncourt novel of the same name.

Texaco is a richly textured novel crammed with historical references spanning over one hundred years from slavery to emancipation to colonialism to *régionalisme*. Chamoiseau weaves within the narrative French and Creole words and quotes about Montaigne, Baudelaire, Claudel, and Césaire. The 1997 English translation by Rose-Myriam Réjouis and Val Vinokurov moves along haltingly as the reader learns how an urban planner, who represents Christ of a second coming and the City, was stoned when he visited the Texaco Quarter. Unexpectantly, the anonymous urban planner receives a helping hand from the Texaco spokesperson, Marie-Sophie Laborieux. Once Marie-Sophie names him *"Oiseau de Cham,"* he is privileged to share her memories when she recites the story of her grandparents and her father Esternome who saved the life of his béké owner from an attack by a *négre marron*, and was given the freedom of being a *négre savanne*.

Esternome joined a white carpenter called Théodorus Sweetmeat from whom he learned the trade and traveled around the island with other freed artisans. After an attack by *négres marrons*, Esternome moved to the northern city of Saint-Pierre where he engaged in an affair with the hot-pepper Osélia and set up house with the political slave woman Ninon. Unfortunately, the couple's happiness was to be destroyed along with thirty thousand others when the Mont Pelée volcano erupted in 1902, reducing the once vibrant Saint-Pierre to a pile of ashes. Heartbroken, Esternome migrated south to Fort-de-France where he gradually got involved with the blind woman, Idoménée, and their union brought forth a daughter Marie-Sophie.

After Esternome and Idoménée's deaths, an oil company purchased a site near the oil reservoirs that would multiply into shacks without roads, schools, electricity, water, and sanitation. Out of this squalor and battle over the Texaco Quarter rose the defiant matadorâ Marie-Sophie, who overcame her grief by engaging in verbal and physical battles with the béké oil company owner and the mulatto officials of Fort-de-France. Coming to her aid were the Haitian Ti-Cirique, who read Marie-Sophie's notebooks; Iréné, the shark catcher; Sonore, the *câpresse;* and Marie-Clémence, the sharp-eyed witness. Meanwhile, the

Texaco shacks were constantly being constructed, destroyed, and rebuilt. Throughout all this activity, we learn from Chamoiseau's inserts about Martinican history, politics, and racial stratification through the Age of Straw, the Age of Crate Wood, the Age of Asbestos, and the Age of Concrete.

For Marie-Sophie the word and the act of storytelling are important. After all, the old Blackman of the Doum told her: "Look for The word, my girl, look for The word." And Chamoiseau, the *marqueur de paroles* (word scratcher), recorded the words of Marie-Sophie's memories in almost four hundred pages of fiction and truth.

Brenda F. Berrian
Williamsburg, Virginia

Fred D'Aguiar, *Feeding the Ghosts*. London: Chatto and Windus. 1997. 230 pages. hc. £14.95.

Fred D'Aguiar uses the voices of the characters to narrate the story of a slave ship, *Zong*, on its beleaguered voyage from Africa to Jamaica. As the story progresses, the details of the journey unfold and the perceptions of the characters are shown through the individual narrations.

At the outset, an omnipresent narrator relates the general details of this voyage: the ship going off its course, the sickness of the slaves, the disposal of the suspected sick, the survival of one woman, and her leadership in an on-board revolt. D'Aguiar's short sentences with repetitive words make the narrative lyrical. Of the slaves' sickness he writes, "Their eyes were black and the whites brown, not muddy. . . They were lubricated eyes, like marbles dipped in oil. Eyes in pain." Despite their illness, each of the selected slaves struggles against his/her death sentence.

Mintah, a young African educated by missionaries and captured in a raid, reacts most sharply to the situation of her fellow Africans. Having nursed the ship's first mate from unconsciousness at the mission, she shrieks out his name and begs for mercy. For her efforts she is brutalized and thrown overboard by the crew. Once plunged into the icy sea water, Mintah demonstrates her determination to scale the ship's rigging. "I have wood in my hands, under my feet and against my body. Nothing can induce me to let go. . ." Indeed, images of wood permeate her entire life. As the daughter of a master woodcarver, she learned to appreciate the qualities of wood. Her brush with death does not quiet her, for after her rebirth from the sea, she leads a revolt. Caught and beaten again on the deck of the ship, she imagines the grains of wood intertwined to make a rope to save her.

After the vessel returns to Liverpool, restitution is demanded for the lost "stock," the legal term for the slaves. Insurance agents representing the investors claim the crew was negligent in their care of their cargo. Despite the crew's testimony, two books are central to the court case. With his ledger in which he kept tally marks of the dead, the captain justifies the disposal of 132 sick slaves. The diary of Mintah, produced by a simpleton, the cook's assistant, however, is the sole voice against the captain's word. The manuscript was created after Mintah had hauled her body up from the sea. For several days she hid in the ship's storeroom where she found ink and a journal. She recorded her perceptions of the events on the ship. D'Aguiar uses her words to express the Africans' perceptions of the situation.

The last chapter is narrated by the chorus, consisting of all those of the *Zong*, including even the "ghosts" of those who had been thrown overboard. They—passengers, crew, and cargo—all speak in unison about their collective need to tell the story in order to heal their wounds.

While D'Aguiar has written a novel which could have been set anytime between 1600, when the Portuguese started the slave trade, until 1807, when the British abolished this institution, there are hints that the story is set shortly after 1807. D'Aguiar places Mintah and her mother as part of an experimental plantation operated by Danish missionaries. These women are members of a group of African laborers who are paid for their work. Historically, after the abolition of the slave trade the Danes planned to convert their African settlements to plantations and believed that they could grow sugar and tobacco in Africa. They also wished to demonstrate that such an operation could be profitable with paid rather than slave labor. In fact, planters and surveyors from St. Croix were selected to implement the details; however, such plans never materialized.

D'Aguiar, raised in Guyana, has written two previous successful novels and three books of poetry. *Feeding the Ghosts* is a powerful book in a time when renewed interest in the slave trade has come to the popular media, for example, through Steven Spielberg's film *Amistad*. While D'Aguiar deals with highly charged subject matter, his prose, resembling poetry, gives the work an enduring quality.

Elizabeth Rezende
St. Croix, USVI

Zee Edgell. *The Festival of San Joaquin*. Portsmouth, New Hampshire: Heinemann. 1997. 155 pages. pb. $13.95.

Luz Marina is the heroine/narrator of this womanist novel that calls to mind the fortitude and resiliency of Simone Scharwz-Bart's Lougandour women (*The Bridge of Beyond*). Like Telumee Miracle, for example, she suffers setbacks that would shatter the resolve of the merely strong, and through her religious anchor and the engine of mother love—that she shared with her mother, and that she holds for her confiscated children—she perseveres through hardships, guilt, and the specter of poverty to reclaim herself from the prison of Salvador Joaquin's mania and the legal prison that incarcerates her for freeing herself from her former cage.

The story, set in the Mestizo community of Belize, opens with Luz Marina's release from prison, having been exonerated for the killing of Salvador, her abusive husband. She returns to her hometown to face the judgment and violence of many who refuse to forgive her for killing a member of a leading family, an act of self-defense they will not recognize. Through flashbacks and waking/sleeping dream-memories, Luz Marina attempts to reconstruct the events of her life to bring clarity to herself, find meaning in her ordeal, and free herself of the guilt that haunts her. Ultimately, her final vision of Salvador's distinctive marks in their children reveals that she has forgiven him and herself, that she has become reconciled to her fate and is prepared to store away their former love in a safe place. But, again, this comes later.

To get to peace she must traverse a path strewn with obstacles that take shape in class exclusivity, domestic violence, and greed. Luz Marina served as au pair and companion to Doña Catalina, the matriarch of one of the most respected families in Belize City. The Doña taught her to read and fueled Luz Marina's dream of a life free from poverty. This dream extended to her parents, who saw her impending marriage to Salvador, one of the Doña's sons, as "a miracle from God." Against the objections of his mother and brothers, who saw the proposed marriage as a gross error given Luz Marina's status, Salvador bolted from the Doña's influence and took Luz as his common-law wife with whom he produced three children. What began as a near-idyllic union soon deteriorated as Salvador transfered his dissatisfaction and disappointment onto Luz, imprisoning her in their home and violently beating her. It was this abuse which progressed rapidly and grew in intensity that lead to Luz Marina's liberatory stroke.

As with the title character of *Beka Lamb,* Edgell explores the connections between Luz Marina's personal struggle and the politics of the region. The same class forces that impinge on Luz threaten the forest lands. Instead of being respected for who/what they are—living, breathing entities whose well-being ensures the nation's welfare—both are considered products whose sale or elimination is of little concern to the wealthy landowners. That Luz, along with other women, joins the activist group which protests against the destruction of the forest reveals Edgell's intention to depict women taking important roles in the shaping of Belizean society.

Through Luz Marina, Zee Edgell explores the struggles of an ordinary woman who on her personal battlefield fights a war, at once local and global, against encroachment on her liberties; and her triumph becomes a victory not only for herself, but, ultimately, over a tyranny whose destructive claws tear into ecologies whose mother-instincts are to sustain us. Edgell uses deft, economical passages to document her heroine's plight ("I ache with pity, looking at the roughness of [Mama Sofía's] fingers, the protruding knuckles of her arthritic hands.)" (92); and she employs proverbs to reveal the folk wisdom of the community, the women's faith in, for example, the circularity of experience, and the women's predicament (". . .sometimes the quickest way to dry road was through the mud" (93). In addition, through flashbacks she skillfully illuminates Luz Marina's story; and through dreams she uncovers her psychological state, and, at times, foreshadows her fate. *The Festival of San Joaquin* is a very fine addition to the canon of novels from the Caribbean by women and to the literature of the region itself.

Marvin E. Williams
St. Croix, USVI

Beryl Gilroy, *Gather the Faces*. Leeds, England: Peepal Tree Press. 1996. 128 pages. pb. £5.95.
Beryl Gilroy, *Inkle and Yarico*. Leeds, England: Peepal Tree Press. 1996. 168 pages. pb. £6.95.

Like many of Beryl Gilroy's novels, *Gather the Faces*, one of her latest works, deals with journeying and the search for identity. It is also a Caribbean romance with a decided spiritual context in which a young woman, Marvella Payne, who has been reared in London, and a young man, Ansel McKay, who has been reared in Guyana, search for and find love and each other. Gilroy sketches the two young people against a background of spirituality and innocence, and creates in Ansel an atypical Caribbean man who lacks the guile, deceit, and irresponsibility of the men found so often in literature and in life.

Indeed, the reader is skeptical about Ansel; he seems too good to be true, and there is the momentary expectation of some dastardly deed such as taking the money Marvella sends him to buy furnishings for their house in Guyana and absconding with it. However, Ansel does what he is supposed to do and prepares a beautiful home filled with the appropriate furnishings and with love for his prospective bride.

Gilroy also employs the extended family as a vital element in the rearing of the young. Marvella's parents, her aunts, Julie and Mavis, her godsister Sherri, and her godmother Monica all buttress and support Marvella in her growing-up years and in her relationship with Ansel.

Several journeys occur in the novel: Marvella and all of her extended family travel from Guyana to Britain looking for the better economic opportunity; Ansel goes to London on an agricultural scholarship which affords him the chance to meet Marvella for the first time. Marvella travels to Guyana for her wedding which is celebrated with all the traditional Guyanese pomp and customs.

Gather the Faces has a happy ending and is written with Gilroy's characteristic clarity of description and fluency of language. Its optimism shimmers, its spirituality glows in the beautiful verses quoted from the Biblical *Song of Songs*, and the reader is revivified as faith in love is restored.

Inkle and Yarico is a novel based on a legend that was popular during the seventeenth and eighteenth centuries concerning a young Englishman, Thomas Inkle. Inkle, who has just become engaged to a young woman named Alice, is shipwrecked on his way to Barbados to manage the family plantation. He comes ashore on an unknown island which is inhabited by Caribs. He is found by Yarico, the daughter of the Carib chief who is himself a shipwrecked African.

In Inkle, Gilroy portrays not just a protagonist, but a metaphor for colonization and enslavement. His self-centered concern and his callousness in dealing with his Carib wife and their children mirror the attitude of the colonizer whose first obligation is to himself. Gilroy heightens the drama by telling the story in the first person male persona and accurately captures the English arrogance, superiority, and selfishness. Yarico is a likable young woman whose love for Inkle is as innocent as she is. She, however, like the rest of the Caribs, just does not understand the nature of the Englishman and how he operates. As far as Inkle is concerned, being non-European is tantamount to being non-human; and although Yarico and her people save his life and allow him to become part of theirs, he is contemptuous of them, and has no problem abandoning Yarico and forgetting the people who for many years were the only family he had.

Inkle's eventual rescue takes him to Barbados where his "natural" prejudices become evident in his treatment of the slaves he acquires and the abolitionists who are seeking freedom for the enslaved. He also mistreats his former fiancée Alice, who is now married to the doctor, who, ironically, saved Inkle's life when he contracted a severe case of syphilis. Inkle is fortunate to earn the love of several women of different social class, race, and economic circumstances, and to live a life relatively untouched by his past actions.

Although Gilroy reworks an old legend, she brings to it her own inimitable style. Her characters live and breathe as the reader is transported back to an earlier time which she meticulously describes. It is evident that Gilroy has done painstaking and accurate research to allow her to recreate Carib society and life in early Barbados. This is a thoughtful, insightful novel written with a delicacy of feeling that clearly puts the reader "in the picture."

Phyllis Briggs-Emanuel
Atlanta, Georgia

Jamaica Kincaid, *My Brother.* New York: Farrar, Straus and Giroux. 1997. 198 pages. hc. $19.00.

This disturbing book, which Jamaica Kincaid insists is *not* a memoir ("A memoir is too generous and big a word," she claimed in a recent interview with Bart Schneider), recounts the death of her brother, Devon Drew, of AIDS at the age of 33. At the outset, predictably, the book describes the young man's shocking physical deterioration. What is not predictable is that his decline, so advanced when Kincaid first sees him, is reversed so dramatically after he begins taking AZT that he goes home free of symptoms, claiming that he is no longer infected with the HIV virus. The other result of his apparent return to health is that the flat statement—"My brother died"—that begins the second half of the book is totally unexpected. Even though we know the death is inevitable, the news of it, as in real life, is jolting nevertheless.

For Kincaid the pain of Devon's death, in January 1996, is compounded by her stormy relationship with her mother, whose presence has dominated her fiction. Kincaid provides evidence that her mother is insensitive, manipulative, and cruel, supporting her claim that "my mother should have never had children." Yet Kincaid also submits for our review evidence that her mother is caring, tender, and loving (yes, the extremes are confounding), supporting her admission that "Her love for her children when they are children is spectacular, unequaled I am sure in the history of a mother's love."

On a similar note, Kincaid's appraisal of her mother country, previously explored in *A Small Place*, is often ambivalent. She describes the hospital as "terrible," with dirty rooms and no medicine. (For a severe headache, Devon is forced to borrow aspirin from an on-duty nurse.) Kincaid observes that in Antigua the same prejudices and shame that exist elsewhere mark the attitudes toward AIDS. Yet, in all fairness, she describes a counseling workshop with "ordinary people in Antigua expressing sympathy and love for one another in a time of personal tragedy and pain, not scorn or rejection or some other form of cruelty."

Although fixed in reality, this non-fictional account is stamped with the distinctive style, subjectivity, and recursiveness of Kincaid's fiction. As in her earlier book *The Autobiography of My Mother*, there is no dialog. Kincaid often reports conversations and quotes selected sentences in parentheses to emphasize the linguistic distance between the kind of English she readily understands and the kind of English her Antiguan relatives speak. For instance, on first seeing her brother she says, "He said he did not think I would come to see him ('Me hear you a come but me no tink you a come fo' true')." This unusual device forces the reader to undergo the strain of translation that Kincaid experiences. A Kincaid trademark is the sad or bitter phrase that becomes a refrain, marking the book as a whole or a passage. The repetition of the phrases "when my brother died" (throughout the book) and "when my father died" (in a two-page passage) echo the recurring plaintive declaration, "My mother died at the moment I was born" that begins and recurs throughout Xuela's recollections in *The Autobiography of My Mother*. Certain painful metaphoric images recur: red ants attack Devon as an infant just as the disease devours him as an adult; his incontinence as an infant and then as an invalid force changing his diapers; and his birth precipitates his sister's leaving Antigua to work and send money for his support just as his death prompts her return and her support.

These images, the subjective style, and the intimate subject matter all give the narrative the unnerving quality of a dream—in this case, a nightmare— as Kincaid relentlessly draws the reader into the grip of this tortured and compelling account of her memories of a family tragedy.

Roberta Q. Knowles
St. Croix, USVI

CONTRIBUTORS

Judith King

Contributors

Opal Palmer Adisa, Jamaican born, is a literary critic, poet, prose writer, and storyteller. Her published works are *It Begins with Tears*, Heinemann, 1997; *Tamarind and Mango Women*, 1992 (which won the PEN Oakland/Josephine Miles Award); *traveling women*, 1989, *Bake-Face and Other Guava Stories*, 1986 and *Pina, The Many-Eyed Fruit*, 1985. Recordings include "Fierce/Love" with Devorah Major, 1992. Her poetry, fiction and essays have been published in numerous magazines. ♦♦♦ **María Elena Alonso** is a professor of Humanities, University of Puerto Rico (Rio Piedras). She has conducted research on postmodern and post-colonial theories and Caribbean culture with special emphasis on women writers and artists. ♦♦♦ **Lilieth Lejo Bailey** was born in Jamaica but has lived in the U.S. for 18 years. She is presently an assistant professor of writing and linguistics at Georgia Southern University. ♦♦♦ **F. W. Belland** was born in Miami, Florida, served with the Marines in Vietnam, and finished his education at Florida State University. He has published two novels *(Fleshwound* and *The True Sea)* and several short stories and now lives in Nicaragua. ♦♦♦ **Brenda F. Berrian** teaches Caribbean and African literature at the University of Pittsburgh. Her bibliographies and work on African and Caribbean women writers have appeared in *Research in African Literatures*, *Sage*, and *Journal of Black Studies*. She has just finished writing the book-length manuscript *Awakening Spaces: French Caribbean Popular Music*. ♦♦♦ **Elizabeth Veronica Best** is a teacher at Harrison College (Barbados) and a part-time lecturer at University of the West Indies (Barbados). She has published her work in *Voices I*, an anthology of Barbadian Writings. ♦♦♦ **Phyllis Briggs-Emanuel** is a professor of English at Clark Atlanta University. Her specialties are British literature, Caribbean literatures, African literature, Caribbean folklore and Caribbean religion. ♦♦♦ **Susan Brown** is the author and illustrator of two books, *Frederiksted Gingerbread* and *Victorian Frederiksted*, and a former teacher in St. Croix. Her writing has been published in *BIM*, *The Caribbean Writer*, *Crescendo*, *GreenPrints*, and two anthologies. Most recently, she was a winner in a Florida poetry competition sponsored by the National League of American Pen Women. ♦♦♦ **Teresa A. Cardinez** is a novice with the Dominican Sisters of St. Catherine of Siena in Trinidad. She is a teacher by profession and an historian by academic training, a graduate of Brown University and the University of the West Indies. Her poetry was published in *New Voices*. ♦♦♦ **Peter Constantine** was born in London and raised in Austria and Greece. He has written six books of poetry and translated literature from Afrikaans, Haitian Creole, Russian, and various southern European languages. His work has appeared in *The New Yorker*, *Fiction*, *Harvard Magazine*, and *The International Quarterly*, and his translations of stories by Félix Morisseau-Leroy are being published this year. ♦♦♦ **Vincent O. Cooper** has published in the area of Caribbean linguistics, and his creative work has appeared in journals and anthologies. He teaches at the University of the Virgin Islands, St. Thomas campus. ♦♦♦ **Nicole Craig**, from Trinidad, is a graduate of the University of the West Indies, (Trinidad) and works as a copywriter for McCann Erickson, Trinidad Ltd. ♦♦♦ **Gayle V. Dancy-Benjamin** has resided in the Virgin Islands for the last 30 years. She is an English teacher at the Charlotte Amalie High School and an adjunct instructor at the University of the Virgin Islands, St. Thomas campus. ♦♦♦ **Gabrielle DiLorenzo** published a book of Honduran folktales after three years spent in Honduras with the Peace Corps. Her work has appeared in various magazines and anthologies. She has received several educational grants and awards and is currently a Spanish teacher at Country Day School in St. Croix. ♦♦♦ **Gene Emanuel** teaches English at the University of the Virgin Islands, St. Thomas campus. ♦♦♦ **M. Lisa Etre** grew up in St. Croix and now lives in St. John. She has a degree from American University and also studied at the University of New Mexico and the Insituto Allende in Mexico. She is currently an art teacher in St. Thomas. Her artwork has been featured in network television and national publications and is available in galleries in the Virgin Islands. ♦♦♦ **John M. Figueroa** has taught at the University of the West Indies, the University of Puerto Rico, in Africa, the U.S. and in England. Most recently, he was with the BBC's Open University in London. He is the author of several works of poetry and short fiction and has edited anthologies and reference works on Caribbean literature. His most recent collection of poems is *The Chase, 1941 - 1989* (Peepal Tree Press, 1991). ♦♦♦ **Joey García** is a native of Belize, Central America, and has been published in various literary magazines and won several awards for her writing, including a contest sponsored by the San Francisco chapter of the Association of American Pen Women. ♦♦♦ **Phillis Gershator's** stories, poems, and reviews have appeared in several journals, including *The Caribbean Writer, Home Planet News*, and *Cricket.* She is the author of eleven books for children. Her most recent children's book, *Sugar Cakes Cyril*, is set in St. Thomas where she has lived for many years. ♦♦♦ **Cecil Gray** was born in Trinidad and has taught at primary, secondary and university levels. He has published two collections of poems, *Woolgatherer* and *Jacob's Kites.* ♦♦♦ **Patricia Harkins-Pierre** teaches English at the University of the Virgin Islands, St. Thomas campus. Her poems and reviews have appeared in various Caribbean journals. ♦♦♦ **Darwin Henderson** is a professor of literacy and children's literature at the University of Cincinnati. ♦♦♦ **David M. Hough,** a long-time resident of St. Croix, was an artist and philosopher. He studied art in Mexico and California and was an adjunct professor at the University of the Virgin Islands. ♦♦♦ **Mirlande Jean-Gilles** lives in New York City. Her poetry has appeared in several magazines, and she is a member of "Words and Waistbeads," a woman's art collective. ♦♦♦ **Simon Jones-Hendrickson,** from St. Kitts, is a professor of economics at the University of the Virgin Islands, St. Croix, but also writes poetry, short stories and novels. He has written two novels, *Sonny Jim of Sandy Point* and *Death on the Pasture*; his most recent volume of poetry is *Of Masks and Mysteries.* ♦♦♦ **Bruce King** has taught in universities throughout the world and is currently working on a literary biography of Derek Walcott. His most recent books are *Three Indian Poets* (1991), *V. S. Naipaul* (1993), and *Derek Walcott and West Indian Drama* (1995). He also edited *New National and Post-Colonial Literatures: An Introduction* (1996). ♦♦♦ **Judith King** has lived on St.

Croix for the past 30 years, and was co-owner of the Gilliam-King Gallery. Currently, she is working in oil painting and silkscreen printing. ♦♦♦ **Rosamond S. King** is a writer and editor who works with non-profit organizations. Her poetry has been published in journals including *Obsidian II*, *Poet Lore*, and *Colored Women Colored Wor(l)ds*. ♦♦♦ **Roberta Q. Knowles** teaches English at the University of the Virgin Islands, St. Croix campus. She co-edited *Critical Issues in Caribbean Literature* (1984) and wrote *Arona Petersen: Famous Virgin Islander (1991)*. ♦♦♦ **Susanne Kort** lives in Venezuela and her poetry has appeared in numerous literary magazines in the U.S. and Canada, including *Seneca Review*, *Literary Review*, and *Northwest Review*. ♦♦♦ **Maria Lemus** was born in Puerto Rico but raised in Venezuela and Miami. She is currently a doctoral candidate in literature at the University of Miami. ♦♦♦ **Laurence Lieberman,** a former professor at the University of the Virgin Islands, St. Thomas campus, has been teaching at the University of Illinois for many years. He regularly travels throughout the Caribbean and the Caribbean remains the primary subject of his poetry. Recent books include *New and Selected Poems* (1993), *The St. Kitts Monkey Feuds* (1995), *Beyond the Muse of Memory* (1995) and *Dark Songs: Slave House and Synagogue* (1996). *Compass of the Dying* and *Regatta in the Skies: Selected Long Poems* will be published in 1998. ♦♦♦ **Sarah F. Mahurt** teaches in the Education Division at the University of the Virgin Islands, St. Croix campus. She has published articles on Caribbean children's literature in the *Journal of Children's Literature* and *The Five Owls*. ♦♦♦ **E. A. Markham** was born in Montserrat but Britain has been his home since 1956. Active in theater and in literature, he is currently professor of creative writing at Sheffield Hallam University, edits the magazine *Sheffield Thursday*, and directs the biennial Hallam Literature Festival. His most recent book of poems is *Misapprehensions* (Anvil, 1995), and of stories, *Taking the Drawing-Room through Customs* (Peepal Tree, 1997). His latest non-fiction work is *A Papua New Guinea Sojourn: More Pleasures of Exile* (1997). ♦♦♦ **Delores McAnuff-Gauntlett** was born in Jamaica where she still lives. Her poems have been published in various journals and she has won awards from the Jamaica Cultural Development Commission. ♦♦♦ **Shara McCallum** emigrated from Jamaica to the U.S. at the age of nine. She is presently pursuing a Ph.D. in poetry and African-American and Caribbean literature at Binghamton University in New York and has published in various literary journals, including *The Iowa Review* and *The Antioch Review*. ♦♦♦ **Irma McClaurin** is an assistant professor of anthropology, University of Florida, specializing in research on gender and the African diaspora. Her latest book is *Women in Belize: Gender and Change in Central America* (Rutgers University Press, 1996). She is also the author of three books of poetry. ♦♦♦ **Christopher Miller** spends his time in volunteer Bible educational work, in addition to constructing Kingdom Halls for Bible education as one of Jehovah's Witnesses. He supports his volunteer work through freelance work with a small business offering computer support services. ♦♦♦ **Eugene V. Mohr** is a professor emeritus at the University of Puerto Rico, Rio Piedras. He is the consulting editor for *Revista/Review Interamericana* and author of *The Nuyorican Experience: Literature of the Puerto Rican Minority*. He has also published widely on linguistics and Puerto Rican and West Indian writing. ♦♦♦ **Hilda Mundo-López** was born in Puerto Rico, but currently teaches at Hostos Community College, CUNY-New York, while working on her doctoral dissertation and researching Caribbean and U.S. Latino literatures. ♦♦♦ **Jeanne O'Day** teaches English at the University of the Virgin Islands, St. Thomas campus. ♦♦♦ **June Owens**, a native of New York, now lives in Florida. Her poems and non-fiction work have appeared widely, most recently in *Amelia*, *The Blue Moon Review*, *Iowa Woman* and *Orbis*. *Willow Moments*, her Cicada Award-winning chapbook was published last fall. ♦♦♦ **Sandra Pouchet Paquet** is a professor of English at the University of Miami where she teaches Caribbean literature and African-American literature. She is the author of *The Novels of George Lamming* and numerous articles on Caribbean literary culture. ♦♦♦ **Mary Gómez Parham** has published widely on Belizean and Latin American literature and teaches Spanish at the University of Houston. Four of her poems recently appeared in *Of Words: An Anthology of Belizean Poetry* (Belize: Cubola Press, 1997). ♦♦♦ **Trevor Parris** is a poet and English professor at the University of the Virgin Islands, St. Thomas campus. His literary publications include a novel for children and *Three Islands*, a poetry collection. ♦♦♦ **Michael D. Phillips** is a professor of humanities at Brigham Young University and the editor of the *Belizean Writers Series*. ♦♦♦ **Geoffrey Philp**, author of *Uncle Obadiah and the Alien*, *Florida Bound* and *Exodus and Other Poems*, has been the recipient of many awards for his work. His most recent collection of poems, *hurricane centre*, was published in November 1997. Born in Jamaica, he now lives in Miami, Florida. ♦♦♦ **Zarina Mullan Plath** spent a semester at the University of the West Indies studying Caribbean literature and she recently won poetry prizes and awards, one sponsored by *Poetry* magazine. She co-edits the journal *Clockwatch Review*. ♦♦♦ **Jennifer Rahim** is a writer of poetry, short fiction and criticism, and a professor of English. She has published *Mothers Are Not The Only Linguists* (1992) and *Between the Fence and the Forest* (1998). Her poems have appeared in Caribbean and international journals and anthologies, including *Creation Fire* and *Atlanta Review*. ♦♦♦ **Raymond Ramcharitar** is a journalist in Trinidad who recently was awarded a fellowship to Yaddo, the writer's colony. ♦♦♦ **Thomas Reiter's** most recent collection of poems, *Crossovers*, was published in 1995 by Eastern Washington State University. He has been a frequent contributor to *The Caribbean Writer*, and in 1995 won the *Daily News Poetry Prize*. He is Wayne D. McMurray Professor of Humanities at Monmouth University in New Jersey. ♦♦♦ **Elizabeth Rezende** has written several works on Virgin Islands history and culture, including *Captured in Time: 1919*, and a children's biography, *D. C. Canegata*. ♦♦♦ **Aneka Janeene Roberts-Griffith** is a freelance journalist with the *Trinidad Express*. ♦♦♦ **Linda M. Rodríguez Guglielmoni** teaches at the University of Puerto Rico, Mayaguez, and has published articles on Puerto Rican and Dominican writers. She is currently working on a twentieth-century history of Spanish Caribbean literature. ♦♦♦ **Elaine Savory**, formerly senior lecturer at the University of the West Indies, Barbados, now divides her time between Barbados and New York where she teaches at the New School for Social Research. ♦♦♦ **Roland B. Scott** lived on St. Croix for twenty-four years. He is a former army officer and a recently retired attorney-at-law. He presently resides in New Mexico where he devotes time to reading historical and biographical works. ♦♦♦ **Ruby Simmonds** teaches English at the University of the Virgin Islands and is also chair of the Humanities Division. She has written book reviews for *The Caribbean Writer* as well as the *Journal of African Children's and Youth Literature* (JACYL). She also writes for the *Virgin Islands Daily News*. ♦♦♦ **Lynn Sweeting** is a Bahamian born poet and writer, and the publisher and editor of *WomenSpeak Journal*. She received the *Isidor Paiewonsky Prize* in 1994 from *The Caribbean Writer* and recently won the *Cassique Prize* in the Bahamas for best writer of 1997. ♦♦♦ **Patrick Sylvain** was born in Haiti, and now works as a bilingual public school teacher in Cambridge. He is also a video-photographer who works as a special researcher for *FRONTLINE*. He has been published in numerous literary magazines, and published three volumes of poetry, a play, a short story collection and a novel. ♦♦♦ **Mark Sylvester** was born in Dominica, but has been a resident of St. Croix since 1980. He is the author of two books of poetry and has received awards for his short fiction in Dominica. ♦♦♦ **Erik Turkman** writes poetry, fiction, non-fiction, and drama. His work often centers around themes relating to his family, which originated in the U.S. Virgin islands. He also works as a jazz musician and photographer. ♦♦♦ **Patricia Turnbull**, author of *Rugged Vessels*, teaches English at the H. L. Stoutt Community College in Tortola, British Virgin Islands. A contributor to *The Caribbean Writer*, she is currently editing an anthology of British Virgin Islands writing. ♦♦♦ **Erika J. Waters** is a professor of English at the University of the Virgin Islands, St. Croix campus, and has published articles and reviews on Caribbean literature. She co-edited *Critical Issues in Caribbean Literature* (1984), edited *New Writing from the Caribbean* (1994) and is editor of *The Caribbean Writer*. ♦♦♦ **Marvin E. Williams**, from St. Croix, teaches at the University of the Virgin Islands, St. Croix campus. His most recent collection of poetry is *Dialogue at the Hearth* and he is currently editing an anthology of Virgin Islands fiction.

ARIEL

A REVIEW OF INTERNATIONAL ENGLISH LITERATURE

Edited by Victor J. Ramraj

A quarterly devoted to the study of literatures in English around the world, *ARIEL* has subscribers and readers in more than fifty countries.

"ARIEL today is at the forefront of the exciting new work being done on the literary and theoretical consequences of colonialism and the postcolonial condition." **Linda Hutcheon, University of Toronto**

Recent Special Issues

South Asian Writings: Postindependence Voices (January 1998)
Postcolonial/Postindependence Children's Literature (January 1997) $12.00
Samuel Selvon: Memorial Tribute (April 1996) $10.00
Writing the New South Africa (January 1996) $12.00
Postcolonialism and Its Discontents (January & July 1995) $18.00
Contemporary North American Native Writings (January 1994) $12.00
New Voices in Caribbean Literature (January 1993) $12.00
Commonwealth Drama (January 1992) $12.00
Literature of Travel (October 1990) $12.00
Post-Colonialism and Post-Modernism (October 1989) $15.00
Nadine Gordimer (October 1988) $10.00

Recent issues include articles on:

Chinua Achebe ○ Paula Gunn Allen ○ Mulk Raj Anand ○ Margaret Atwood ○ Paul Bowles ○ Dionne Brand ○ Erna Brodber ○ Hugh Brody ○ Roy Campbell ○ Canadian Ethnic Anthologies ○ Bruce Chatwin ○ George Elliott Clarke ○ Michelle Cliff ○ Joseph Conrad ○ Isabella V. Crawford ○ Beatrice Culleton ○ David Dabydeen ○ Anita Desai ○ Marian Engel ○ Timothy Findley ○ Roy Fisher ○ Janet Frame ○ Eduardo Galeano ○ Allen Ginsberg ○ Goan Novels ○ Nadine Gordimer ○ Wilson Harris ○ Samuel Hearne ○ Jewish-Canadian Poetry ○ Rudyard Kipling ○ C. J. Koch ○ Hanif Kureishi ○ Sonny Ladoo ○ George Lamming ○ Doris Lessing ○ Roger Mais ○ David Malouf ○ Lee Maracle ○ Kamala Markandaya ○ Daphne Marlatt ○ Pauline Melville ○ V. S. Naipaul ○ Ngugi wa Thiong'o ○ Michael Ondaatje ○ Rexford Orotaola ○ Philippine Writing in English ○ Caryl Phillips ○ Jean Rhys ○ Salman Rushdie ○ George Ryga ○ Olive Senior ○ Leslie Marmon Silko ○ Sistren Theatre (Jamaica) ○ Wole Soyinka ○ Gayatri C. Spivak ○ Randolph Stow ○ Graham Swift ○ Mary TallMountain ○ Ned Thomas ○ Derek Walcott ○ Recent Welsh Poetry ○ Albert Wendt ○ Zoë Wicomb

Individual $22.50   Student $15.00   Institution $32.50
(Any one special issue is available at half the cover price with a one-year subscription)

*ARIEL, Department of English, University of Calgary, Calgary NW, Alberta, Canada T2N 1N4
(403) 220-4657   FAX (403) 289-1123   E-MAIL ariel@acs.ucalgary.ca
Web Site: http://www.acs.ucalgary.ca/~ariel/*

BLACK RENAISSANCE NOIRE

CALLALOO

A Journal of African-American and African Arts and Letters

Charles H. Rowell, Editor

EMERGING WOMEN WRITERS

Elizabeth Alexander, from DIVA STUDIES (drama) • Katherine Clay
Bassard, THE DAUGHTERS' ARRIVAL: THE EARLIEST BLACK
WOMEN'S WRITING COMMUNITY (article) • Edwidge Danticat, from
THE JOURNALS OF WATER DAYS, 1975 (fiction) • Ellen Gallagher,
PORTFOLIO (paintings) • Farah Jasmine Griffin, TONI CADE
BAMBARA: FREE TO BE ANYWHERE IN THE UNIVERSE (essay) and
TEXTUAL HEALING: CLAIMING BLACK WOMEN'S BODIES, THE
EROTIC AND RESISTANCE IN CONTEMPORARY NOVELS OF SLAVERY
(article) • Saidiya Hartman, SEDUCTION AND THE RUSES OF POWER
(article) • Allison Joseph, SUMMERS ON SCREVIN and others (poems)
• Helen Elaine Lee, from BLOOD RESIDENCE (fiction) • Opal Moore,
ENTER, THE TRIBE OF WOMEN (essay) • Audry Petty,
CONSTELLATIONS, TRACES, and SUGAR (fiction) • Patricia Powell,
from THE PAGODA (fiction) • Lorna Simpson, PORTFOLIO (photog-
raphy) • Sharan Strange, FIRST SIGHT and others (poems) • Natasha
Trethewey, ACCOUNTING and others (poems) • Judith Wilson,
SNIFFING ELEPHANT BONES: THE POETICS OF RACE IN THE ART
OF ELLEN GALLAGHER (article) • Beryl J. Wright, BACK TALK:
RECODING THE BODY (article) • *and more.*

Prepayment is required. **Annual subscriptions:** $35 (individuals); $75 (institutions). **Foreign postage:** $9.00 (Canada & Mexico); $18.35 (outside
North America). **Single-issue prices:** $9 (individuals); $19 (institutions).

Send orders to: **The Johns Hopkins University Press**,
P.O. Box 19966, Baltimore, MD 21211-0966, U.S.A. To place an order using
Visa or MasterCard, **call toll-free 1-800-548-1784,** FAX us at (410) 516-
6968, or send Visa/MasterCard orders to this **E-mail address:**
jlorder@jhupress.jhu.edu

WORLD LITERATURE TODAY

Founded in 1927 as Books Abroad

World Literature Today is the oldest continuously published international literary quarterly in the USA. It is the only periodical which regularly provides systematic and comprehensive coverage of current literary activity in all the major and many of the "minor" languages of the world. The "World Literature in Review" section of each quarterly issue contains some 300 reviews in English, evaluating the latest in poetry, fiction, drama, biography, and criticism from more than 50 languages.

A Section of Articles and Commentaries balances the breadth and diversity of the reviews with analyses of important writers, works, movements, and trends and with informative surveys of contemporary writing in areas as prominent as Paris or as distant as Kyrgyzstan.

Special Issues focus on individual figures such as Edouard Glissant of Martinique, Raja Rao of India, Elizabeth Bishop of the U.S., and Octavio Paz of Mexico, or on topics such as Literature and Revolution in Eastern Europe, Native American Literature, and the literatures of Australia, South Africa, and Central Asia.

Some of our Contributors Past and Present—Vassily Aksyonov, Dámaso Alonso, John Ashbery, Elizabeth Bishop, Jorge Luis Borges, André Brink, Michel Butor, Peter Carey, Julio Cortázar, Assia Djebar, Odysseus Elytis, Carlos Fuentes, Nadine Gordimer, Seamus Heaney, Kenzaburō Ōe, Thomas King, Harry Levin, Thomas Mann, Czeslaw Milosz, Toni Morrison, Mudrooroo, Les Murray, Octavio Paz, Marjorie Perloff, Francis Ponge, Raja Rao, Severo Sarduy, Gerald Vizenor, Derek Walcott, Yevgeny Yevtushenko.

World Literature Today also administers the biennial Neustadt International Prize for Literature and the Puterbaugh Conferences on World Literature.

Individual subscriptions $35/year, $60/two years,
Institutional subscriptions: $45/year, $70/two years; Single copy $10
Foreign postage $10/year in Canada, $15/year elsewhere.

WORLD LITERATURE TODAY / 110 Monnet Hall / University of Oklahoma
Norman, OK 73019-0375 USA
Phone: (405) 325-4531 / Fax: (405) 325-7495

SUBMISSION GUIDELINES

Submit poems (5 maximum), short stories, one-act plays and personal essays. Only previously unpublished work will be accepted. If self-published, give details. Include brief biographical information. Put name, address, telephone number, and title of manuscript on separate sheet of paper. Only title on manuscript. Please note that manuscripts will not be returned unless they are accompanied by a self-addressed, stamped envelope. Only authors of accepted works will be notified.

Mail submissions to
The Caribbean Writer
University of the Virgin Islands
RR 02, Box 10,000
Kingshill, St. Croix
USVI 00850
OR
Submit electronically to **qmars@uvi.edu**

Company Street, Christiansted, St. Croix   David M. Hough

ANNOUNCEMENTS

Prizes Awarded for Volume 11

Lorna Goodison
The Daily News Prize
for poetry

José Raúl Bernardo
The Canute A. Brodhurst
Prize for short fiction

Phebus M. Etienne
The Charlotte and Isidor Paiewonsky
Prize for first-time publication

TWO NEW PRIZES

The Una Marson Prize ($500) will be awarded for either a poem, short story, essay or play by an author who is a resident of the Caribbean. Residency is defined to mean the author must have lived in the Caribbean for at least one year and must be submitting his/her work from the Caribbean. The prize is named for Jamaican-born Una Marson (1905-1965), one of the earliest women writers. She was a poet, playwright and life-long advocate for Caribbean literature.

The Marguerite Cobb McKay Prize ($100) will be awarded for a poem, short story, essay or play by an author from the Virgin Islands.

All submissions are considered for all prizes.